Also by Mark Kleinman

Housing, Welfare and the State in Europe
European Integration and Housing Policy (co-editor)

A European Welfare State?

European Union Social Policy in Context

Mark Kleinman

palgrave

First published 2002 by
PALGRAVE
Houndmills, Basingstoke, Hampshire RG21 6XS
and
175 Fifth Avenue, New York, N.Y. 10010
Companies and representatives throughout the world

ISBN 0–333–69891–6 hardback
ISBN 0–333–69892–4 paperback

This book is printed on paper suitable for recycling and made from fully
managed and sustained forest sources.

A catalogue record for this book is available from the British Library.

Library of Congress Cataloging-in-Publication Data
Kleinman, Mark.
    A European welfare state? : European Union social policy in context/
Mark Kleinman.
        p. cm.
    Includes bibliographical references and index.
    ISBN 0–333–69891–6 (cloth)—ISBN 0–333–69892–4 (paper)
    1. European Union countries—Social policy. 2. European Union
countries—Economic integration—Social aspects. 3. Welfare state. I. Title.
HN373.5 .K54 2001
361.6′1′094—dc21
                                                                    2001032763

10   9   8   7   6   5   4   3   2   1
11   10   09   08   07   06   05   04   03   02

Copy-edited and typeset by Povey–Edmondson
Tavistock and Rochdale, England

Printed in China

Contents

For Lois and Sam

Preface

Over the last 15 years the pace of economic integration in Europe has been rapid, symbolised by the adoption of the single currency by 11 of the 15 member states of the European Union in January 1999. Increased economic integration has inevitably raised important and difficult questions about political integration, particularly the relationship between the member states and the European Union as a supra-national tier of governance. But what about the *social* aspects of integration? Does increased economic and perhaps political integration imply a European welfare state? What do we mean by the 'European Social Model'? What has been, is and should be the proper role of the European Union in social policy?

European economic integration in particular, and the process of globalization more generally, raise questions about the role not just of the EU, but also of the member states. Are welfare states in Europe becoming more similar to each other? Can *national* welfare states continue to be effective in an economically integrated Europe and under conditions of globalization? Will welfare in the future become primarily a European rather than a national responsibility?

This book sets out to answer these questions. It does so by describing and analysing the social policy of the European Union in the context both of the process of economic integration in Europe and of the development, diversity and challenges of national welfare states in Europe. The book is therefore about European social policy in two senses – both the social policy of the European Union itself, and in general terms, the social policies of the member states. It is also about the relationship between the social policies of the member states and that of the EU, and it explores European social policy in the context of the crucial political debates within Europe today: What is the future for European integration? What is meant by European citizenship? Should Europe have a fully federal political system?

In this book I am concerned with social, economic and political issues. Understanding European social policy requires an examination of the process of *economic* integration which has been the driving force of the European project. But the ultimate goal has always been political integration and political union, raising issues about citizenship, accountability and democracy. Moreover, in modern European countries, the politics of the welfare state is one of the main battlegrounds between competing parties, even though the social policies of left and right have in fact become far more similar since the 1980s. Hence the social, political and economic aspects of the modern European welfare state are closely linked.

The structure of the book is as follows. In Chapter 1, I look first at what we mean by social policy, and go on to examine what has happened to European welfare states since the 1970s. In Chapter 2 I analyse the different types of welfare state in Europe and consider the question of whether there is a 'European social model'. In Chapter 3 I examine in detail the impact of globalization on the welfare state.

The next two chapters are concerned more directly with the social policy of the European Union. In Chapter 4 I trace the historical development of European social policy, and examine how social policy is formulated and implemented. In Chapter 5, I consider how we should understand European social policy at present and assess the prospects for a European welfare state.

Chapters 6 and 7 are concerned with the interface between economic integration and social policy. In Chapter 6 I look at the social consequences of European economic integration, in particular the impact of the creation of the Single European Market and then the single currency. In Chapter 7 I look at the most important social and economic issues facing Europe – the rise in unemployment and social exclusion.

In Chapter 8 I examine the relationship between citizenship and welfare, and in particular, between the European citizenship bestowed by the Maastricht Treaty and the concept of European welfare. Finally, in Chapter 9 I draw some conclusions.

My aim in this book is to consider the past, present and future of European welfare in a broader perspective, which links it both to the economics of integration and to the continuing challenges faced by national welfare states. This book does not provide a comprehensive checklist of every piece of European social legislation or action – there are other sources from which such information can be obtained. It is intended, rather, to help the reader understand the key issues and complexities of European social policy and European welfare through analysis and explanation, and in the context of a wider political economy of social policy.

In order to explore the current and future role of the European Union in social policy, one needs at the same time to look at the development of the different national welfare states in Europe, and at the broader political, constitutional and democratic issues raised by the process of European economic integration. In this book, I do not treat the social policy of the European Union in isolation, but consider European Union social policy as part of a three-way relationship with the social policies of the member states and the wider process of European integration and policy-making.

'Europe' is a topic that raises passions and prejudices, often generating more heat than light. I have tried as much as possible to maintain an objective approach to the material I discuss, but my own views will also emerge from the text. At the outset, then, I should make it clear that I am a supporter of European integration, but a critical supporter. The first few years of the twenty-first century will be a turning point in the European project. Establishing a Europe that is more accountable, more democratic and closer to the concerns of its citizens will be crucial. The social policies, both of the member states and of the European Union, will be a critical component of that process.

This book is the product of many years of research, teaching and discussion of European welfare issues with colleagues and students. I would like to thank in particular, Julian Le Grand, Steen Mangen, David Piachaud and Monika Zulauf for helpful discussions of European social policy. I would also like to thank participants at various seminars at which I have presented some of these ideas, including the International Relations Seminar at the London School of Economics; the European Network of Housing Research Conference 'Social Housing Policy' at Nunspeet, the Netherlands in 1999; and the conference on 'The Role of Private and Public Sectors in Welfare Provision' in Kyoto, Japan in August 2000. Finally, my thanks go also to Steven Kennedy at Palgrave for both constructive criticism and editorial support.

MARK KLEINMAN

1

Crisis? What Crisis? Continuity and Change in European Welfare States

What is social policy?

Before we can discuss European social policy we have to define what we mean by social policy itself. Moreover, how we define social policy will affect how we interpret and understand the role of the European Union in social policy: the broader the definition, the more the EU can be defined as being actively involved (Leibfried and Pierson, 1995).

Very broadly, one can distinguish 'Anglo-Saxon' and 'continental' definitions of social policy. In the British empiricist tradition, social policy is identified closely with the collective provision of social services: education, health care and personal social services, social security and perhaps housing (Kleinman and Piachaud, 1993). The main issues in social policy in this tradition are therefore the effectiveness and efficiency of service provision, who provides the services, and to whom service providers are accountable. Elsewhere in Europe, the term 'social policy' has been identified more with institutions and relations pertaining to the labour market, and in particular with the rights of workers and the framework for agreements between employers, unions and government – the 'social partners'.

In this book, I assume a broad definition of social policy: 'government interventions that are designed to affect individual behaviour or command over resources or to influence the economic system in order to shape society in some way' (Kleinman and Piachaud, 1993, p. 3). I include within this definition all policies that are designed to prevent, mitigate or alleviate the social consequences of economic developments. This is perhaps a rather Anglo-Saxon definition, – but it is also broadly consistent with Leibfried and Pierson (1995), who define social policy as all activities that modify market outcomes, including policies on industrial relations, education and vocational training, the family, social security and many others.

If defining social policy is difficult, so too is agreeing on what we mean by the 'welfare state'. *The Encyclopaedia Britannica* defines a welfare state as a:

> concept of government in which the state plays a key role in the protection and promotion of the economic and social well-being of its citizens. It is based on the principles of equality of opportunity, equitable distribution of wealth, and public responsibility for those unable to avail themselves of the minimal provisions for a good life.

Esping-Andersen (1990, p. 19) refers to the 'common textbook definition' that a welfare state involves 'state responsibility for securing some basic modicum of welfare for its citizens' – a formulation with strong echoes of T. H. Marshall. Marshall defined the social rights of citizenship (see Chapter 8) as including a whole range from 'the right to a modicum of economic welfare and security to the right to share to the full in the social heritage and to live the life of a civilised being according to the standards prevailing in the society' (Marshall, 1950, p. 11). The problem is vagueness at both ends of the range. How is 'the life of a civilised being according to the standards prevailing in the society' to be defined (and by whom)? Alternatively, almost any modern government provides a *modicum* of welfare. Too broad a definition runs the risk of making the concept of 'welfare state' operationally meaningless. Veit-Wilson (2000, p. 2) argues that 'the adjective "welfare" has become devoid of all explanatory or discriminatory meaning. It becomes interchangeable with any word referring to modern industrial states'.

A further difficulty is that the term 'welfare state' carries with it normative as well as descriptive baggage. Initially, this was pejorative. The term *Wohlfahrstaat* was a term of abuse by right-wing critics of the social-democratic Weimar Republic in the 1920s (Glennerster, 1995, p. 1). Thirty years later, at the height of the post-war consensus, the term 'welfare state', in Britain and elsewhere, took on an almost mythic quality: 'The Welfare State, it was believed, reached its perfect form in 1948. Like some Greek temple it had logical, intellectually satisfying proportions' (Glennerster, 1995, p. 8). A further thirty years and the wheel had turned once more: at the height of the New Right insurgency in the 1980s, it appeared that the welfare state was to blame for all modern ills, from low productivity to lone parenthood.

Social policy involves government intervention, but this may take one or more of several forms: principally regulation, finance or subsidy, and direct provision. Social policy, in its broad definition, is concerned not only with workers but also with all members of society (including non-citizens). Social policy can be defined in terms of its purposes or goals; the mechanisms or activities undertaken to obtain those goals; and the outcomes or effects of policy. There are a wide variety of purposes towards which social policy is directed, but they can be grouped under the following headings:

- risk management and insurance against interruptions in earnings;
- redistribution over the life-cycle;
- redistribution across households:
  - from richer to poorer;
  - from capital to labour;
  - from non-families to families;
- provision of public goods which the market will not supply;
- remedying externalities which would otherwise result in under-provision;
- provision of merit goods;
- state-building;
- promotion of 'social peace' or cohesion across groups; and
- development or promotion of certain values.

In order to try to achieve these social policy goals, governments intervene in three main ways:

- through fiscal policies (taxing and spending) which redistribute income across groups, areas, or through time;
- through regulation, which sets minimum standards or determines the provision of welfare goods by private or non-profit agencies; and
- through direct provision.

What gets defined as social policy differs across countries, and changes across time within the same country. However, a schematic list, in no particular order, would include:

- social protection: pensions, unemployment and disability benefits;
- family and child welfare policies;
- social care;
- anti-poverty and social inclusion policies;

- provision of services: health services, education, personal social services and housing;
- regulation of the labour market, working conditions and industrial relations;
- public health; and
- equal opportunities and anti-discrimination policies.

In addition, one might include some newer issues currently at the margins of social policy:

- urban policies;
- environmental protection and ecological issues; and
- consumer protection.

Across European countries, the balance between these different components varies. In few countries would *all* of the above items be seen as comprising part of social policy. Moreover, there are differences between European countries in: the *mechanisms* used to achieve policy goals; the *institutional frameworks* for formulating and delivering social policy; and the *functional relationships* between the state, the private sector, the individual and social groups.

The grounds for intervention can be grouped into three main categories, based on arguments about efficiency, equity and solidarity (Kleinman and Piachaud, 1993).

In terms of *efficiency* there are two senses in which social policy intervention can be justified. The first refers to the level of provision of particular services such as health care or education. For any given society, there will be a socially efficient level of provision of each of these services; this point is reached when social benefits and social costs are equated at the margin. Market forces alone will lead to sub-optimal provision, because of the existence of externalities, imperfect information and supply inelasticities. True public goods will not be provided at all by the free market. There will thus be under- or even zero provision of some welfare services, and intervention is needed to remedy this.

Second, sub-optimal provision will have an impact on productivity and output in the economy as a whole. Modern economies require a well-trained, healthy workforce – which implies adequate education and health provision. Maximising economic output – that is, maximising national product subject only to the technical capacity constraints of the economy – requires a high and stable level of effective demand. This in turn implies stabilisation policies including a social security system that maintains household incomes during periods of unemployment and sickness. In other words, efficient economies require effective education, health, housing and social security policies. Underprovision of social policy lowers the productivity of industrial capital, thereby leading to both output and profits being below what is technically feasible.

State intervention in social policy can also be justified in terms of *equity* or distribution. Equity may be considered generally or specifically: the concern may be with an overall distribution of income that is in some sense, 'fair', or it may be concerned with the distribution of, say, health care or educational opportunities: that is, the concern may be with opportunities or it may be with outcomes. While allocative efficiency can be defined in reasonably exact terms (measurement is quite another question), the definition of equity involves more than just technical considerations – although technical issues are also relevant (Le Grand, 1991). Despite the difficulties and ambiguities, the promotion of equity is perhaps the most common ground on which social policy is justified. Intervention on equity grounds implies some kind of decision rule or rules about distributional outcomes. In liberal democracies, such decision rules are arrived at, in principle at least, through the electoral process, via the mechanisms of representative democracy and universal suffrage. However, parliamentary democracy is neither a necessary nor a sufficient condition for equity-based social policy intervention. Benevolent dictators or enlightened aristocrats could decide to provide social policy on equity grounds. Moreover, such policies could in theory lead to outcomes that are superior on some equity ground to those obtained through democratic processes.

Third, social policy can be justified in terms of *solidarity*. This is a term that is more commonly used in continental than in British discussion of social policy. In Anglo-Saxon debate the term 'community' sometimes plays a broadly equivalent role. 'Solidarity' is, however, a key part of the European vocabulary. For example, in her response to questions from the European Parliament, the incoming Commissioner for Employment and Social Affairs, Ms Anna Diamantopoulou, said in 1999 that 'Reforming the European social model does not imply reducing solidarity. On the contrary, it means reinforcing it.'

Solidarity is a term that is capable of a range of interpretations and applications (Spicker, 1991). For example, it might refer to the promotion of co-operation and altruistic behaviour; to the provision of welfare services as merit goods; or to the building of a sense of community, whether at local, national or European level. Citizens can decide for themselves that they wish to co-operate rather than to compete in order to provide certain goods or services collectively. Co-operation as well as competition is an aspect of human behaviour.

To some extent, welfare services can be considered to be merit goods – that is, state provision can be justified beyond the level that consumers would freely choose in a completely decentralised system. For example, compulsory education with a common curriculum may promote a sense of solidarity. Taking this further, social policy can be used deliberately to create a sense of identity or solidarity – the extension and development of social policy was a key part of nation-building in national welfare states. Social policy used in this way is a tool of both social inclusion and social exclusion. By defining who is entitled and who is not entitled to social benefits, or who is able and who is unable to enforce social rights, social policy at the national level played a major role in defining and policing the boundary of the nation, creating solidarity for those within the boundary, but at the same time excluding those beyond it. Whether the creation of a form of social citizenship at the *European* level is desirable and/or practical will be discussed in Chapter 8.

Whatever the grounds for intervention, questions will arise about the *level of government* at which policy formulation and implementation are appropriate. Should policy be made at local, regional, national or European level? In particular, what is the case for supranational policy? Some arguments can be advanced in terms of externalities and imperfect information. In an economically integrated Europe, there is a case to be made for social regulation in areas such as education and training, working conditions and so on, to prevent free-riding and under-investment. It is frequently argued that in the absence of European (or ideally global) regulation, nation states will compete fiercely with each other in reducing the extent and generosity of their welfare states in order to attract highly mobile capital and moderately mobile skilled labour – a process known as 'social dumping'. It is further argued that the outcome will be competitive deregulation and a 'race to the bottom' in welfare provision. In this and subsequent chapters we shall examine whether the evidence supports such claims.

The criteria of efficiency, equity and solidarity can be applied to the consideration of the spatial level of intervention as well as to the grounds of intervention themselves (see Kleinman and Piachaud, 1993). The results are not clear-cut. In terms of *efficiency*, the existence of cross-border externalities and generalised information problems suggests some reasons for a European social policy. On the other hand, there is no a priori reason for uniformity of social policy throughout the EU. Indeed, diversity, by encouraging innovation, experimentation and comparative research might well strengthen the dynamism and technical efficiency of social policy. On *equity* grounds, the case for a European social policy might be stronger, particularly if it is the case that European economic integration is increasing inequalities throughout the EU. Finally, a *solidarity* objective inevitably implies consideration of the extent, scope and desirability of notions such as European citizenship and European identity.

What's Happening to Welfare States?

A look along the bookshelves suggests that welfare states have been in 'crisis' since at least the mid-1970s. This is unlikely, not least because the word 'crisis' itself means a 'turning-point or decisive moment' (*Pocket Oxford Dictionary*) – by definition, a moment, and not a prolonged process. With the benefit of hindsight, it is easy to see that such a description of the welfare state in the 1970s and 1980s was an exaggeration. As we shall see, continuity rather than violent change has been the dominant characteristic of European welfare states.

If the notion of a 'welfare state crisis' seems exaggerated, how should we characterise the development of the welfare state in the post-war period? Until comparatively recently, the dominant approach to welfare state research was one in which rising welfare state expenditures were explained primarily as the consequence of economic development and socio-economic convergence across countries (Wilensky *et al.*, 1987). It was argued that industrialisation makes social policy both necessary – because pre-industrial modes of social organisation are destroyed; and possible – through the rise of modern bureaucracy. Hence, 'this approach is inclined to emphasize cross-national similarities rather than differences; being industrialized or capitalist over-determines cultural variations or differences in power relations' (Esping-Andersen, 1990, p. 12).

Convergence entails more than mere similarity. It conveys the idea of a causal process by which the systems of different countries necessarily become more alike over time. Indeed, the older concept of convergence was grounded in the theory of industrialism; it implied the view that industrialisation is the motor of social change, and that all industrial societies will converge towards a similar form of mixed economy with substantial state intervention (Harloe and Martens, 1983). Convergence theory implied that the logic of industrialism would lead not to class conflict, but to elite leadership and mass response (Goldthorpe, 1984). Pluralistic industrialism would generate convergence, as there were, in effect, no ideological choices left.

In the 1970s and 1980s, this 'end of ideology' argument lost force. In the first three decades after 1945, the success of Keynesian demand management techniques seemed to guarantee continued high economic growth, and with it the ability for states to meet the costs of a continuous expansion in welfare services from increased output without having to make difficult choices. But from the mid-1970s onwards this historic social compromise gave way to a more uncertain and conflictual period in all Western European countries.

The slowdown in economic growth in Western economies after 1973, and the consequent pressures on welfare state spending and social policies, undermined the idea that continuing expansion of the welfare state was inevitable. However, as we shall see, the idea that the period since the mid-1970s has seen an erosion of European welfare states is wrong. Nevertheless, the end of the 'long boom', and with it the reduction in what might be called welfare state optimism, has led to increased attention being given to the contingent and specific reasons behind the emergence of particular welfare states.

Since the 1980s, there has been an enormous increase in the range of studies of the welfare state. In Britain, for example, until the early 1970s, studies of the welfare state or of social policy were more or less dominated by a Fabian, social administration approach that stressed amelioralism, the inevitability of gradualism, and constant if unspectacular improvements in social conditions. This was seen as resulting from greater awareness of problems through policy-orientated research; from enlightened government action: and via implementation through trained professionals and disinterested bureaucrats.

From the 1970s much of this began to change. The traditional or mainstream approach came under attack from three directions. First it was attacked from the Left, initially through a neo-Marxist critique of the role, limitations and organising principles of the welfare state (Gough, 1979, O'Connor, 1973), later from anti-racist and feminist critiques (Ginsburg, 1992, Williams, 1989). Second, it was attacked from the New Right, who shared the belief of the neo-Marxists that there was a fundamental conflict between the ability to sustain a competitive and profitable capitalist economy and the pressures for ever-rising social expenditure. The terminology differed, but the underlying argument was similar: in neo-Marxist terms, there was a contradiction between the accumulation and legitimation functions of the state; in the New Right's framework, the danger to capitalist prosperity lay in the threat of productive activity being 'crowded out' by non-productive activity. The growing influence of public choice theory meant that the Fabian image of the disinterested social administrator was replaced by a new vision of the 'budget-maximising bureaucrat', a far less reassuring figure. Third, and perhaps most significantly in the long run, there was the critique from mainstream economic theory and applied economics. Increasingly, the tools of applied economic analysis – means/ends rationality; the distinction between efficiency and equity goals; cost-benefit analysis; methodo-logical individualism and consumer sovereignty – were applied to social policy. As a result, many of the traditional assumptions about the scope, role and forms of intervention of the post-war welfare state came under scrutiny, and what had been the policy consensus was put on to the defensive.

In addition, the growth of comparative studies of welfare states since the 1980s has undermined 'culture-specific' or insular ap-proaches. A range of welfare states has arisen for specific reasons, as the result of different social forces, and with different institutions, assumptions and rationales. The growth of comparative studies increased awareness of both strengths and weaknesses of different forms of the welfare state and, above all, of the range of possible arrangements.

Finally, the collapse of much of 1960s' and 1970s' 'grand theory' (Mishra, 1990) paradoxically created the conditions for a more usable and appropriate theoretical framework for empirical studies of the welfare state. The inadequacies of ultra-empirical social amelioralism combined with the irrelevance and obscurity of much grand theory have together opened up a space for a theoretically informed empiri-cal approach in which both structural factors and theoretical frame-works on the one hand, and the specificities of actual existing systems on the other, can play their part.

However, in the late 1980s and 1990s, convergence theory reap-peared, albeit in a different guise. This was a profoundly different type of convergence from the earlier version. It was not convergence *upwards* around the inevitability of an expanding welfare state, but convergence *downwards*, a convergence of retrenchment in which nation states supposedly had no choice but to adapt to the demands of the free market. Now it was no longer the logic of industrialism, but rather the logic of 'globalization' that was supposedly the driving force, pushing welfare states on to a path of downward convergence.

In this chapter I look at these two versions of convergence, and then go on to examine the evidence for convergence and the issues raised by it. Consideration of downward convergence involves analysing both external and internal factors affecting welfare states. One of the main external influence on welfare states – globalization – will merit a chapter in its own right (Chapter 3). This chapter will therefore focus mainly on internal factors, although we shall also consider the extent to which European integration itself is a force promoting convergence of welfare systems.

The Old Convergence Model

In the old convergence model, the emphasis is on notions of the inevitability or irreversibility of the welfare state. Welfare states could be explained as the logic of industrialism. The social and economic processes of industrialisation and modernisation created the need for greater state activity to ensure the social reproduction of the labour force, and hence the introduction of welfare states (Wilensky, 1975). Industrialisation and modernisation led to the weakening of family and community ties, a rise in the number and relative proportion of the elderly, and increased participation in the formal, industrial economy. At the same time, the business cycle intensified with periodic mass unemployment (Kloostermann, 1994). As a result, large-scale intervention by the state became necessary to preserve stability and economic life.

Moreover, modernisation implied a political as well as an industrial revolution; that is, a social and political process in which subjects become citizens (Pierson, 1991). The expansion of the franchise de-emphasised class politics through the granting of social concessions and shared citizenship status. Following Marshall (1950), it was argued that modernisation implies a general expansion of citizenship rights from the civil and political to the social. The welfare state was a key component of this historic accommodation. Welfare state development could be explained mainly by reference to economic factors:

'economic growth and its demographic and bureaucratic outcomes are the root cause of the general emergence of the welfare state' (Wilensky, 1975, quoted in Pierson, 1991). Given this common underlying explanation, the expectation was that welfare states, not just across Europe but also across the world, would become more similar over time. Hence the 'old convergence' hypothesis was essentially a *functionalist* argument (Ginsburg, 1992).

The emphasis in this type of explanation was on the universality of the welfare state. Markets require states – the failure of markets to secure human reproduction requires private (family) or public provision (Pierson, 1991, Therborn, 1987). The welfare state is therefore seen as in some sense irreversible, a functional necessity (Pierson, 1991).

This general position became more difficult to sustain in the 1970s and 1980s when the end of the long boom signalled an era of higher inflation, slower growth and more difficult public policy choices. Most advanced countries entered a more uncertain period, in which the triumph of modernist welfare states no longer seemed so assured. In the literature a new wave of comparative research on welfare states emphasised political, historical and sociological factors, as well as the level of economic development, as explanatory variables (for example, Baldwin, 1991, Castles, 1982, Flora, 1986, Therborn, 1987). Many of these studies continued to use the level of social expenditure as their measure of welfare state activity, but attempted to relate it to political as well as structural variables. For example, Castles (1982) looked at expenditures on education, income maintenance, and health care in eighteen OECD (Organization for Economic Co-operation and Development) countries, finding that political factors – mainly party political strength – were relevant explanatory variables.

Other writers (Esping-Andersen, 1990, Leibfried, 1993) developed classifications of welfare state ideal types or 'welfare state regimes', which emphasised the differences rather than the similarities between countries. We shall look at these in more detail in the next chapter.

The logic of the convergence school comprised three distinct steps. First, that some measure such as social expenditure as a proportion of gross domestic product (GDP) captured the essence of a welfare state and that the relevant data were adequately consistent across countries. Second, that the prime or even sole cause of this was the level of economic development. Third, and often implied rather than stated, that over time international levels of development will converge, leading to (and indeed logically entailing) convergent welfare states.

Both the convergence school and their 'politics matters' opponents were therefore agreed in looking at the 'welfare effort' – quantitative measures of social expenditure – as their explanandum. The critique of the convergence theorists by the 'politics matters' school was focused on the second of these three steps. With regard to the first step, more recent comparative work has focused attention on the form and content of welfare state expenditure, and not just its level – what type of welfare state regime is implied? Are contributions and benefits redistributive or status reflecting? What is assumed about the division of paid and unpaid work? Welfare states with similar levels of expenditure may not be at all convergent in terms of their distributional, institutional and social characteristics. In regard to the third step, whether or not social convergence is a logical conclusion from economic convergence, one should not assume that economic convergence is inevitable. Most evidence to date suggests that economic integration, whether in federal states or through increased trade between independent nations, leads to some convergence in gross national product (GNP) and in living standards. At the same time, there is considerable evidence that economic growth and increased economic integration is quite compatible with increased inequalities across individuals, households and geographical areas (see Chapter 6).

New Convergence and Welfare Retrenchment

The old type of welfare convergence was essentially born of optimism: welfare states were inevitable, given industrialism and modernisation, and gradually all nations would develop welfare states, which would over time become more similar. New convergence, by contrast, is born of pessimism – the belief that everywhere the welfare state is being reduced or 'retrenched' in the face of the growing power of markets, the desire of politicians to reduce state expenditure and public borrowing, and the unwillingness of citizens to fund welfare expenditure through either taxes or contributions. Rhodes and Meny (1998) refer to the 'era of welfare pessimism', which they identify as being driven by three factors: the erosion, or at least weakening, of the social contract; the impact of population ageing and its effect on the generational contract; and the impact of globalization: 'rightly or wrongly globalization is perceived as the core of the problem' (ibid., p. 8). External constraints – both globalization and increased European integration – have reduced the national scope for action.

Governments have lost faith in their capacity to intervene, and the belief that high levels of welfare and economic growth are incompatible is prevalent, despite the inconclusive evidence.

In practice, most authors see a complex process in which there are both continuing national differences in welfare provision, institutions and ideology, alongside trends towards greater convergence. In Taylor-Gooby's (1996) view, this amounts to a process of 'fragile' convergence:

> the impact of political complexion is not great when compared to level of development and the trend to convergence. Everywhere programmes of benefit curtailment and retrenchment are on the agenda, and the differences are of degree and of the vigour with which these policies are pushed home. (p. 214)

The processes of change are not consistent across all countries. For example, changes in the British welfare state since the 1980s have been of a different and more radical order than elsewhere (Taylor-Gooby, 1996, Clasen and Gould, 1995), and differences of emphasis and substance can be found elsewhere too. So, with new as with old convergence theory, politics *does* matter. Outcomes differ across countries, and these differences can be related both to the configuration of political forces, and to institutional factors within the welfare state that act as a brake on policies of radical retrenchment. Evidence suggests that continuities are greater in welfare states where there are strong organisational interests in the status quo.

Overall, however, the dominant pattern is one of continuity. The politics of the welfare state remain largely the politics of the status quo – by and large, the old social contract is standing its ground (Rhodes and Meny, 1998). As a result, there is little evidence of radical change but rather a 'frozen' welfare landscape (Esping-Andersen, 1996).

The attention given to the supposed welfare state crisis in the late 1970s and early 1980s was perhaps a reflection of Anglocentric bias in the literature, rather than of the underlying reality (Pierson, 1995). It is the continuities rather than discontinuities in welfare states and welfare expenditures that are, in fact, most apparent. Nowhere has welfare been replaced by pure market mechanisms, and the ratio of social expenditure to GNP has remained almost unchanged (Falkner and Talos, 1994, Scharpf, 2000). The 'growth party' may be over, but muddling through rather than radical change is the norm (Pierson,

1995). However, although the welfare 'crisis' of the 1970s was much exaggerated, since that time the legitimacy of expanding welfare provision has been challenged, and there has been a loss of faith in bureaucracies, perceived as being inefficient and ineffective (Rhodes and Meny, 1998).

Although it is incorrect to speak of welfare state convergence, it is clear that there have been a number of common trends in welfare development. These include (Falkner and Talos, 1994; Jordan, 1998; Rhodes and Meny, 1998, Taylor-Gooby, 1996):

(i)   The role of the state in social policy is connected more closely with prevailing economic conditions. In much of the literature, there is an exaggerated concern with 'globalization', often poorly understood (see Chapter 3). What is undoubtedly true, however, is that governments have become more concerned to align their policies on welfare expenditure to domestic economic conditions.

(ii)   There is a changed relationship between the 'three factors of social reproduction' – state, market and family. The shift to market- and family-based welfare has been encouraged by the inactivity and withdrawal of the state.

(iii) There has been increased decentralisation of responsibilities. As well as loss of power upwards to 'Europe' or to 'world markets', nation states have also devolved powers and responsibilities downwards to regions and municipalities.

(iv)   There have been increased pressures on social expenditure, driven both by the increased real costs of providing welfare services, and the desire of governments to placate both voters and financial markets by reducing, or at least slowing the growth of, taxes and borrowing. These domestically-derived pressures were compounded in the 1990s by the need for European governments to meet the deflationary Maastricht convergence criteria.

(v)   Governments have tried to generate additional income, other than taxes and social security contributions, to pay for welfare expenditure.

(vi)   There is a continuing programme of managerial reform of public services ('modernisation') to reduce costs and increase efficiency.

(vii) Selectivity has increased, in some cases leading to problems of social exclusion and increased risk of poverty.

This listing is mainly descriptive, referring to the observed similarities in policies, rhetoric and perceived problems across countries. At a more analytic level, we can identify seven key structural factors behind increased similarities across European countries at the start of the twenty-first century. Five of these are internal to nation states, two are external.

Internal and External Drivers of Change

Internal Factors

Slower growth   The key difference between the first three decades after the Second World War and the following twenty-five years is, of course, the much lower levels of economic growth in the advanced economies in the latter period. Why this happened is the topic of many hundreds of books, although it may well be that the most accurate answer is, in Paul Krugman's words 'We don't know.' But the key point is that, after three decades in which both state-financed welfare and private consumption could expand together, there were now harder choices for both citizens and governments.

In addition, there was, at least for the northern European welfare states, the problem of maturation – welfare states had already expanded to consume considerable proportions of GDP. Further expansion – for example, to cover the costs of social care for an increasing population of the very elderly – will be relatively expensive. Maturation also meant that citizens have become used to a comprehensive and complex welfare system, taking it for granted as a non-heroic, even mundane aspect of modernity. This can be contrasted with the immediate post-war period, where the achievement of a welfare state was seen as the culmination of a prolonged struggle against war, economic depression and political inequality.

Changes in labour markets   Welfare state expansion in the post-war period was closely linked to the principle of full employment, and to the use of broadly 'Keynesian' methods of demand management by governments in order to achieve it. Since the 1970s, there have been significant changes both in European labour markets and in the policy goals and mechanisms of European governments. Changes in employment patterns and the functioning of post-industrial labour markets are a complex phenomenon, varying considerably across countries. Nevertheless, there are some common trends. All European countries are moving towards being service economies, although this transition is more difficult in some countries than others. There has been a decline in traditional, full-time, permanent (usually male) employment with explicit or implied social protection. Employment growth has been concentrated in part-time, temporary and fixed-term contracts, and in sectors and occupations that have traditionally been identified as 'female'. Employment rates in Europe are lower, and unemployment rates higher, than in the USA or Japan, although this pattern varies considerably across European countries (see Chapter 7).

At the policy level, equally important was the retreat in the 1980s and 1990s from the commitment of European states to the principle of full employment. This principle was the bedrock of all types of welfare state. Beveridgean, conservative-corporatist and social-democratic welfare states, in different ways, all take as their premise a working society. But this principle gradually gave way, first in the UK, later throughout the EU, to a changed ideological position in which the control of inflation, and the reduction of public expenditure and public debt was prioritised over other goals of macroeconomic policy. This shift in policies and in underlying ideology occurred both at the level of the nation state and at the European level. The prioritisation of counter-inflationary policy over the maintenance of full employment was both reflected in and reinforced by the key EU agreements of the 1990s: the Maastricht and Amsterdam treaties, and the Stability Pact.

The absence of full employment creates enormous pressures for welfare states. The growth in unemployment causes both expenditure on welfare payments to rise, and income from taxation to fall. Consequently, both public expenditure and public borrowing as a proportion of GDP will rise, creating further pressures for cutbacks in expenditure and entitlements. Rising unemployment, and associated social exclusion, also leads to increases in social costs from increased crime and other social pathologies.

Furthermore, permanently high unemployment affects the nature of the welfare state. The rise of long-term and youth unemployment in particular is associated either with growth in social assistance and means-testing in some systems, or alternatively, with outright exclusion from the social protection system. Social assistance is qualitatively different from social insurance. In a social assistance welfare state, social exclusion and social division increase. In addition, social assistance is expensive and complex to administer.

Hence the effects of structural changes in labour markets and changes in the commitment of governments to full employment are profound. A welfare state in which full employment is abandoned, and in which welfare is left increasingly to the market or to stigmatised social assistance is one in which the contractual commitments between individuals, and between the individual and the state have been weakened. This weakened commitment itself then becomes a factor in the complex of variables determining the future trajectory of the welfare state. This is what is meant by path dependency. It is *not* the case that outcomes are determined inevitably by past events. Rather, the path is constrained by what has already taken place.

This seems to be a very important aspect of 'new convergence'. Labour markets may or may not be less secure than in the 'Golden Age' of the post-war boom. Globalization may or may not be a qualitatively new phenomenon (see Chapter 3). But in the first three decades of the post-war period, welfare state growth and full employment were closely connected, with lines of causality in both directions. Inevitably, then, the abandonment, or at least weakening, of the full employment goal by governments will have major consequences for the direction of social policy.

Demographic changes The ageing of European populations and changes in family structure are well known. As with changes in labour markets and the international division of labour, one needs to separate firm evidence from the more apocalyptic interpretations. Predictions of a 'demographic time bomb' have been exaggerated, but clearly the shift in the age structure does impose strains on welfare expenditure, particularly the funding of pensions and health care services. The European population aged over 60 is estimated to grow by 70 per cent between 1960 and 2020, reaching about 27 per cent of the total by the latter date (Hantrais, 2000, p. 148). While there are important differences between member states in the rate and extent of this process, it is a process that is common to all. By the late 1990s, spending on old age was the largest item of social expenditure in all member states except Ireland. This problem of increased dependency was exacerbated by policies in the 1980s and 1990s in most member states of forced or voluntary early retirement, or partial retirement. Economic activity rates begin to decline as much as ten years before the official retirement age (Hantrais, 2000).

Given the broad similarities in this social change across countries, population ageing is a force for convergence across national boundaries. Moreover, while the expenditure implications are less than catastrophic, coupled with prevailing attitudes among both elites and voters towards reduced public expenditure, taxes and contributions, the net result is to produce considerable pressures for retrenchment and reduced entitlement.

The other main demographic change is in terms of family structure. Fertility rates have converged across Europe, mainly because of very rapid falls in fertility in Southern Europe. By the late 1990s, fertility rates in the EU were below those in the USA and, together with those in Japan, were the lowest in the world (Hantrais, 2000, p. 99). Marriage rates also fell, from almost 8 per 1000 in 1960 to 5 per 1000 in the late 1990s. Births outside marriage rose in all countries, but at very different rates, so that the gap between those countries with the highest rates, and those with the lowest (broadly between Northern and Southern Europe) widened considerably (Hantrais, 2000, pp. 100–1). The pattern is similar with respect to divorce: an increase in divorce rates everywhere, but a sharp division between Northern and Southern Europe. Partly as a consequence of this, there are clear differences in terms of the numbers of single-parent families, which by the end of the 1980s comprised 15–17 per cent of all families in the UK and Denmark, but only 5–7 per cent in Greece, Italy and Spain.

Hence the evidence in terms of family trends is more mixed. While there is clearly reduced fertility and a move away from marriage almost everywhere, traditional family structures remain more important in Southern Europe. This difference in social organisation will both underpin and be supported by differences in welfare state arrangements between Southern and Northern Europe. The general conclusion is that demographic trends provide some impetus towards convergence in terms of the expenditure effects of an ageing population and some commonality in family and household trends. But important differences remain, particularly between Southern and Northern Europe, reinforcing arguments for taking southern European welfare states to be a distinct variant (see Chapter 2).

Mass attitudinal change   European citizens continue to display strong support for the welfare state – at least in terms of expressed opinions. Eurobarometer data show that EU citizens believe by a two-thirds to one-third majority that social protection must be maintained, even at the cost of higher taxes. Support for expanding provision is strongest in the lower-spending countries such as Greece,

Portugal, Spain and the UK, and weakest in the higher-spending countries (Taylor-Gooby, 1996). An analysis of data from seven European countries – Germany, Britain, Italy, Austria, Ireland, Sweden and Norway – for 1985 and 1990 shows that the great majority of citizens in most western European nations support the welfare state and at least say they believe in paying a fair share of taxes (Newton, 1998). Most believe that the rich pay too little and the poor too much. Citizens are supportive of greater income equalisation but not radical equalisation. They do discriminate between different public policies and programmes, being more in favour of welfare programmes, less so culture and environmental spending, and still less law and order and defence. Within the welfare budget, citizens distinguish between different programmes and policy instruments.

Newton (1998) concludes that European citizens are more sophisticated than many theories allow. The pattern is consistent across the countries studied – national variations are relatively minor, so there is a common 'West European' view on the welfare state, in contrast to a more varied pattern in regard to trust in government and political participation. Core services of the welfare state – health, education, housing, and provision for old age, illness and unemployment – are regarded as a government responsibility by more than 90 per cent of the public.

However, in their voting patterns, European citizens seem much less reluctant to support parties and candidates that would increase expenditure and taxation. There is no evidence that political attitudes have swung sharply to the right since the 1980s in Europe. Rather, what appears to be happening – and this is a worldwide rather than a specifically European phenomenon – is that citizens have experienced a loss of faith in the institutions of government, and indeed in collective institutions generally. All forms of deference to established authorities are in decline. European citizens have become more pragmatic, less invigorated by the broad vision. Citizens increasingly evaluate policies and programmes of governments and parties in terms of the specific effects on themselves and their families, rather than in terms of broader concepts. Citizens state that they support the welfare state in principle, but in practice are reluctant to sanction tax increases unless they are strongly convinced of the link with improved services.

Moreover, as advanced economies have become predominantly service economies, expectations of welfare state services have increased greatly:

Expectations of what to expect from a service provider are thus driven by the cutting edge of the capitalist system – banking and financial markets, supermarkets and malls, fashion and personal services. The things people care about most are, however, still schooling for their children and care when they are sick or old. So, when they take their children to school or hospital they expect the kind of environment and response, at the very least, they can expect in the bright, colourful, child-friendly and consumer-hungry supermarket where they do their weekend shopping. (Glennerster, 1999, p. 9)

This is a very widespread trend, and while its direct effects on welfare state convergence may be limited, in the medium and long term it is a very potent force that, while not determining a specific course of action by governments, constrains the options that are open. If politics is the art of the possible, attitudinal change among European citizens has limited the scope of what is deemed to be possible in the welfare field, and hence the scope of welfare politics.

Elite attitudinal change   More significant has been a clear shift in attitudes among political, economic and financial elites. In this world view, the scope for government action is seen as being relatively limited, markets are to be supported and perhaps guided, but certainly not replaced, and the control of inflation rather than the elimination of unemployment is the main economic goal:

Mainstream public choice theories have been fused with market theories and converted into a powerful new ideology which has become politically dominant over the last two decades. This new ideology has overthrown or undercut the previous dominant ideology often described as the Keynesian welfare state ... The new ideology ... argues the general beneficence of markets and the many failures of politics ... Unfortunately there is as yet no good name for this new composite ideology. 'Government by the market', suggesting the dominance of a market-based view of the role of politics and government, perhaps adequately conveys its meaning. (Self, 1993, p. 56)

As a result, policies of economic management have become increasingly similar across European states, so that it mattered relatively little whether the government was nominally socialist or conservative.

In Europe, the paradigmatic episode was the experience of the socialist French government of 1981–3. Once the experiment with 'Keynesianism in one country' had failed, the French state embarked on a course of economic and financial orthodoxy to which it has by and large held true ever since. This involved prioritising the control of inflation and the maintenance of a strong currency, and via these first two, full economic and monetary union with a single currency over the costs in terms of unemployment and loss of social cohesion. The French Keynesian experiment, its failure and the resulting U-turn in policy had profound consequences, not only for France itself but also for the broader project of European integration. Despite the rhetoric on both sides, the European integration project has been anchored firmly in prevailing economic orthodoxy.

The orthodox doctrine is reinforced relentlessly by official reports and pressure from the major international organisations such as the OECD as well as the European Commission. These reports stress continually the need for structural adjustment, for reductions in wage costs, for cuts in public expenditure, and for greater flexibility in labour markets. This implicit consensus over the proper conduct for economic and social policies became explicit, and indeed mandatory, with the Maastricht Treaty. The Treaty prioritised monetary and fiscal convergence criteria, with no reference to variables in the real economy. Subsequently, the Amsterdam Treaty and the Stability Pact reinforced this orthodox line.

External Factors

Two main factors are commonly cited as external influences on convergence of European welfare regimes. The first, *globalization*, is the subject of Chapter 3 below. The second key external factor is the process of European integration itself.

European integration as a convergence factor   Greater integration in Europe creates pressures for convergence in social policies along both economic and political vectors. As I shall discuss in more detail in Chapter 6, there is no clear separation between the different 'stages' of economic integration – customs union, common market, monetary union – and it is not possible to have economic integration without political and social implications. Indeed, given the pervasive nature of government intervention in all modern economies, creating a barrier-free internal market implies some degree of convergence or harmonisation between social policies. This is because government interventions in areas such as training, education, pensions, transport, social provision and so on, have essentially similar effects to trade barriers, tariffs and other direct border interventions.

If cross-border externalities exist, then diversity of social policies will lead to inefficient outcomes. For example, inter-country differences in education and training create incentives for countries to 'free-ride' by poaching the educated and trained workforce of the others. In this version, the pursuit of national self-interest by each country will lead to under-investment in education and training across Europe as a whole – convergence downwards. Alternatively, member states may agree to intergovernmental or supranational arrangements that bind them to providing minimum levels (convergence upwards, or at least to a social minimum).

There are also equity considerations pointing in the direction of greater convergence. First, there is the fact that there are considerable differences in income levels, in levels of provision of public services, in social protection, and in minimum standards between member states. If the Maastricht Treaty is taken seriously, that is, that 'every person holding the nationality of a Member State shall be a citizen of the Union', then it can be argued that differences between citizens who happen to reside in different member states should be reduced. However, a stronger equity argument relates to the consequences of economic integration. If European integration leads to widening disparities and inequalities both within and between member states, then there is an argument for social policy intervention – at the European level – to try to remedy these inequalities. Such intervention might be through a process of 'levelling up' existing national social policies, or through a specifically European (supranational) social policy.

Additionally, convergence in social policies may come about not because of the consequences of integration, but as a precondition for it to happen. The efficiency gains that the European Commission saw as being the main reason for completing the single market rest on the reallocation of productive factors to their most efficient use. Similarly, equity considerations imply that citizens of the Union should have equal, or nearly equal, access to the economic advantages arising from a single market and economic union. Both of these imply at the very least similar active labour market policies to help unemployed or underemployed workers to retrain and obtain new jobs, and perhaps also similar levels of education, health provision and social protection in different member states in order to aid labour mobility.

Furthermore, there are, of course, pressures for convergence along more directly political vectors. The growing volume of European social legislation binds the member states to common standards or arrangements in areas such as health and safety, labour standards, non-discrimination and so on (see Chapters 4 and 5). However, in recent years, the European Commission has moved back from the earlier, maximalist vision of seeking to 'harmonise' social policy (in practice, mainly social protection systems) towards the more limited goal of convergence.

Also important are less direct mechanisms of policy convergence. European works councils bring together employers' organisations and trade unions in European-level corporatist arrangements. Interest groups organise increasingly on a Europe-wide basis to lobby Brussels and Strasbourg – FEANTSA (Fédération Européenne d'Associations Nationales Travaillant avec les sans-Abri) the European coalition for the homeless; and CECODHAS (Comité Européen de Coordination de l'Habitat Social), European social housing grouping, are two examples. Conferences, academic and professional research studies, and twinning arrangements between professional organisations are further examples. All these developments increase awareness of policy-makers, professionals and service deliverers in each country to policy and practice elsewhere. In the long run, this enhanced consciousness of alternatives, and practical experience of seeing other systems in operation may have more effect than specific EU directives. Most important of all may be the indirect effects of measures taken by the EU, not specifically to further social policy goals, but in order to complete the single market, to create an economic and monetary union in Europe and to bring about a single currency.

Until relatively recently, European integration could be taken to be a straightforward force for greater convergence, if not outright harmonisation, across European welfare states. From the late 1980s, however, there has been greater uncertainty over the European project, increased political scrutiny of European institutions, a more pragmatic attitude by citizens to public policy, and taxpayer resistance to increasing the scope of government at whatever level. As a result, increased 'top-down' pressures for convergence for the sake of the European project may provoke a centrifugal reaction, leading to demands for greater divergence and diversity in the future.

What Is the Evidence on Welfare Retrenchment?

What impacts have these internal and external factors had on European welfare states? Have governments in different European countries responded to these pressures in similar or in different ways? In particular, what evidence is there for welfare state retrenchment – that is, what evidence is there of downward welfare convergence? If there has been a process of downward convergence, we would expect to find this reflected in data on expenditure levels; we would expect to find that welfare regimes have become more similar; and that there has been a common shift in political sentiment towards retrenchment of the welfare state. Have these developments, in fact, occurred?

Table 1.1 shows trends in social protection expenditure in EU member states over the last twenty years. The trend has emphatically *not* been one of downward convergence. First, there is no downward movement in the proportion of GDP spent on social protection. Across the EU as a whole this proportion rose from 24.3 per cent in 1980 to 28.2 per cent in 1997. Moreover, this increase was not caused solely by the accession of three relatively high-spending new members: social protection expenditure among the expanded EU of 15 members continued to rise between 1990 and 1997. In all countries except Ireland and Luxembourg, the proportion was higher in 1997 than in 1980. Secondly, there is no evidence of convergence across countries. By and large, relativities are preserved over time. High spenders in 1980 remain high spenders in 1997, and low spenders remain low spenders.

TABLE 1.1   *Social protection expenditure in the EU member states as a percentage of GDP 1980–1997*

Country	1980	1990	1997	Country	1980	1990	1997
Belgium	28.0	26.7	28.5	Luxembourg	26.5	22.6	24.8
Denmark	28.7	29.7	31.4	Netherlands	30.1	32.5	30.3
Germany	28.8*	25.4	29.9	Austria	–	26.7	28.8
Greece	9.7	23.2	23.6	Portugal	12.8	15.6	22.5
Spain	18.1	19.9	21.4	Finland	–	25.5	29.9
France	25.4	27.7	30.8	Sweden	–	33.1	33.7
Ireland	20.6	19.1	17.5	United Kingdom	21.5	23.2	26.8
Italy	19.4	24.1	25.9	EU-15	24.3**	25.4	28.2

*West Germany (1980)
**EU-12 (1980)
Sources: Eurostat 1996, Eurostat 2000.

Similar results are obtained in a study of 18 OECD countries over the period 1970 to 1997 (Scharpf, 2000). Taxes and social security contributions as a proportion of GDP rose across the OECD through the 1970s. But this rise slowed in the early 1980s, and from 1985 to 1995 the proportion remained roughly constant. Moreover, with one exception, this pattern held true also for individual countries:

> [T]here seems to be no convergence over time. Instead, the stagnation of tax revenues seems to have had more or less the same constraining effect on Scandinavian high-tax countries, Anglo-Saxon low-tax countries and the Continental welfare states with their intermediate levels of taxation. (Scharpf, 2000, p. 200)

A wide-ranging study of social expenditure for thirty-nine countries, of varying stages of development, found that, as far as crude spending ratios were concerned, there was no evidence of a race to the bottom – the average spending ratio increased over time. There was also no tendency to convergence, but rather a slightly increased dispersion. However, analysis of these data also suggests that there was some evidence of a trend to lower social spending relative to a given level of wealth – that is, big spending welfare states moved closer to the trend line of 'expected' spending, given national wealth (Alber and Standing, 2000).

Between 1960 and 1994, total government spending in the OECD countries doubled, so that government expenditure constituted more than half of GDP in the early 1990s (Garrett, 2000). Total public spending, taxation and deficits increased most rapidly during recessions, because of the well-known effect that recessions both increase demand-led expenditure ('entitlements') such as unemployment benefits, and depress tax receipts. But 'of more interest is the fact that the public economy did not subsequently contract during economic recoveries' (Garrett, 2000). Furthermore, among OECD countries, the standard deviation around the mean for government spending – that is, the degree of divergence between countries, shows a long-term rising trend from the 1960s to the 1990s, although admittedly, there was some convergence in the 1980s. However, even this period was 'preceded and followed by (recession) periods when cross-national differences in fiscal policy increased' (Garrett, 2000).

Stephens *et al.* (1996) use cross-national data on measures of social expenditure and a number of case studies to examine the extent to which there has been a rollback of welfare state entitlements and the extent to which party political differences in social policy have been eroded. The quantitative data cover eighteen advanced nations, including eleven members of the EU. Data cover the period 1958–89 and measure 'welfare effort' as government expenditure or revenue as a percentage of GDP. This study does not therefore include any observations for the 1990s. The authors argue that their results are consistent with the hypothesis that there are three distinct periods: from the late 1950s to around 1971; from 1971 to 1979; and from 1979 to the late 1980s:

> Governments first responded to the economic difficulties by following traditional formulas which entailed maintaining or increasing entitlements and expenditure in an effort to fight recession and unemployment and mitigate their social consequences. After a decade of 'fumbling', government after government regardless of political color embarked on new policies which often involved reining in the increase in expenditure and increasing revenue. (Stephens *et al.*, 1996, p. 6)

These authors also find that party political influences on welfare expenditure and revenue were strong in the 'Golden Age', weaker in the 1970s, and almost non-existent in the 1980s. The analysis of the quantitative data therefore suggests some convergence in policies across countries, and a weakening of direct partisan political differences. But in their case study analysis, they find considerable differences in the policy trajectories followed in social-democratic, liberal and Christian-democratic countries. Despite some cutbacks in the most recent period, social democratic nations such as Sweden, Norway and Finland 'are still and will continue to be very generous welfare states' (Stephens *et al.*, 1996, p. 12). In Britain, by contrast, they argue, the structure of social spending has been shifted 'away from the Beveridge ideal towards a more thoroughly residualist model'.

They conclude that, with the exceptions of the UK and New Zealand, there were very few cases where benefits were in fact lower in the mid-1990s than in 1970. Moreover, in almost all cases, the basic institutional features of the different welfare states were maintained – and hence the variation across them. The two exceptions, Stephens *et al.* argue, are the UK and New Zealand, where there was a substantial move towards an 'essentially residualist' system.

The overall conclusion of these authors is that, while there have undoubtedly been pressures on welfare states, since the 1980s in particular:

> we are dealing with a political constraint here, not an inexorable economic constraint. Societies still have political choices regarding

the types of welfare states they want to maintain, though these choices are more constrained than in the Golden Age. (Stephens *et al.*, 1996, p. 21)

However, as we saw earlier, there has been no general shift to the right in voter attitudes to the welfare state. Welfare states in Europe retain broad political support. Citizens express preferences for, or at least pay lip service to, the principle of maintaining tax levels in order to pay for welfare services. However, there is at the same time evidence of falling levels of trust and confidence in government generally.

Conclusions

The often repeated view that European welfare states are being dismantled structurally through a process of downward convergence is unfounded. The empirical evidence is consistent with an alternative view which stresses *stability* of expenditure levels and continued *divergence* in the extent, form and content of the welfare state in different European countries. The functionalist theory is shown to be wrong; the 'logic of globalization' has no more eliminated the structural and institutional differences between welfare states than did the 'logic of industrialism' decades before.

Nevertheless, there are forces pushing for some convergence in social policies. In part these are simply a consequence of economic integration in Europe – with the maturation, or perhaps 'growth to limits' of the Northern welfare states, and the expansion of the relatively underdeveloped Southern welfare states, there will be greater similarities between European welfare states. This process is being reinforced by actions at the European level – both direct European social policy measures and indirect consequences of the process of economic integration. In addition, there are common pressures in the form of structural changes to labour markets, and changed patterns of fertility and demography. Finally, there are some common political trends at both elite and mass levels – in particular, greater scepticism about the potency and efficacy of government action.

But European welfare states remain distinctive. The evidence of this chapter suggests that nation states and their institutions remain important; that there is no 'logic of globalization' driving welfare states downward; and that the key determinant of domestic welfare states remains the political choices of citizens and their politicians. We now go on to examine these propositions in more detail.

2

One Social Model or Many?

Typologies of Welfare States

At present, there is no European welfare state. What do exist are fifteen separate welfare states within the European Union. These welfare states have both similarities and differences. The first wave of comparative analyses of welfare states emphasised the similarities rather than the differences between them. The dominant explanatory model was that of convergence: welfare states could be explained as the logic of industrialism. More recently, the focus has shifted to the differences rather than the similarities between welfare states. Some studies used a historical perspective in order to explore the roles and importance of class politics and social structure on the origins and development of particular welfare states (Baldwin, 1991; Skocpol, 1992). Other authors have sought to establish typologies, consisting of a limited number of welfare models or 'welfare state regimes', based on ideal-typical classifications of actually existing welfare states (Esping-Andersen, 1990; Abrahamson, 1992; Leibfried, 1993). This 'welfare modelling business' (Abrahamson, 1999) takes as its starting point the assumption that welfare states cluster around certain distinct regimes.

Given the generally insular nature of the British social administration tradition, it is ironic that Richard Titmuss of the London School of Economics has left such a lasting impression on the comparative study of welfare states. Many of the current typologies of welfare states contain strong echoes (whether deliberate or not) of Titmuss's famous threefold classification of social policy models (Titmuss, 1974). Titmuss's classification comprised; first, the Residual Welfare model, in which needs are met by the state only when the private market and family have clearly failed, and then only temporarily. Second, there is the Industrial Achievement–Performance model in which social needs are met on the basis of merit, work performance and productivity. In this model social welfare functions as an 'adjunct' to the economy, hence Titmuss's alternative name, the

28

'Handmaiden Model'. Finally, there is the Institutional Redistributive model, in which social welfare is seen 'as a major integrated institution, providing universalist service outside the market on the principle of need' (Titmuss, 1974, p. 31).

However, despite the superficial similarities, there are two important differences between Titmuss's approach and more recent classification schemes. These differences are specific to the British tradition, of which Titmuss was both architect and symbol. First, Titmuss's primary focus was on the provision of services, reflecting the traditional British social administration concern with service delivery and social policy implementation. Second, he was perhaps above all concerned with values. While his three models were only approximations of ideas about social policy, they were approximations which 'serve to indicate the major differences – the ends of the value spectrum – in the views held about the means and ends of social policy' (Titmuss, 1974, p. 32).

More recent comparative studies of social policy say little about values, adopt a more 'scientific' approach to the analysis of social institutions, and focus on *means* rather than ends as the operational method for classifying welfare state regimes. This 'welfare modelling' approach can be distinguished not only from the more value-driven Titmussian attitude, but also from the 'logic of industrialism'/modernisation approach to comparative social policy, discussed in the previous chapter. If the development of welfare states is seen essentially as an aspect of modernisation, it is a small step to classify welfare states into leaders and laggards. If it is assumed that eventually all welfare states will converge, the empirical question then becomes the level of progress attained by different countries. Hence, countries could be ranked on a continuum from 'residual' to 'institutional' forms of social welfare, with the clear implication that the institutional form was more advanced:

> This way of arguing has been labelled the modernisation thesis, and it anticipates a move from residual to institutional welfare state structuring. We can say that the explanatory variable is maturity or degree of industrialisation, and the most commonly used measure was welfare state size indicated by total social expenditure relative to GDP. (Abrahamson, 1999, p. 396)

But in the welfare modelling approach, there is much less emphasis on the idea of linear development from less advanced to more advanced welfare states. Rather, differences across countries are seen as alternative approaches, rooted in institutional, political and historical specificities. Hence, although measures of social expenditure as a proportion of GDP remain important, a more complex way of classifying welfare states than simple quantitative indicators is used.

The most influential comparative study in recent years has undoubtedly been Esping-Andersen's *The Three Worlds of Welfare Capitalism* (1990). Esping-Andersen bases his typology on two key concepts: the de-commodification of labour; and the welfare state as a system of stratification. Esping-Andersen argues that, in capitalist societies – that is, those where markets become universal and hegemonic – workers become commodified. The workers' material welfare becomes entirely dependent on the sale of their labour. But with modernisation and citizenship, 'the introduction of modern social rights implies a loosening of the pure commodity status. De-commodification occurs when a service is rendered as a matter of right, and when a person can maintain a livelihood without reliance on the market' (Esping-Andersen, 1990, p. 22).

De-commodification is a feature of all welfare states, but to differing degrees. Esping-Andersen relates the degree and extent of de-commodification to each of three basic types of welfare state. In those welfare states dominated by social assistance, the low level of benefits and means testing severely weaken the amount of de-commodification. Indeed, in these countries (mainly, according to Esping-Andersen, the Anglo-Saxon world) the effect may be to strengthen the market by increasing the desirability of private welfare for those who can afford it. In the second group of countries, there is compulsory state social insurance with relatively good benefit entitlements. But this too does not bring about substantial de-commodification, as benefits depend strictly on contributions, and hence on work and employment. The third, Beveridge-type model, offers the possibility of full de-commodification, but in practice, such schemes have rarely offered benefits to a level that represents a real option to the formal labour market.

Hence, Esping-Andersen's test of de-commodification is a strong one. He states that a *minimal* definition of de-commodification is one where 'citizens can freely, and without potential loss of job, income, or general welfare, opt out of work when they themselves consider it necessary' (Esping-Andersen, 1990, p. 23). This is, in fact, an astonishingly *maximal* definition of de-commodification. It is hard to imagine any welfare state in which it would be either desirable or feasible for citizens to opt out of work of their own volition without *any* loss of income or welfare.

Second, Esping-Andersen emphasises the role of the welfare state in social stratification. He dismisses the naive view that social policy must inevitably lead to greater equality and redistribution. Rather, each type of welfare state gives rise to a particular type of stratification system. Hence the poor-relief tradition, and its 'contemporary offshoot' the social assistance state, were designed explicitly to maintain social stratification. The social insurance corporatist state was promoted by conservative welfare reformers such as Bismarck both to consolidate class differences among wage earners and to tie loyalties more directly to the central state authority. Social democrats sought to build an equalitarian welfare state on universalistic principles. But in practice this has foundered on the problem of the generally low levels of flat-rate universal benefits. With greater prosperity, the result is another kind of dualism, that is, a particular type of social stratification, in which better-off households rely increasingly on the market, through private insurance and fringe benefits, and eventually only the poor rely on the state.

Within this conceptual framework, Esping-Andersen then analyses international variations in de-commodification and welfare state stratification. He argues that the variations revealed in this way are not linearly distributed, but tend to cluster around three models. The first cluster is the liberal welfare state, characterised by means testing and modest universal transfers or social insurance, strict entitlement rules, and state encouragement of the market. Examples include the USA, Canada and Australia. The second cluster comprises conservative-corporatist regimes, in which social rights are deeply enshrined, but in a way that preserves status differences. Private insurance and occupational fringe benefits are marginal; family policy stresses traditional family arrangements, and social insurance typically excludes non-working wives. The principle of subsidiarity preserves important roles for the church and the family. Examples include France, Germany, Italy and Austria. The third and smallest cluster comprises the social-democratic regimes in which the principles of universality and de-commodification are extended to the middle classes. Hence services and benefits are 'upgraded to levels commensurate with even the most discriminating tastes of the new middle classes' (Esping-Andersen, 1990, p. 27). Family and market hence play more minor roles. These regimes are committed to the full employment guarantee and are in fact dependent on its attainment. Examples are the Scandinavian welfare states.

In his typology of welfare states and welfare regimes, Esping-Andersen breaks not only with the earlier 'logic of industrialism' school but also with those who see the welfare state as a straightforward corollary of the extension of the franchise and the growth in working-class political power. Rather, in each country the welfare state arises in a different way, and for differing reasons. This links Esping-Andersen's typological and cross-sectional approach with the institutional and sociological histories of specific welfare states such as those by Baldwin (1991) and Skocpol (1992). As Esping-Andersen points out, in many cases it was the conservatives rather than liberals or socialists who first attacked the commodification of labour. The development of welfare states has in some cases been sought explicitly in order to preserve stability and block the socialist threat by rewarding loyalty and discouraging collective action by wage earners (Esping-Andersen and Korpi, 1984).

Abrahamson (1992, 1999) and Leibfried (1993) use similar typologies to Esping-Andersen, but derive four categories of welfare state, or four social policy regimes in the European Union. For Abrahamson (1992) these are: the Scandinavian model; the liberal model; the corporate model; and the Latin model. Abrahamson argues that the issue is no longer one of state socialism versus market liberalism. All states are in practice engaged in some form of welfare pluralism, and hence comparisons across different European welfare states are about classifying regimes according to the specific combinations of elements in the welfare mix. The three basic elements in the mix are the state, the market and civil society, which comprise the 'welfare triangle'. Furthermore, Abrahamson argues, European welfare systems are converging towards one particular model, the corporate model, which implies a dualistic or stratified rather than universal, egalitarian welfare state:

> Dualisation in this sense means a bifurcated welfare system where the (labour) market takes care of the 'well-to-do' workers through various corporate arrangements and leaves the less privileged groups in society to predominantly local institutions, either in the form of municipalities or private charity. (Abrahamson, 1992, pp. 10–11)

Leibfried (1993) adopts a similar typology, with four types of welfare state: Scandinavian, Bismarckian, Anglo-Saxon, and 'Latin rim'. Scandinavian welfare states have 'modern' welfare regimes, are characterised by full employment, with the welfare state as employer of first resort (especially for women), and imply a right to work.

Bismarckian welfare states have institutional welfare regimes in which the welfare state is compensator of first resort. Both Scandinavian and Bismarckian welfare states have institutionalised concepts of social citizenship. Anglo-Saxon states have residual welfare regimes, with the welfare state as compensator of last resort. The individual's right is to income transfers rather than either to work or to non-means-tested social insurance. Finally, 'Latin rim' countries embody rudimentary welfare regimes in which the welfare state is only a 'semi-institutionalised promise'.

Whether three or four separate models are identified in Europe largely comes down to the question of how to classify the welfare states of Southern Europe. One view is that these welfare states are incomplete or immature versions of the corporatist model (Abrahamson, 1992; Castles, 1995; Kastrougalos, 1996). The clear implication is that over time and with continuing economic development, these welfare states will become full members of the continental-corporatist 'family'. Castles (1995) argues that Southern European countries are 'quite typical members of the Conservative family of nations, which happen to spend less than others in the grouping only because they are poor and have relatively youthful populations'. However, others disagree, and argue for a distinctive South European or Mediterranean model of welfare (Ameda and Sarasa, 1996; Ferrera, 1996; Guillen and Matsaganis, 2000), pointing to specific characteristics of the social and political systems of Southern Europe (see below for further discussion).

Castles and Mitchell (1993) use a different approach. They derive a typology of eighteen OECD countries according to household transfers as a proportion of GDP and 'average benefit equality'. This yields a fourfold classification which groups Canada, Japan, Switzerland and the USA (broadly the 'Anglo-Saxon' or liberal world); Austria, France, Germany, Italy and the Netherlands (the corporatist world); Belgium, Denmark, Norway and Sweden (social democratic); but also a fourth category, comprising Australia, Finland, Ireland, New Zealand and the UK. This latter category fits least well into the Esping-Andersen category, and is termed 'radical'. In an earlier article, a 'radical' welfare regime was defined as one in which 'the welfare goals of poverty amelioration and income equality are pursued through redistributive instruments rather than by high expenditure levels' (Castles and Mitchell, 1990, quoted in Abrahamson, 1999).

Castles and Mitchell (1993) are critical of Esping-Andersen's decision to give relatively low scores to means-tested programmes. They point out that means-tested programmes can, and in some cases do, provide relatively generous replacement ratios and can therefore promote de-commodification. However, this criticism seems misplaced. Esping-Andersen draws a distinction between institutional and Bismarckian regimes which avoid means-testing, and liberal regimes which do not. He does so in order to develop a classification scheme based on *means* rather than *ends*. This classification schema can be kept quite separate from the question of how redistributive or egalitarian each regime is in practice.

In another variant, Glennerster (1999) adds a category of 'labourite selectivist', derived from the work of Castles and Mitchell, to the three Esping-Andersen categories, defining this as 'selective social security with a good safety net and universal health and education which, in total, has a redistributive outcome' (Glennerster, 1999, p. 11). His main point is that the UK has moved from a social-democratic but low-tax model pre-Thatcher, to a liberal model under Thatcher and a labourite selectivist model under Blair.

Inevitably, any attempt at classifying welfare states in this way will be criticised, both in terms of ignoring relevant factors and of eliding differences between states. One of the most important criticisms is made by Lewis (1992). She argues that the key relationships include not just that between work and welfare, but also those between paid work, unpaid work and welfare. The provision of informal care is an important omission, both from Esping-Andersen's typology and from Titmuss's earlier work. While it is untrue to say that Esping-Andersen ignores gender entirely, once gender issues are considered, his typology begins to break down (Lewis, 1992). For example, the Norwegian system's treatment of women primarily as wives and mothers takes it closer to the UK than to its Scandinavian neighbour, Sweden (Leira, 1992).

Esping-Andersen's typology is very much based on the characteristics of the social insurance system in each country. What happens if we look at other aspects of the welfare state? If the focus is on social care, gender issues and the role of women in providing care become central. Nevertheless a basically similar typology emerges if we classify countries according to their social care characteristics (Anttonen and Sipila, 1996). With child benefit, a somewhat different clustering becomes apparent (Gornick *et al.*, 1997; Ditch *et al.*, 1998; Abrahamson, 1999). In my own study of housing policy in Britain,

France and Germany (Kleinman, 1996) I found that ironies abounded. Britain – supposedly the residualist welfare state – had the largest social rented sector; French economic policy was the most orthodoxly neo-liberal; and corporatist Germany had gone furthest in privatising social housing. But none the less, on balance I concluded that the broad distinction between 'Anglo-Saxon' British policy and corporatist French and German policy was a useful one, not only in terms of describing the policies in each country, but also in terms of relating policy and its outcomes to broader political, social and institutional factors.

All the above criticisms are perhaps an unavoidable part of any system of classification. Typologies mean selecting key characteristics that are shared by group members, and ignoring, or downplaying, other characteristics where group members differ. Inevitably, then, there are questions of judgement involved. These various typologies each comprise a set of ideal types. In practice, existing welfare systems may combine elements from more than one ideal type.

A more fundamental attack on the entire welfare modelling business is mounted by Veit-Wilson (2000), who attacks the 'diverse and imprecise meanings' attached to the term 'welfare state'. Veit-Wilson argues that the term welfare state is used as a synonym for all modern industrial states, all of which provide some measure of welfare for their citizens. By contrast, Veit-Wilson is concerned to emphasise the *welfare* part of the welfare state – 'but how much and for whom, the rich or the poor, is to define the distinction between welfare and unwelfare states?' (ibid., p. 5). Following Wedderburn (1965) and Briggs (1961), Veit-Wilson leans towards a 'British' definition of the term, emphasising 'coverage, a minimum real income or the highest standards of provision for *all*' (Veit-Wilson, 2000, p. 12). The defining characteristics of a welfare state should include 'policies to prevent poverty arising for everyone as well as those providing relief for such poverty as occurs' (ibid., p. 11).

If these criteria are applied, the accepted typologies for classifying welfare states are far less relevant. For example, Veit-Wilson quotes an empirical study of OECD countries by Eardley *et al.* (1996), which focused on the range of benefits and services available to guarantee a minimum level of subsistence to those in need. These authors found seven patterns of social assistance schemes and concluded that 'the social assistance regimes tentatively outlined here bear only a distant resemblance to Esping-Andersen's typology of welfare regimes' (Eardley *et al.*, 1996, p. 170).

Veit-Wilson raises a key issue: are welfare state typologies mainly about the *state*, and hence a tool of political science for classifying versions of modern capitalism? Or are they mainly about *welfare*, and the lack of it – a currently unfashionable view, and one that harks back strongly to Titmuss and the importance of values as well as means or even outcomes in social policy. Veit-Wilson is unapologetic in rejecting a value-neutral definition of the welfare state, challenging theorists of the welfare state not just to clarify their definitions and analysis, but also to explain 'what is their use of the term "welfare" and their knowledge *for?*' (Veit-Wilson, 2000, p. 22).

Europe's Four Types of Welfare State

In considering the role of European Union social policy, and the possibility of a European welfare state, it is important to acknowledge the range of existing types of welfare state in Europe. Continuing differences between welfare systems in Europe point to the real political, social and economic underpinnings of individual national welfare states, and are thereby highly relevant to the continuing discussions about the future role of European social policy. With some caveats, it does seem useful to classify the fifteen welfare states in the European Union into four categories: conservative-corporatist; social-democratic; Mediterranean; and Anglo-Saxon.

Conservative-corporatist Welfare States

This first group of countries comprises Germany, France, Italy, Belgium and the Netherlands. In these countries, there is a Bismarck-ian tradition of a strong state managing and incorporating social groups. Contributory social insurance is at the heart of this model. Benefits are financed by contributions from employers and employees as well as from taxation. Status, occupational and income differences are reproduced in the pattern of benefits for unemployment, sickness or old age. Correspondingly, there is relatively little emphasis on redistribution as a goal of social policy.

Service organisation and delivery are pluralistic – that is, non-state or para-state organisations predominate in the administration and distribution of insurance funds, and in providing services. Conserva-tive-corporatist welfare states reflect the influence of Catholic social teaching, particularly the principle of subsidiarity – welfare arrangements should only fall to the state in the absence of adequate measures at some lower or intermediate level, be that through the family, the community, the occupational group or some other aspect of civil society. In other words, there is a hierarchy of solidarities: 'Subsidiarity means that solidarities are hierarchically ordered; the main source of solidarity, or mutual responsibility, is the family, secondarily a community, and so forth; only at a distance are there responsibilities to the state, the international community or "humanity" '(Spicker, 1991, p. 6). In general, then, the model reflects and supports an organic, hierarchical and integrationist view of society, in which family, church and occupational forms of welfare are supplemented by the state, not replaced by it.

Germany is often taken to be the paradigmatic case. In Germany, the social state (*sozialstaat*) is underpinned strongly by the social market economy: 'the state's general commitment to providing income and employment security is complemented by an emphasis on the obligations of private associations or groups (above all employers and trade unions), families and individuals to support themselves' (Ginsburg, 1992, p. 68). Redistribution through the welfare system is mostly horizontal (within occupations and status groups) rather than vertical. Pensions and unemployment benefits reflect occupational and income differences. The short-term unemployed with a full contribution record receive 68 per cent of previous take-home pay for a year (*Arbeitslosengeld*). Those not eligible for this benefit are means tested for *Arbeitslosenhilfe* giving 58 per cent of net pay; the means test is, however, quite severe. A third group are dependent on the much lower levels of flat-rate benefit payable through social assistance (*sozialhilfe*), while it appears that 15–25 per cent of the registered unemployed in the 1980s were not in receipt of any benefit (Ginsburg, 1992, pp. 76–7).

While the core, insurance-based social benefits are relatively generous, social assistance is both harshly means-tested and carries considerable stigma (Mangen, 1991). This has become increasingly important since the 1980s with the rise in unemployment and increased numbers of those who for various reasons, including long-term unemployment and lack of attachment to the labour force for other reasons, do not have contribution records and hence are dependent on social assistance. This is an important aspect of the growth in social exclusion, and the creation of what is often referred to as a 'two-thirds society'; that is, one in which a third of the population is excluded.

Family policy is conservative, generally supporting traditional gender roles. The majority of women with children aged under five are not in the labour force (Ginsburg, 1992) and provision of day care and nursery facilities has traditionally been poor (Lawson, 1996). Moreover, 94 per cent of German schoolchildren finish their school day at 1 pm, with obvious implications for the ability of mothers to go to work (Lawson, 1996). In the past, socialised child care tended to be associated with the state collectivism of the German Democratic Republic, and hence West German social policy reflected a desire to respect the privacy of the family and to bolster traditional values.

Housing policy reflects the principles of the social market economy (Kleinman, 1996). The government takes responsibility for ensuring an adequate standard of housing for all, but this is to be achieved primarily through market rather than state mechanisms. Social housing comprises less than 7 per cent of the housing stock in the western part of Germany, and a major deregulatory measure in the 1980s effectively privatised much of the social rented stock (Harloe, 1995; Kleinman, 1996). More than 40 per cent of houses are rented from private landlords and the owner-occupied sector is much smaller than in Anglo-Saxon countries.

Despite some moves towards neo-liberalism, traditional conservative influences in German social policy remain strong (Mangen, 1991). While there are new pressures on the social system from the rise in unemployment, from demographic changes and from increased social exclusion, the response has been adaptation of the German model, in which social insurance remains the centrepiece, rather than radical reform (Clasen and Gould, 1995; Lawson, 1996). The unemployment and pension insurance schemes were heavily relied upon to manage the social costs of unification, while the introduction of a new compulsory insurance to finance the costs of long-term care in old age, by providing non-means-tested benefits in cash or kind, attests to this. In general, there is an acceptance of, and trust in, the 'social state' in Germany; additionally, there are institutional and organisational features that promote stability, such as the independent corporatist funds and the strong role of the unions, as well as political factors (Clasen and Gould, 1995).

Germany remains a relatively large welfare spender, with considerable public support for a positive state presence in social policy. The German 'middle way' persists, but there are also tensions and pressures. First, the German social state has always been underpinned to some degree by the use of non-citizen migrant labour – *Gastarbeiter*, or 'guestworkers'. Germany has failed to develop a long-term policy towards immigrants and their descendants. Importantly, the Anglo-Saxon term 'ethnic minorities' is rarely used. Even those born in Germany are referred to as *Auslander* ('foreigners'), a term with pejorative connotations and almost exclusively used to refer to non-whites. Until very recently, citizenship was not generally extended to the 4.5 million foreigners in Germany, who represent about 7.5 per cent of the population. Only a very small proportion of foreign workers have become naturalised German citizens. Children of foreigners remained foreigners, and the barriers to naturalisation and citizenship were higher than in other European countries. Nationality was by *jus sang* and not *jus soli*. However, during the 1990s, the situation began to change somewhat. The 1990 Immigration Law made right of abode easier for long-settled foreigners, but without bestowing citizenship. In January 2000, a new citizenship law was passed, which granted German citizenship to all those born in Germany, whatever their parents' status.

More generally, the last two decades of the twentieth century saw a broad process of increased social differentiation in Germany, Unemployment and social exclusion increased, there have been greater regional differences since unification, and the population has become more diverse ethnically. Increased social division has led to greater concerns about the creation of a 'two-thirds, one-third' society.

Crucially, German post-war social policy was founded on the importance of a strong economy. Ludwig Erhard, economics minister from 1949 to 1963 and one of the architects of the post-war German social market system believed strongly that the 'best social policy is an effective economic policy' (quoted in Mangen, 1991, p. 108). For four decades after 1945, the German 'economic miracle' supported by a consensual political system and the *realpolitik* of the Cold war was able to deliver both economic growth and a generous and inclusive social system in the Federal Republic of (West) Germany.

But after 1989, Germany was confronted by a series of new challenges – primarily, of course, unification with the former German Democratic Republic, but also the challenges of globalization and European integration. Economic growth, previously almost a norm, became much more problematic, and unemployment rose. Unemployment reached almost 12 per cent in 1997, before falling to 10.4 per cent in October 1999 (PricewaterhouseCoopers, 2000). OECD projections suggest that unemployment will remain above 8 per cent into 2001 (OECD, 1999a). Containing the costs of the German pensions and health care systems remain key political issues, and there has been some shift towards labour market flexibility and a greater emphasis on active labour market measures (OECD, 1999a).

After sixteen years of Christian Democrat rule under Chancellor Kohl, an SPD–Green coalition was elected in September 1998, with Gerhard Schroder as Chancellor. Schroder has sought to move the SPD in the same general direction as New Labour under Tony Blair – that is, away from interventionism and tax-and-spend policies and towards a more market-orientated and business-friendly approach. So, for example, the June 1999 budget contained measures 'to slash state spending, squeeze pensioners and the unemployed, and give tax breaks to business' (*The Economist*, 26 June 1999). Schroder has echoed directly the 'Third Way' rhetoric of Blair and President Bill Clinton by talking about '*die neue Mitte*' (the 'New Middle') in Germany. However, Germany's corporatist institutions, coalition-based politics and federalist system of checks and balances makes radical change more difficult than in the UK.

The welfare state displays many similar features in France: corporate rather than national solidarity, horizontal rather than vertical redistribution, occupationally based welfare, and plural service delivery (Hantrais, 1996). There is a strong emphasis on social integration, and social security is the centrepiece of social policy arrangements. Recently – that is, since the early 1980s – there has been a move towards greater targeting and redistribution.

The three independent funds (*caisses*) for old age, sickness and family allowances are co-ordinated centrally, but organized regionally. They are run by elected representatives from employers and beneficiaries (Chamberlayne, 1992). Local, regional, religious, occupational and political solidarities are stressed. The system of social protection is very complex, with more than 500 different social security institutions. Moreover, the state's influence on the employers and employees who run these institutions varies considerably (OECD, 1994).

About one in six of French housing stock is social housing, provided by independent HLM (*habitations à loyers modérés*) organisations, which include both government-sponsored (local and regional) and independent companies. Social housing is funded partly by a payroll tax as well as by state direction of savings funds (Kleinman, 1996). Traditionally, the French state played a major role in both setting the price and determining access to loans for owner-occupiers. In the 1980s and 1990s, however, the system moved towards a greater reliance on free market mechanisms.

Family policy has always been very important in France. It has a dominant role within the social security system, and has clear goals: to compensate parents for the costs of children and thereby to promote a high birth rate. French policy has traditionally been pro-natalist, with an emphasis on good mothering, but in the 1970s and 1980s there was an increasing concern with vertical rather than horizontal redistribution, via means testing and reducing the importance of family benefits (Lewis, 1992).

While insurance-based benefits, as in Germany, are relatively generous, until the introduction of the RMI (*Revenu Minimum d'Insertion*), there was no national social assistance safety net (Collins, 1990). Prior to this, individuals without a contribution record, or who had exhausted insurance benefits, had to fall back on local, family, church or charitable support. The RMI provides a basic income, but takes the form of a reciprocal undertaking rather than a welfare benefit. Two-thirds of the target group are childless, and most are men, 'a reminder of the pre-emption of much poverty in France by family policy' (Chamberlayne, 1992, p. 313).

As with Germany, one of the dominant trends since the mid-1970s has been the growth in unemployment, in less secure forms of work (*précarité*) and in other types of social exclusion. New poverty is linked to the issues of intermittent wages, long-term unemployed who fall out of the insurance based system, and the problems of the young unemployed without an adequate contribution record. Typical of the French importance given to social integration are the mechanisms accompanying RMI, which stress solidarity, reciprocity, and contractual commitments. Housing policy too has traditionally been characterised by notions of social housing acting as an integrating or acculturating force, rather than as the response to a legally recognised need.

More generally, the specifically French concepts of republican citizenship and identity are important in understanding French social policy. The state is an active force, not just in the economy, but in civil society too, promoting integration and acculturation to a clearly defined, even monolithic, French identity: '[French] ideology emphasizes the assimilation of regional, national and religious cultures into a distinctive conception of citizenship and national civilization actively promoted by the state. Republicanism is far more intolerant of diversity in public life than American pluralism' (Silver, 1993, p. 346).

Since 1983, when the Mitterand government abandoned 'Keynesianism in one country', the French state has pursued orthodox monetary and fiscal policies rigorously, based around the notions of the *'franc fort'* and competitive disinflation. This strategy, aimed at the twin goals of domestic competitiveness and low inflation, and externally, the attainment of the Maastricht convergence criteria, has been adhered to despite the human and political costs in terms of permanently high unemployment and stagnant living standards for the majority of French citizens: 'The leader who deserves the monetarist palm is François Mitterand ... Mr. Mitterand's Socialist government allowed real wages to rise by less than 6 per cent between 1983 and 1989 ... Perhaps the main policy legacy of the 1980s will turn out to be neither "Reaganism" not "Thatcherism", but "Mitterandism"' (*Financial Times*, 20 April 1990, quoted in Halimi *et al.* 1994).

In terms of the economic and social policy of the European Union, this has indeed turned out to be true. The French experience of the failure of domestic Keynesianism and the subsequent turn towards economic orthodoxy and the market had a profound effect on EU economic and social policies over the next twenty years. Domestically, the result in terms of social policy has been a more differentiated system in which there are three tiers of people:

> the employed in secure jobs, covered by comprehensive insurance schemes and earning additional cover from contributions to mutual societies' higher occupational pensions; those employed in less secure jobs without additional schemes to top up benefits; the long-term unemployed or never employed dependent on a minimum income or national assistance which fall through the insurance net. (Hantrais, 1996, p. 68)

The French economy, after a poor performance in the early 1990s, grew strongly after 1996. In 2000, the OECD commented that 'France has not enjoyed such a favourable economic situation for ten years ... the French economy benefitted from rapidly growing activity, low inflation and growth that was richer in jobs ... This stems from continuing wage moderation, the policies of cutting social contributions for unskilled workers, and the development of more flexible contracts of employment.' (OECD, 2000). Nevertheless, unemployment remains high, only recently falling below 10 per cent and remaining close to 9 per cent at the end of 2000. Reducing structural unemployment is a key priority. The socialist government of Lionel Jospin has consistently defended the 'European social model' and rejected American, or even New Labour, solutions of promoting free markets and labour flexibility. However, in practice, the French approach has been a judicious mix of traditional state-centred social and economic policies with more deregulatory measures. Since coming to power in June 1997, Jospin totally or partly privatised more companies than his four predecessors combined: 'The trends are clear: privatisation, decentralisation, entrepreneurship, multiculturalism, a weaker state, lower taxes, a pared-down public sector, and a more collegial European identity in place of *l'exception française* and the universal sense of mission that have heretofore defined France's place in the world' (*Time*, 12 June 2000). France has become more 'liberal', even more 'Anglo-Saxon' in terms of its economic and business orientation, while at the same time concerned to defend its social policy and welfare system: 'No one now contests the free market, but we still need rules and institutions. We say the free market is okay, but it's still not okay for society to be organized only by the market' (former Finance Minister D. Strauss-Kahn, quoted in *Time*, 12 June 2000).

Italy occupies a somewhat ambiguous position, sometimes included in the group of conservative-corporatist nations, and sometimes included with the Mediterranean or 'Latin rim' nations. It is usually, included in the corporatist camp, perhaps because of its status as one of the founding six EEC nations. As we saw above, this ambiguity poses no problems for Castles (1995), as he includes the Mediterranean countries within the conservative 'family' of nations. Perhaps part of the answer lies in the regional variation within Italy itself; that is, in the political and economic differences between the 'core' north and the peripheral Mezzogiorno.

The Italian welfare state comprises a very fragmented system, with strong clientelistic attributes (Saraceno and Negri, 1994; Niero, 1996). Social security is occupationally based, while local authorities are responsible for providing means-tested social assistance. However, a national health service financed by a combination of taxation, contributions and user charges was set up in 1978. Under a combination of internal pressures for reform, and the external constraints imposed by the Maastricht Treaty and convergence criteria, attention has been focused in recent years on improving administrative capacity, and promoting greater efficiency and value for money.

Social Democratic Welfare States

In these welfare states, the principles of universalism and de-commo-dification of social rights were extended to the 'new middle classes'. The welfare state was to promote not equal but minimum needs, as elsewhere, but rather equal and high standards of welfare for all: 'This implies, first, that services and benefits be upgraded to levels commensurate with even the most discriminating tastes of the new middle classes; and, second, that equality be furnished by guaranteeing workers full participation in the quality of rights enjoyed by the better-off' (Esping-Andersen, 1990, p. 27). Social democratic welfare states are hence characterised by high levels of services and benefits in which manual workers participate fully, having the same rights as white-collar employees. The costs of parenthood are socialised, women are allowed to choose to work outside the home, and there is a consequent heavy social service burden to allow this to happen.

Work and welfare are closely connected in this model. There is a guarantee of full employment, not just because the system is committed to it politically, but also because the system in fact depends on having as high a proportion of the adult population as possible working, in order to maximise revenue and minimise outlays. In addition, of course, the state's responsibilities for provision of child care and other social services increases demand for labour, especially for female labour in order to staff, administer and manage these services.

There is no single pure case of the social democratic model, although the Scandinavian countries are closest to it. Furthermore, there are also important differences between Scandinavian countries. For example, Norway and Finland have lower expenditure than Sweden and Denmark (Parry, 1995), and as we saw above, there are differences between Norway and Sweden in terms of assumed gender roles.

Sweden has attracted considerable research attention for several decades 'because of its pioneering role in promoting state welfare while preserving a benign climate for industrial capitalism.' (Parry, 1995, p. 384). The four pillars of the Swedish approach have been identified as:

(A) a tradition of broad popular social entitlements – coming from the force of an independent peasantry – instead of segmented corporatist rights or charity concern with poverty, (B) a sharp segmentation between high personal and low corporate taxation, (C) cautious and competent state management and (D) employer-union co-operation. (Pfaller *et al.*, 1990, p. 269)

In Sweden, the social democratic project became the national project (Heclo and Madsen, 1987). Social Democratic governments were in power from 1932 to 1976. Bourgeois coalitions elected in 1976 and 1979 had little impact on the welfare state, and Social Democrats were returned in 1982, 1985 and 1988. In the 1980s, those on social insurance benefits continued to have high living standards. Coupled with housing benefits and subsidised social services, this meant that Swedish pensioners were no worse off in retirement compared with when they were working (Gould, 1996).

Other social services were provided to a high standard. Child care was subsidised, and parental leave included insurance at an income replacement level of 90 per cent. Four out of five adult women were in the labour force, and their pay rates were only 15 per cent below those of men. Health indices were very good (Gould, 1996). Unemployment remained very low, unemployment benefits were good, and active labour market policies assisted those without jobs into finding them.

As a result, tax levels in Sweden were extremely high, the public sector employed more than 30 per cent of the workforce, and represented 60 per cent of GDP. In 1990, Sweden was still the most decommodified welfare state in Europe. Events then began to catch up, with recession, inflation and sharp losses in manufacturing employment (Gould, 1996). In 1991, the Social Democrats lost power to a Bourgeois coalition committed to a 'system shift'. However, in practice, political and institutional factors meant that incremental rather than drastic change was the fate of the Swedish welfare state (Clasen and Gould, 1995; Gould, 1996). This meant cuts in services and benefits, and greater welfare pluralism instead of universal state provision. As a result, the high income replacement levels of social insurance have fallen from 90 per cent to 80 per cent, and eligibility has been tightened. There has been growth of private, semi-private and co-operative provision of social services. Inequality has increased as a result, but not to the degree found elsewhere in Europe.

By the end of the 1980s, Sweden's economy had recovered and its generous and extensive welfare state had survived. The turnaround in the Swedish economy in the 1990s was achieved by modifying not abolishing its welfare state, which remains extremely generous (Hirst, 1998). Sweden has thus been able to maintain an expanding economy and high labour force participation rates as well as comprehensive and institutional welfare provision.

Overall then, there have been some substantial changes, but no fundamental alteration to the basic welfare model. Why has this been? Clasen and Gould (1995) point to four factors. First, the Centre–Right coalition was never itself strong enough to implement fundamental changes. Second, there were objections from the Minister of Health and Social Affairs. Third, the Swedish system of three-year mandates (now extended to four) makes radical change difficult. Fourth, and most importantly, social democracy has become part of the fabric of the Swedish nation. The state is seen as a natural providing agency: 'Scandinavians do not, in fact, have many feelings towards the state at all ... The state ... is a tool' (B. R. Andersen, quoted in Clasen and Gould, 1995). Unlike both the *laissez-faire* (Anglo-Saxon) or subsidiarity (conservative) traditions, both of which require justifications for state intervention, the tradition in Sweden is solidaristic. Support for the 'Swedish model' remains strong, even if the economic environment has become more hostile.

Denmark started later than Sweden on the path of social democratic welfare but at the time of writing has an equally high level of welfare. In the 1980s it too experienced high unemployment, sluggish growth and some cutbacks in welfare state provision (Hirst, 1998). But since the early 1990s, there has been a strong economic recovery and public support for the welfare state remains high. Hirst (1998) points to several relevant factors. The welfare system supports economic flexibility by combining high out-of-work benefits with relatively low employment protection. In addition, because unemployment benefits and basic pensions are funded out of general taxation, the Danish system avoids some of the drawbacks of corporatist welfare systems that link benefits closely to an individual's existing job. The universalism of the benefits system also sustains broad political support, avoids the social exclusion associated with more residualist systems, and enabled Denmark to resist the trend towards greater income inequality in the 1980s and 1990s.

Perhaps most importantly, these different aspects of the system support and reinforce each other. In effect a high expenditure/service equilibrium can be sustained:

> The Danes have a very high level of collective and public service consumption – for example, the widely available public day care that enables dual-income families to function, and good public

transport. Given a high level of income equality and ready access to good public services and universalist benefits, most citizens irrespective of income or occupation are consumers of public services and benefit from them. Hence the viability of a high-tax high-service regime. (Hirst, 1998)

Additionally, the diffused nature of political power makes radical change to the welfare system difficult, in contrast with both the UK and New Zealand, which have 'first-past-the post' and centralised political systems. In a universalist and politically decentralised system such as this, solidaristic behaviour is not self-sacrificing altruism, but rather 'a rational choice' (Hirst, 1998).

In the Netherlands, the welfare state has been shaped by the relationships between classes and religious groups (Terhorst and van den Ven, 1997). In the nineteenth century, these cleavages led to political stalemate that later gave way to a unique political and social solution called 'pillarisation'. This term refers to the fact that each major secular and religious group developed its own structure of social service, within an overall state framework but retaining a considerable degree of independence (Harloe, 1995, p. 26). Pillarisation both implies and depends on social and religious consensus:

> the religious map of the Netherlands has been spotted like the skin of a panther. Religious minorities have been scattered over the country ever since the Reformation preventing a territorially based solution to the 'social question'. The only alternative then was pillarisation. But pillarisation can only be successful if there is an agreement on a variety of interrelated fields. There must not only be consensus between 'pillars' but also between classes because the higher classes have to agree with a progressive tax system. (Terhorst and van der Ven, 1999, p. 16)

In the 1980s, the Netherlands fell victim to 'Dutch disease': unemployment (including hidden non-employment) reached 27 per cent of the labour force, state finances were deteriorating rapidly, and the country slid from sixth to sixteenth position in the OECD ranking of per capita income (Terhorst and van der Ven, 1999). The Netherlands appeared to be 'a classic example of the defects of a continental welfare model' (Hirst, 1998). But since then the situation has changed rapidly. In the 1990s the country has experienced strong and steady economic growth, the highest jobs growth in the EU, declining unemployment, a falling ratio of public debt to GDP, growing private sector profitability, and a lower tax burden (Terhorst and van der Ven, 1999). How has this come about?

Several factors are relevant (Visser and Hemerijck, 1997; Hirst, 1998; Terhorst and van der Ven, 1999). At the end of 1982, capital and labour agreed the 'Wassenaar Accord' under which labour agreed to moderate demands for higher wages as long as large-scale unemployment prevailed. State expenditure was cut, although in a controlled manner so that there were no concentrated severe impacts on specific social groups. Reforms were undertaken to reduce labour market rigidities.

Employment growth in the Netherlands averaged 1.8 per cent between 1983 and 1993, compared to only 0.4 per cent average in the EU (Hirst, 1998). Most of the new jobs were temporary, part-time or less than 35 hours; most were in services. The female participation rate grew, with women's employment rising from 35 per cent of the labour force in 1983 to 55 per cent in 1996; hence 'the Netherlands has switched from a single breadwinner family-centred employment pattern to a 1.5 jobs per family pattern' (Hirst, 1998).

As with Denmark and Sweden, the Netherlands has experienced modifications to, rather than abolition of, the basic social-democratic welfare model:

> although these policies meant a clear break with the past, they did neither result in a demolition of the welfare state nor in a fast transition of 'organised' to 'disorganised' capitalism. The transition from Keynesianism to monetarism took a longer time in the Netherlands than in many other countries, was less celebrated by its victors and less hard on its victims. (Terhorst and van der Ven, 1999, p. 25)

The Mediterranean Model

The term 'Mediterranean model' is preferred to that of 'Latin rim', as the latter is somewhat patronising and also inaccurate. Core and periphery may be appropriate terms to use when analysing the economic development of Europe, because geographical proximity to markets and factors of production is one important variable (although only one among several) affecting the level and pace of economic development. However, the terminology is inappropriate when categorising welfare states. This is not a question of political correctness, but of good research practice. To use the term 'rim' immediately implies that such welfare states are peripheral (to what? other welfare states? their own citizens?), and that they are backward with respect to other welfare states in Europe. It is a short step from here to the notion that these are primitive or embryonic welfare states that will in time develop into fully-fledged welfare states of another type. This notion may, in fact, be true – but it is a hypothesis to be investigated, not an *a priori* truth, and the nomenclature should reflect that.

This is, in fact, Leibfried's (1993) hypothesis. He argues that the welfare states of Spain, Portugal, Greece and 'to some extent (southern) Italy' can be characterised as 'rudimentary welfare states'. While many of these countries have made strong promises of a modern welfare state in their constitutions, these constitutional commitments are not backed by legal, institutional or social implementation. Leibfried concludes that the 'Latin rim' is characterised by 'catching up; welfare state as semi-institutionalised promise'. Furthermore, 'The development of "normal welfare systems" seems most likely – normal in the sense of the Northern European or German welfare model' (Leibfried, 1993, p. 142). However, more recent studies argue for the existence of a specifically Mediterranean model of welfare (Ferrera, 1996) and specifically criticise the traditional view of social welfare in southern Europe as being 'rudimentary' (Guillen and Matsaganis, 2000).

What are the characteristics of the Mediterranean model? First, in terms of income maintenance, these welfare states are not only highly fragmented, especially Italy and Greece, but are also characterised by strong internal polarisation (Ferrera, 1996). That is, while there is no minimum income scheme in Italy, Spain, Portugal or Greece, retirement benefits for those who do qualify are extremely generous. As a proportion of income, these benefits are, in fact, the highest in Europe. So in these welfare states there is a class of 'hyper-protected' workers, including public employees, white-collar workers and private sector workers on full contracts that exists alongside large numbers of underprotected individuals, particularly informal and irregular workers, the young, and the long-term unemployed. Hence the notion of these welfare states as being rudimentary or underdeveloped is only part of a more complex picture. The family is an important institution in this context. The southern European family acts as a 'social clearing house' – it is important that at least one family member is employed in the 'guarantismo' (protected) sector, for the good of all family members (Ferrera, 1996).

Second, in Mediterranean welfare states there has been some departure from corporatism through the creation of national health systems on universalistic principles. All four countries have reformed health care in this direction since the 1980s, with the most successful being Italy. None of these countries, however, have health systems financed through taxation along the lines of the UK and Scandinavia. Instead, they rely on contributions, although all four countries have stated the objective of shifting the burden away from contributions. In practice, then, there are occupationally – and territorially – based differences in health care.

Third, there is a low degree of state activity in the welfare sector. Moreover, state activity has not led not to a reduction in private-sector activity, but rather to 'public/private collusion', often involving massive waste and inefficiency.

Fourth, these welfare states are clientelistic and particularistic. This includes straightforward political corruption, but more typically political clientelism, trading favours for votes. These can be distinguished from the 'pork barrel' politics that, of course, exist almost everywhere, because of the individual nature of the arrangements. State transfers are exchanged for party support, often via trade unions. There is strong evidence for this in Italy, and while systematic comparative evidence does not exist, there are indications that the situation in similar in the other three countries (Ferrera, 1996, p. 27).

Ferrera (1996) concludes that the southern European welfare state is a distinctive model. While formally it resembles other 'corporatist' (and Catholic) countries, there is a different 'socio political etiquette'. These welfare regimes are not embedded in open universalistic political cultures with solid, impartial Weberian state bureaucracies. They are closed, particularist cultures with relatively weak state apparatuses. The reasons for this particular development are several: persistent economic and political 'backwardness'; sectoral and territorial dualism; amoral familism; a strong Catholic church and a weak political left; weak state institutions, especially in regard to bureaucratic professionalism and autonomy; the prominence of political parties in the absence or atrophy of other institutions of civil society; and ideological polarisation with a maximalist and divided political Left.

In Greece and Spain since the 1980s social policy has been expansionary, in terms both of expenditure and measures. Guillen and

Matsaganis (2000) explain this by reference to three main factors: the legitimation needs of government in the period of transition to democracy; the fact that Left-wing parties were in office for long periods in both countries; and the impact of EU recommendations and 'demonstration effects'. The Southern European welfare model is not a 'lagging' version of continental corporatism, but rather is characterised by serious imbalances, inequities and inefficiencies. While coverage is patchy, there are classes of 'overprotected' workers, and hence a sharp distinction between insiders and outsiders. In these circumstances, it is not useful to think in terms of 'expansion' versus 'retrenchment'. Rather, 'reform is not necessarily a threat to glorious past achievements but becomes an opportunity to promote social justice and a more inclusive society' (Guillen and Matsaganis, 2000, p. 141). The period of welfare state expansion has now come to an end, and current issues are more about *qualitative* change.

In Spain in the early 1980s, the main areas of provision were cash benefits, health care, social housing, and education, with only limited social care services (Almeda and Sarasa, 1996). Social security was earnings-related and contributory, and organised entirely though central government. Social insurance rights depended on occupational status, as in the Bismarckian model, so that different types of worker received different benefits. The regime was regressive, in that workers on average incomes subsidised the benefits and services of better-off groups. In addition, specific categories such as clergy and international civil servants were incorporated on favourable terms; 'an indication of the importance of "clientelist" social relations in Mediterranean welfare regimes' (Almeda and Sarasa, 1996, p. 156).

Family policy sought to bolster and protect the traditional family, with the assumption that married women should not work outside the home. Hence there were benefits for wives who did not work outside the home, maternity benefits, child benefits and 'birth awards', which rewarded large families. In addition, families under financial pressure could get additional benefits. As a result, for some working-class families, benefits through these schemes might be greater than earned income (Almeda and Sarasa, 1996).

Health care was provided through four systems: social insurance, private, occupational and charitable. The result was a mixed and uncoordinated system. Reforms in the 1980s sought to rationalise and co-ordinate provision more.

Spain suffered badly in the 1970s recession. In the 1980s, the Socialist government moved towards orthodox neo-liberal economic policies to reduce inflation, increase profitability and liberalise the economic system. Inflation fell and the external balance of payments improved, but unemployment rose rapidly. Spain has a chronic unemployment problem. The unemployment rate rose to 24.1 per cent at the end of 1994, before falling to 15.4 per cent in November 1999. However, this remains the highest unemployment rate in the EU (PricewaterhouseCoopers, 2000). Fertility rates have fallen rapidly, so that Spain now has the lowest fertility in Europe. Marriage rates have also fallen, but, unlike most of the rest of Europe, this has not been offset by increases in cohabitation. There are relatively few unmarried mothers and other lone parents in Spain in comparison with other European countries.

Between 1980 and 1990, social spending grew more rapidly in Spain than the EU average. Universal pensions and health care were established, education and unemployment benefits were improved, and a national social assistance schemed began to be created. Emerging problems were similar to the rest of Europe: persistent long-term unemployment, and increased flexibility of labour markets leading to various forms of insecure work, and hence lack of social insurance rights and the consequent need for social assistance. Further strains are being imposed by the perceived need to meet the Maastricht criteria.

The demographic changes caused by rapidly falling fertility rates in Spain and other southern European countries are having profound effects. As well as the immediate impacts on, for example dependency ratios and pension financing, the continuing 'demographic deficit' means that these southern European states are now countries of immigration, not emigration. Whereas in previous decades, southern Europe exported its surplus labour to the more prosperous economies to the north, now it is importing labour from the less developed countries to the south and east. Southern Europe countries are in the process of adjusting to becoming more diverse and multi-racial, a process with long-term and important changes, not just for social policies but also more widely for the politics and social practices of these countries.

The Anglo-Saxon Welfare State

In practice, within the EU this effectively means just the United Kingdom. The Republic of Ireland has some similarities with the UK

– unsurprisingly, given the colonialist history and continuing close contacts between the two countries. But in other respects it might be included with the Mediterranean countries (smaller role for state welfare, rapid economic growth within the EU) or with the corporatist countries, as does Esping-Andersen (1990, p. 85).

However, defining the UK as an 'Anglo-Saxon' welfare model, in the same category as the United States, is to ignore significant differences between the UK and the USA. Britain, as both Esping-Andersen (1990) and Abrahamson (1992) allow, represents something of a hybrid or anomalous case in the typology of welfare states. The British welfare state was, of course, founded on the universalist principles of the Beveridge model. There is a wide range of contributory benefits, the National Health Service (NHS) has since 1948 provided a tax-financed universalist service, and there is an almost unique system of publicly owned council housing that at its peak accommodated one in three of the population. Expenditure on social protection in the UK in 1997 was 26.8 per cent of GDP, only slightly below the EU average (28.2 per cent). Using OECD definitions, total UK government spending was 40.1 per cent of GDP in 1998, much lower than most OECD countries, but well above the US figure of 30.5 per cent (Institute for Fiscal Studies 1999?). Given these facts, it is over-simplistic to categorise the British welfare state simply as a minimalist, liberal safety net.

However, in practice, the real value of contributory benefits have been eroded, and entitlement has been reduced progressively, so that larger and larger proportions of the population have become dependent on various forms of social assistance. Indeed, the insurance element in British social security has become almost entirely fictive, with National Insurance contributions effectively becoming part of the tax system (a regressive part in fact).

Poverty and social exclusion have grown rapidly in Britain since the 1980s. The proportion of the population living in households below 50 per cent of average (mean) income rose from 10 per cent in 1979–80 to 25 per cent in 1996–7 (Department of Social Security, 1999). In particular, there has been a large increase in the numbers of working-age households where no one is working, with the proportion doubling between the end of the 1970s and the end of the 1990s. This has been driven both by a fall in male unemployment rates and by a rise in single adults, including lone parent families. In the UK almost 20 per cent of children are growing up in households with no working adults, compared with 10 per cent or less in Spain, the

Netherlands, France, Germany, Italy, Greece and Portugal. Teenage birth rates are higher and education participation rates lower by comparison with other EU countries (Department of Social Security, 1999, p. 30). Income inequality rose faster in the UK between 1977 and 1990 than in any other country except New Zealand (Rowntree Foundation, 1995).

In education, universal – and, from the 1960s, comprehensive – education coexisted with a small, but politically and socially significant private sector, to which most of the political and economic elite sent their children. Private health care grew, and more importantly, inequalities in health care provision, both geographically and across specialisms, persisted. In housing, the council housing sector, which in the inter-war and immediate post-war period housed skilled workers and other intermediate social groups, became increasingly residualised, housing only the poorest and those with no other choice (Kleinman, 1996)

Hence, there has always been a strong element of 'latent dualism' in the British system. Esping-Andersen (1990) sees one cause of this, ironically, as being the Beveridge principle of flat-rate universalism:

> with growing working-class prosperity and the rise of the new middle classes, flat-rate universalism inadvertently promotes dualism because the better-off turn to private insurance and to fringe-benefit bargaining to supplement modest equality with what they have decided are accustomed standards of welfare. Where this process unfolds (as in Canada or Great Britain) the result is that the wonderfully egalitarian spirit of universalism turns into a dualism similar to that of the social-assistance state: the poor rely on the state, and the remainder on the market. (Esping-Andersen, 1990, p. 25)

This latent dualism pre-dates and cannot be reduced to, 'Thatcherism'. Unlike other EU countries, the extent and direction of change in Britain since the 1970s are probably sufficient for it to be described as a regime shift in the direction of a liberal, residual welfare state. There have been cuts in national insurance benefits, the abolition of the link between the state pension and average earnings, incentives to transfer to private pensions, and cuts in entitlements to unemployment and disability benefits. From 1995, unemployment benefit was replaced by a 'Jobseeker's Allowance', limited to six months and with strong behavioural conditions: 'As a result of these changes, claimants of working age have been shifted towards the large assistance scheme and retired claimants toward the private and occupational sector' (Taylor-Gooby, 1996, p. 210).

In terms of pensions policy, the growth of private and occupational schemes, the cutting of the link of the basic state pension to earnings and the incentives given to people to leave SERPS (state earnings-related pension scheme) and take out private pensions, have together combined to shift pensions increasingly from the public to the private sector. By the mid-1990s, over half of all pension income was private (Glennerster and Le Grand, 1995).

Clasen and Gould (1995) compare changes in Britain with changes in the paradigmatic corporatist and social democratic states of Germany and Sweden. In Britain, they argue, there has been a system shift, with changes in health care, education and social care, from the principles and practices of the Beveridgean welfare state set up after the Second World War. There has been a move to a liberal welfare system. By contrast, in Germany and Sweden there has been a retrenchment but no system shift. Welfare institutions, characteristics and structures are more robust in these countries than in Britain (Clasen and Gould, 1995). Ironically, the lack of pluralism in the British welfare system – its state-centric nature – has made it more rather than less vulnerable to radical change. The different trajectory of the British welfare state since the 1980s is therefore no accident, but rather is linked to specific characteristics of the British polity: centralisation, the Westminster model, first-past-the-post elections, the two-party system, and the lack of countervailing regional, association and institutional sources of power.

But is it accurate to speak of *regime change* in Britain? Can a country in which the government spends around 40 per cent of GDP, most of it on the welfare state; in which a quarter of the population live in social housing; and in which health care is still (mostly) free at the point of use really be described as a 'liberal welfare regime'? British social policy in the 1980s was dominated by radical rhetoric from government. In practice, there were as many continuities as radical shifts. Certainly, with the single exception of the sale of council housing, the main policy trend in the 1980s and 1990s was not true privatisation, but rather the introduction of quasi-markets. Quasi-markets refer to a form of welfare pluralism in which the state pays for and regulates social services, while provision is undertaken by a range of private and voluntary organisations (Le Grand and Bartlett, 1993; Glennerster and Le Grand, 1995).

Internal markets were introduced into the National Health Service and into the provision of social care. Under the Conservatives, schools were encouraged to 'opt-out' of local authority control, and a National Curriculum was introduced. Both of these measures strengthened the influence of central government. Much of post-16 education was moved out of local government control to independent management with a strong representation of business interests. But at the same time, state influence over the universities, both directly in terms of funding and indirectly in terms of curriculum, was increased. In housing policy, true privatisation occurred with the sale of a quarter of the council housing stock to its tenants. For the remaining social rented sector, transfer to independent, but non-profit, landlords was encouraged in a variety of ways (Kleinman, 1996).

In general, then, the effect of the 1980s reforms in the British welfare state has been to create quasi-markets rather than to privatise. A significant development has been the growth of the 'unelected state' or 'quangocracy' in the Thatcher and Major years, by which functions and spending were transferred from democratically elected local bodies to unelected quangos appointed by, and responsible to, government ministers. By the 1990s, there were over 17 000 members of UK appointed bodies, including NHS purchasing agents and trusts, housing action trusts, training and enterprise councils, grant-maintained schools and many others, compared with approximately 25 000 elected local councillors. Moreover, the appointed bodies accounted for about 20 per cent of all public expenditure, compared with 25 per cent by local authorities (Skelcher and Stewart, 1993).

With the election of New Labour in 1997, there was a complex pattern of continuities with, and differences from, the previous administration. Public spending in the first three years was kept under tight control, with Chancellor of the Exchequer Gordon Brown proving himself to be, if anything, more fiscally orthodox than his conservative predecessors. Public spending fell from 41.2 per cent of GDP in 1996–7 to 38.9 per cent in 1998–9 and is planned to fall further to 36.9 per cent in 2001. Spending over the term of New Labour's first Parliament will average 39.4 per cent of GDP, compared with 43.0 per cent over the Conservative administration of 1992–7 and 44.0 per cent over the period 1979–97 (Institute for Fiscal Studies, 1999). But the IFS cautions that this does not provide concrete evidence that the New Labour government is a low spender: the role of government has changed, with some expenditure transferred from the public to the private sector; the impact of the economic cycle distorts the figures; and the distinction between government spending and tax relief is not always clear. Moreover, in its second Comprehensive Spending Review, the government indicated a more generous approach to public expenditure, with particular emphasis on raising real spending on health and education. On these projections, total public spending will rise to 40.5 per cent of GDP by the end of the review period in 2003–4.

A very strong theme of the New Labour government is the imposition of target setting, performance measures and evaluation of both outputs and outcomes on the public sector. Hence increases in expenditure on welfare services are linked to the achievement of specified targets, and to demonstrated efficiency and economy in meeting need. Schools, hospitals and other organisations are expected to 'compete' in terms of having their performance measured against that of their peers, and, increasingly, having funding streams dependent on successful performance.

The British welfare state is a distinctive model. It is certainly important to distinguish it from the other three models we have considered. However, whether it can be described as unproblematically an 'Anglo-Saxon' or a liberal welfare regime is, at the very least, debatable. Glennerster (1999) argues that the Thatcher governments shifted the UK from a social-democratic regime to a liberal one, but under Blair, the UK is shifting again to a 'labourite selectivist' regime, akin to Australia and New Zealand. Putting the UK in a category with Australia and New Zealand suggests, of course, an 'Anglo-Saxon' regime, but in a somewhat difference sense to that intended by Esping-Andersen and others.

Is There a 'European Social Model'?

In Chapter 1 we saw that there was no evidence that European welfare states were converging downwards. Here we have seen that European welfare states retain distinctive characteristics and can, to some degree at least, be grouped into sets whose members bear a family resemblance. A clear conclusion is that institutions still matter 'tremendously' and are an important countervailing, divergent force against the common pressures from demographic, economic, family and labour market changes in welfare states (Esping-Andersen, 1996). In most cases, there have been only modest rollbacks in the welfare state, and social expenditure levels have remained fairly stable. There has not been radical change, but rather a 'frozen' welfare state landscape. Most Northern European welfare states have not deregulated radically, but have trimmed benefits at the margin, stabilised expenditure and cautiously introduced greater flexibility. Southern European welfare states have expanded in both coverage and expenditure. The notion of a welfare state crisis has been exaggerated. There has been no general trend to scale back spending, although the 'steering capacity' of the state has been constrained (Rhodes, 1995, 1998).

Developments in several European countries have confounded the views of 'welfare pessimists'. In several of the highest-spending social-democratic countries, after a period of recession and welfare cutbacks, economic recovery has been combined with the maintenance of reformed, but nevertheless generous and extensive, welfare states. This very quick review of the outlines of different European welfare states demonstrates the importance of history, values and institutions in understanding the trajectories of national welfare states. These differences are difficult to capture in schematic typologies. Nevertheless, it seems useful to indicate the main family groupings – there is a point to the welfare modelling business.

It follows from our analysis that one cannot speak of a single 'European Social Model'. Rather, there is a range of different European social models in existence. As there is no single European model, it logically follows that the idea that European Social Policy is about 'defending' a European Social Model against, say, globalization, is logically inconsistent. Rather, what European (supra-national) social policy seeks to do is to *create* a European social model – either by synthesising aspects of all four models or (more realistically) by imposing one model on all. In an analogous way to the national myths that create and sustain both nationalism and nations, the idea of a 'European Social Model' should be considered perhaps as a founding myth which helps to create (not defend) the concept and reality of 'Europeanism' and a politically integrated Europe.

3

Globalization and the Welfare State

Understanding Globalization

Globalization is often referred to as a key factor promoting both retrenchment of welfare states and their convergence. As we saw in the previous two chapters, there is little evidence for either retrenchment or convergence of European welfare states. Globalization does add an additional constraint on the ability of national governments to formulate and implement welfare systems – but it is one factor among a series of internal and external constraints. Despite the supposed importance of globalization as a causal factor, an exact definition of the term is often lacking. Atkinson (1998a) identifies at least six possible meanings:

(a) the globalization of capital markets and free movement of capital;
(b) the spread of technology and the transfer of production to newly industrializing countries (NICs);
(c) increased competition from NIC imports;
(d) increased competition between OECD countries;
(e) greater pressure on *national* governments from fiscal and other policies of their neighbours; and
(f) greater homogeneity of consumer tastes.

In practice, much of the debate around globalization and the welfare state seems to be concerned mainly with the growth of competition for goods and services on a world scale, and the increased mobility of capital facilitated both by the lowering of national economic and financial barriers and the development of new technologies. These phenomena, it is often argued, create pressures on social protection systems in two ways.

First, it is argued that social protection imposes costs on domestic producers (either through taxes or through employer contributions), which raise the price of manufactured products above that prevailing in countries with less generous social protection systems. Domestic producers hence lose their share both of world and (no longer protected) home markets. This leads to reduced profits, and ultimately to loss of economic activity and higher unemployment. Second, countries with high taxes and/or highly regulated labour markets are less attractive to footloose international capital, and hence will suffer a relative, and eventually absolute, decline in investment. Conversely, countries with lower taxes and a deregulated labour market possess a 'competitive advantage' and will enjoy high levels of inward investment, lower unemployment and greater economic activity. As a consequence of both these factors, states are now engaged in a game of what is called in this literature 'competitive retrenchment', in which social protection systems are bid down by the market pressure of international competition:

> [it] remains true that the social market model – in both the Japanese and the European variant- is under threat from globalization ... It appears that a purely *national* defence of the achievements of social reforms won during the golden age is no longer sufficient ... in a globalized economy, governments must be lean and mean. The competition to become more competitive, in short competitive austerity, means a downward slide in standards of social protection. (Mishra, 1998)

> Countries striving for comparative advantage [*sic*] in sectoral niches of an encompassing international market tend to treat their *social regimes* as part of an economic infrastructure that they may find necessary or expedient to revise in support of their respective productive specialization. (Streeck, 1999)

This argument has been repeated so often that it is now almost a commonplace. However, as Stephen Jay Gould once wrote, 'Few arguments are more dangerous than the ones that "feel" right but can't be justified' (Gould, 1981, p. 157). Globalization, and in particular the increase in trade with newly industrialising (low-wage) economies, has been held responsible for several of the problems afflicting the major advanced nations. In particular, it is often argued – or more commonly, simply assumed or implied that:

(i)   in a globalized system, the prosperity of Europe depends on the 'competitiveness' of its national economies;
(ii) 'unfair competition' from low-wage countries is responsible for rising unemployment, lowered prosperity and increased wage inequality in Europe and the USA; and
(iii) globalization makes generous welfare states of the European type unviable because they undermine 'national competitiveness'. In an effort to enhance 'competitiveness', countries engage in 'social dumping', leading to a process of competitive deregulation – a 'race to the bottom'.

In this chapter, I aim to show that each of these statements is incorrect. First, the level of economic welfare in Europe (or anywhere else) depends fundamentally on productivity not on 'competitiveness'. Indeed, it is by no means clear exactly what is meant by *'national* competitiveness', as distinct from the competitiveness of *firms*. Great care should be taken in the use of terms such as these. Moreover, whatever the relationship between globalization and national economic welfare, the welfare of individuals and of households will depend not only on the growth of GDP, but crucially also on its distribution. The distribution of welfare will continue to be influenced strongly by domestic political choices about alternative economic and social policies. Hence, even if it were true that the prosperity of European countries were determined by something called 'national competitiveness' (which it is not), there would still be an important role for national (and European) social policies in determining the distribution of welfare.

Second, competition from Third-World countries is not, and cannot be, a fundamental cause of increased economic inequality and rising unemployment in Europe. In general, increased trade raises average welfare in both participating countries. But, around a rising average, there can and will be sharp changes in the distribution of welfare. In particular, increased trade between rich and poor countries (which remains a relatively small component of international trade) will disadvantage the position of less skilled workers in the rich countries. It is not inevitable that this should result in higher unemployment and increased inequality – there is no 'logic of globalization' that decrees it. The increases in unemployment, poverty and inequality that many (but not all) OECD countries have experienced since the 1970s are primarily a result of the failure of their economic and social policies to adjust to a new set of circumstances in a way that includes all members of society. This failure is a betrayal of some of the core principles of the welfare state – in particular, full employment and social security. Blaming international trade or a vaguely defined process of 'globalization' is little more than a convenient way of avoiding the difficult domestic political choices that a sustained assault on unemployment and inequality would imply.

Third, and most importantly, globalization – or, more strictly, internationalisation – does not close off policy options and political choices. Internationalisation does not impose an iron logic on welfare states and, in practice, responses differ strongly across different types of welfare regime. There is no evidence of any convergence of spending and taxation across regime types. It remains a domestic choice about what to spend national income on – that is, the balance between public and private spending; about whether and how to defer consumption across the life-cycle (pensions, family support); about the level of insurance against unemployment, sickness and disability, and whether and in what combination this is provided by private and public sectors; and about the degree of redistribution across households. Politics matters, and will continue to matter for the welfare states of the twenty-first century.

Critical examination of the 'social dumping' argument is particularly important in the context of European social policy as it is used frequently as a reason for the need for more European social legislation. That is, it is argued that social policy at the European level is necessary to prevent social dumping, competitive deregulation and a 'race to the bottom' in social standards. It is therefore important to analyse both the theoretical arguments and empirical evidence about social dumping. In the next section I therefore look in very general terms at theory and evidence on the links between international trade and welfare, and in the following section I consider in more detail the effect on inequality. I then go on to look more specifically at the relationship between internationalisation and the welfare state in the context of European social policy. We are then in a position to consider whether globalization establishes a ground for intervention at the supranational level. Finally, in the last section I draw some conclusions.

It is extremely important to be clear about these matters, for two reasons. First, because so much that is written or asserted about globalization and the welfare state is muddled, self-seeking or just plain wrong. Second, because the growth of external pressures on welfare states, and the supposed inability or ineffectiveness of national governments to respond to these pressures is one of the key arguments in support of the extension of trans-national welfare and, implicitly, a federalised European welfare state.

Welfare, International Trade and 'Competitiveness'

While the term 'globalization' includes more than just the economic aspects, it nevertheless makes sense to begin with an economic definition. For example, most definitions of economic globalization, or more accurately, internationalisation, would include at least three component parts: the growth in world trade; increased capital flows and deregulation of finance markets; and the shift away from managed exchange rates.

Is there anything new about globalization? The answer to this question depends in part on the time period studied. In the 1980s and 1990s, the level of international trade and economic interdependency was far higher than in the first three post-war decades. But this degree of globalization was not unprecedented, and in many ways represented a reversion to the international trading economy of the pre-1914 era. In 1919, J. M. Keynes wrote:

> What an extraordinary episode in the economic progress of man that age was which came to an end in August, 1914 ... The inhabitant of London could order by telephone, sipping his morning tea in bed, the various products of the whole earth, in such quantity as he might see fit, and reasonably expect their early delivery upon his doorstep; he could at the same moment and by the same means adventure his wealth in the natural resources and new enterprises of any quarter of the world, and share, without exertion or even trouble, in their prospective fruits and advantages ... But, most important of all, he regarded this state of affairs as normal, certain and permanent. (Keynes, 1919)

World merchandise exports as a percentage of world GDP rose from 5.1 per cent in 1850 to 11.9 per cent in 1913. The proportion then fell to 7.1 per cent in 1950, only recovering to its 1913 level in 1973. By 1993, it had risen to 17.1 per cent (Wes, 1996, p. 5). The *composition* of trade had changed considerably, however. For example, in 1913, the United Kingdom mainly imported raw materials and exported manufactured goods. In 1992, British imports and exports both largely consisted of manufactured goods. In 1955, only 5 per cent of exports from the developing world were manufactured goods, but by the 1990s this had risen to almost 60 per cent (Wes, 1996, p. 6). Nevertheless, the growth of manufacturing exports from the Third World remains a relatively small part of European and other developed economies. In 1990, the advanced industrial nations spent only 1.25 per cent of their combined GDPs on imports of manufacturing goods from newly industrialising countries (NICs) (Krugman, 1996, p. 55).

What effect does international trade have on living standards and economic development generally? The key principle here is that of *comparative advantage*, first introduced by the nineteenth-century economist David Ricardo. Like all great insights, the principle of comparative advantage is deceptively simple. It can be stated in a few sentences, and was derived with reference to an economy far less complex than that of the twenty-first century. Yet it remains a powerful tool for understanding the costs and benefits of international trade and an interdependent world.

The principle of comparative advantage rests on the notion of differences in the productivity of labour between countries. It is obvious that where there are differences in the absolute level of productivity in different sectors between countries, there will be opportunities to gain from trade. So if country A is efficient in producing clothes, and country B is efficient in producing food, both will gain if country A specialises in clothes production, and country B in agriculture, trading the surpluses with each other. Each country could be self-sufficient, producing all its own clothes and food, but both countries will be better off if specialisation and international trade occur.

But the principle of *comparative* advantage is more subtle. Here it is argued that countries will gain from trade even where one country has an absolute advantage in the production of *all* goods, that is, where labour productivity in country A is higher in all sectors. Why is this so? The answer lies in the fact that while country A may be more productive than country B in all sectors, the margin of its superiority will differ across these sectors. That is, its *comparative* advantage over country B will vary between sectors, and both countries will gain if country A specialises in production of the commodity where it has the highest *comparative* advantage.

'Comparative advantage' therefore means something entirely different from 'competitive advantage' – the latter being a far more difficult term to define. The principle of comparative advantage – the key axiom of international trade theory – is that *all* countries (or regions) have a comparative advantage in the production of some (tradable) good or service, even if they have an absolute advantage in none of them. Thus specialisation and international or inter-regional trade will bring benefits to both parties, even if one nation or region is 'under-developed' – that is, it does not have an absolute advantage in *any* tradable good or service. Places and firms cannot 'get' or 'enhance' *comparative* advantage. Like Molière's character who found he'd been speaking prose for forty years without realising it, firms and places *always* have a comparative advantage in something. This distinction between comparative and competitive advantage is crucial, yet confusion between the terms abounds in the literature, including in some surprising places. The basic principles of the Ricardian model hold just as much for today's economy as in previous periods – and as we saw above, the world economy has experienced earlier periods of integration and internationalisation.

It is often argued that common labour standards and/or wage rates need to be imposed to prevent unfair competition from low-wage countries:

> Labor unions, human-rights activists, and some governments in the North, argue that market access in the North should be conditioned on upgrading of labor standards in the South, to prevent 'social dumping' and a 'race to the bottom' on such standards. Sanctions on trade in response to violations of labor standards are sometimes referred to as a 'social clause'. Other Northern governments, notably the United Kingdom, and nearly everyone in the South are much more skeptical of the benefits of a social clause, viewing it mostly as protectionism, even if sometimes well-intentioned. It should also be noted, however, that this is not exclusively a North–South issue, narrowly defined. Some relatively high-income European countries' interest in social harmonization in the European Community may derive from fears about competition from accession to the European Union by lower-income countries. (Golub, 1997, p. 5)

Most current arguments against the extension of trade with newly industrialising economies are thus simply modern versions of the old 'pauper labour' fallacy. Differences in international wages do not preclude mutually beneficial trade between countries. In fact, the reverse is likely to be true – the greater the economic diversity, the greater the potential benefits from trade:

> The fear that high-wage countries are unable to compete with low-wage countries … confuses the fundamental distinction between comparative and absolute advantage … overall differences in productivity (absolute advantage) determines wages, while sector-specific variations in productivity and costs determine trade patterns. (Golub, 1997, p. 9)

From the point of view of economic competitiveness – that is, the competitiveness of firms based in different countries – the key comparison is not between wage rates, but between unit labour costs – that is, the cost of producing a comparable unit of output. Productivity in low-wage countries will be below that in high-wage countries for a variety of reasons, including lower levels of investment in physical and human capital. In theory, one would expect differences in productivity largely to offset differences in wage rates, so that unit labour costs across countries would vary far less than either productivity or wage rates. In 1993, labour cost in the textile industry, for example, varied from 2 per cent of the US cost in Bangladesh to 200 per cent in Japan. But unit labour costs in manufacturing as a whole, allowing for productivity, varied far less across a range of countries, from about 70 per cent in Korea to about 106 per cent in the Philippines. In fact, unit labour costs in some newly industrialising countries were above those in the USA – the productivity gap exceeded the wage gap (Golub, 1997).

Hence the popular notion that globalization is undermining the prosperity of the advanced economies is incorrect on both theoretical and empirical grounds:

> The truth, however, is that fears about the economic impact of Third World competition are almost entirely unjustified. Economic growth in low-wage nations is in principle as likely to raise as to lower per capita income in high-wage countries; the actual effects have been negligible … The world economy is a system – a complex web of feed-back relationships – not a simple chain of one-way effects. In this global system, wages, prices, trade, and investment flows are outcomes, not givens. (Krugman, 1996, pp. 51–3)

Does this mean that from a welfare point of view, we should stop worrying and embrace globalization wholeheartedly? Unfortunately, it is not as simple as that. International trade, as free trade generally, is not entirely benign. While the principle of comparative advantage shows that trade will increase total economic welfare, distributional outcomes can, and often do, worsen. That is, the principle does not predict any particular pattern to how the gains from trade in the form of increased output will be shared. With specialisation, output and employment in some sectors will fall, while in others they will grow. In theory, capital and labour will shift from the declining sectors to the growth sectors in response to the higher returns that can be earned in these expanding sectors. But, in practice, adjustment is unlikely to be smooth, as labour, housing and (to a lesser extent) capital markets have imperfections.

Moreover, there can be longer-term effects on development options and on social values. For developing countries, specialisation in sectors where they currently enjoy comparative advantage, may lock them into niche roles in the world economy which close off other development opportunities in the future. In the real world, nations may eventually specialise in particular sectors not through any 'natural' facility, nor through a smooth process of rationally guided utility maximisation, but perhaps because of war, conquest, under-development or even pure chance. The policy question that then arises is whether countries (or regions, or cities) should accept where their comparative advantages lie, and stick with these sectors, rather than trying to change their fates by specialising in growing industries. As Begg (1999) puts it, 'Is it better to be active in the right sectors than competitive in the wrong ones?'

Furthermore, the growth of international trade brings into sharp focus differences in social norms as well as living standards between countries. Lower production costs in one country can be associated not just with specialisation or efficiency, but also with the widespread use of child labour, low or non-existent health and safety standards, repression of workers' rights, and political oppression. Trade has implications for domestic norms and social arrangements. Rodrik (1997) argues that free trade between countries with different domestic practices requires either the acceptance of erosion of standards in the country with higher social regulation, or some degree of harmonisation or convergence. This is rather a pessimistic view, as it does not allow for a third possibility of convergence *upwards* as part of the process of economic growth in the less developed partner – an outcome for which (as we saw in the previous chapter) there is a certain amount of evidence from the experience of the welfare states of Southern Europe. However, Rodrik is certainly correct to state that a concern with social arrangements and social norms can be distinguished from a position of outright protectionism.

There is no reason why, in general, free markets and free trade cannot be combined with a principled position on labour standards and social protection. First, the empirical evidence suggests that foreign investment is not highly responsive to weak labour standards (Golub, 1997). Second, it is clear that the legitimacy of the global economic system is badly damaged by perceptions of unfair practice. Even at the purely economic level, any short-term gains from holding down labour standards and repressing workers' rights are likely to be far outweighed by the negative consequences of a retreat from open markets and a flight to protectionism. More broadly, the case for universal core labour rights and social standards is overwhelming – although at a practical level it has to be recognised that the labour standards of developed countries are as yet unattainable for most of the world's people (Golub, 1997).

One of the most commonly heard views is that, because of globalization, countries are in a head-to-head battle over something called 'competitiveness' that will determine both the fate of a country and the living standards of its inhabitants. Raising national (or regional or local) competitiveness then becomes an obsession. Although this view, or something like it, is repeated often by politicians, commentators and academics, it is fallacious. The concept of 'national competitiveness' has no strict meaning. Nations do not compete; firms compete. If trade barriers are reduced, and low cost imports arrive, there may well be detrimental effects on domestic producers and their workers, as discussed above. On average, living standards would rise, however, as the lower imported prices would lead to higher real wages, all other things remaining constant.

Living standards are not determined through some gladiatorial contest between countries. They are determined fundamentally by the productivity of domestic workers. If productivity rises by 1 per cent, then in general, living standards will rise on average by 1 per cent. If productivity in other countries rises by more than 1 per cent, domestic living standards are unaffected – although national pride may be wounded and those making trips abroad may return envious of other countries' achievements.

Krugman (1996) expresses this most clearly, and is worth quoting at length:

> The idea that a country's economic fortunes are largely determined by its success on world markets is a hypothesis, not a necessary truth; and as a practical, empirical matter, that hypothesis is flatly wrong. That is, it is simply not the case that the world's leading nations are to any important degree in economic competition with each other, or that any of their major economic problems can be attributed to failures to compete on world markets. The growing obsession in most advanced nations with international competitiveness should be seen, not as a well-founded concern, but as a view held in the face of overwhelmingly contrary evidence ... Even though world trade is larger than ever before, national living standards are overwhelmingly determined by domestic factors rather than by some competition for world markets ... the major industrial countries, while they sell products that compete with each other, are also each other's main export markets and each other's main suppliers of useful imports. (Krugman, 1996, pp. 5 and 9)

So can we entirely leave aside notions of competitiveness? No, for two reasons. First, while it may not make sense to think of countries competing with each other, domestic firms certainly do compete with foreign firms. Higher wage costs for domestic firms will indeed affect their competitiveness and will affect the location of new investment. In response to this, governments will face considerable pressure to reduce these costs. Second, and perhaps most importantly, the view that countries do and must compete with each other is extremely influential among politicians and policy-makers. So whether or not it makes economic sense, if politicians behave as if welfare states are corporations and need to be made 'leaner' and 'more efficient' through reducing costs, firing workers and increasing insecurity, this will increase pressure on welfare states. I am leaving aside here the vexed question of whether strategies of this type do or do not make firms more efficient, and also leaving aside what exactly is meant by efficiency. If politicians in all European countries, and among all parties, come to hold similar beliefs about this, then these pressures will result in greater convergence. This leads us on to considering the more specific arguments about the impact of globalization on the welfare state.

Globalization and Inequality

Granted that international trade (and indeed inter-regional or inter-city trade) allows specialisation and hence increased economic output, it might nevertheless be the case that one result is increased unemployment, wage inequality and social exclusion. With a growing volume of trade and the removal of tariff and other barriers, previously protected domestic markets become subject to international competition. Domestic producers will lose market share and may eventually be forced out entirely. Alternatively, they will have to cut costs and increase productivity through new investment and the replacement of labour with capital. Other sectors may be growing through an increase in the size of the total market, but this is of little comfort to the workers in the declining sectors who lose their jobs, nor to the shareholders in declining sectors whose investments are losing value.

In principle, then, increased trade can lead to hardship – falling wages, falling employment and growing unemployment – in particular sectors. How bad this will be depends on the speed and scale of adjustment. In theory, in a perfect world, capital and labour would shift from the declining to the growing sectors of the economy, so that there would be no net costs. But in practice, market failures, lagged adjustments, and the social and individual costs of adjusting to economic change mean that the picture will be far more messy. Globalization affects the distribution between particular groups in the population, and in particular between skilled and unskilled workers: 'Economic theory also suggests that, even though the North as a whole gains from trading with low-wage countries, imports of labor-intensive products are likely to be harmful to unskilled workers in the North' (Borjas and Ramey, 1995). So it is at least theoretically possible that increased trade has led to greater inequality in the advanced economies. In the deregulated and flexible labour markets of the USA, the outcome would be increased wage inequality, while in the more regulated labour markets in the European Union, with greater social protection and employment protection, the outcome would be increased unemployment, and a greater division between insiders and outsiders in the labour market.

It is certainly the case that, in recent decades, European unemployment has increased. In the USA, unemployment is lower, but wage inequality is much greater than in Europe, and has increased. But is trade responsible for these trends? Broadly speaking, most economists believe that trade has played a role, but a relatively minor one, in the increase in unemployment and inequality since the 1980s. Having reviewed the major studies, Wes (1996) concludes:

> The literature on trade and wages is increasingly reaching a consensus that globalization has exerted a downward pressure on wages in OECD countries particularly for unskilled workers. However, although trade with NIEs may play a role in explaining recent labour market trends, many economists emphasise that the impact is still relatively minor. (Wes, 1996 p. 40)

Most studies in the 1980s, based on factor content of trade (FCT) analysis conclude that any loss of jobs in the North through increased competition from newly industrializing economies have been offset by additional employment created in skill-intensive industries (Wes, 1996). Wes quotes studies by Murphy and Welch (1991) who argue that trade was not a main cause of increased wage inequality in the 1980s, although it contributed to it; and by Borjas *et al.* (1992), who estimate that the joint effect of trade and immigration into the USA in the 1980s accounted only for between 8 per cent and 15 per cent of the increase in the differential between the wages of those with a college education and those with only high-school education.

A contrasting view is given by Wood (1994), who argues that most studies using the FCT approach underestimate the effects of trade. Wood's own calculations show that trade is responsible for a 20 per cent decline in demand for less-skilled workers, accounting for virtually all the observed labour market trends (Wes, 1996, p. 31)

The main alternative explanation by those economists who reject trade as a major cause of increased unemployment and inequality in the advanced countries is technological change. As Wes (1996) points out, regardless of whether trade or technology is seen as the main driver, the policy prescriptions advocated are remarkably similar: reducing the supply of unskilled labour through education and training; boosting demand for less skilled labour through public works or employment subsidies; and using taxes and transfers to redistribute income. Neither group of economists advocates protectionism.

Globalization and the Welfare State

What impact is globalization having on national welfare states? At the extreme, it is asserted that globalization effectively means the end of the welfare state. Countries are powerless in the face of vast international economic forces. Competitive pressures inexorably force down the level of social protection and welfare provision, as each nation engages in a 'race to the bottom' under the pressure of competitive deregulation. Throughout the history of European social policy such concerns have been expressed about social dumping and downward convergence. But, as we saw in Chapter 2, there is no evidence of downward convergence in social expenditure levels across the EU or the OECD.

The social dumping argument within the EU rests on the idea that economic and monetary union will lead to increased competition, favouring low wage/low social wage countries and setting off a levelling down process as firms use increased competition and the threat of relocation to bargain down workers' wages and conditions. In addition, workers will migrate from South to North, weakening unions and driving up unemployment. However, there are several problems with this argument (Adnett, 1995).

First, there is the need to distinguish comparisons of wage costs or social wage costs from comparison of unit labour costs. Much discussion focuses on differences in wage costs between different parts of the EU, whereas the correct measure is unit labour costs. In fact, unit labour costs in 1990 were in general fairly similar across EU countries. Using the UK as the base index of 100, unit labour costs were 107.9 in Germany, 101.3 in France – and 236.6 in Portugal. Moreover, there is no evidence that the relative position of the 'high social welfare' economies has deteriorated, and hence there is no evidence that member states with high levels of social protection have been at a disadvantage (Adnett, 1995).

Second, while in the USA, for example, regional labour market adjustment takes place mainly through labour mobility, in the EU, labour mobility is, and will continue to be, far lower. Third, although capital mobility is close to perfect, productivity cannot always be reproduced: there are skill bottlenecks, limits on managerial transferability, and different production technologies. Fourth, costs are not the only, nor necessarily the main, driver of location. Proximity to markets will also be important.

In terms of both theory and practice, the social dumping argument is weak (Adnett, 1995). A high social wage is prevalent in Northern Europe because of high productivity. In effect, highly productive workers are choosing to take the return on their labour in the form of greater social protection and better working conditions. Employers

similarly prefer the benefits of such a regime, including fewer acci-
dents and lower absenteeism and turnover. Despite widespread fears
about social dumping in an integrated Europe, the evidence is less
than convincing. Were the theory to be true, one would expect to find
widespread examples of social dumping in Southern Europe since the
accession of European countries to the EU. In fact, there is no
evidence of competitive retrenchment in these countries (Guillen
and Matsaganis, 2000). Since the 1980s, the less developed welfare
states of Southern Europe have *expanded* provision in an attempt to
emulate Northern welfare states. Growth in social policy expenditure
and activity was related to the legitimation needs of government in
the transition to democracy: 'If anything, "catching up with Europe"
in terms of social as well as economic standards seems to have been
elevated to something of a national ideal, shared by both government
and opposition' (Guillen and Matsaganis, 2000, p. 120). What one
could term the 'strong' form of the globalization argument – that
globalization inevitably leads to competitive deregulation, and conversely, that the welfare state is necessarily a constraint on economic
growth, productivity or 'competitiveness' finds little backing. Empirical studies of the relationship between the extent of the welfare state
and the rate of economic growth tend to inconclusive results (Esping-
Andersen, 1994; Atkinson, 1995, 1998; Gough, 1996).

Divergence of institutions across welfare states leads to a divergence in responses to common issues (Esping-Andersen, 1996). As we
saw in Chapter 2, some European countries have been able to
combine relatively generous welfare states with economic growth.
Similarly, in Chapter 7 we shall see that some countries are able to
combine welfare generosity with high employment levels. So the
relationship between welfare and economic growth is complex. Welfare states can work with, rather than against, the grain of economic
growth by easing adjustment to economic and industrial change
through, for example, the provision of unemployment insurance
(Atkinson, 1998). Several smaller European countries combine extensive welfare states with open economies (Hirst, 1998, Rodrik, 1997;
Katzenstein, 1985). These two aspects are complementary rather than
conflictual: the state's commitment to providing security for all
reduces citizen resistance to economic change and industrial adjustment: 'Very open economies are more exposed to external shocks and
must develop means to cushion their firms and workers against them'
(Hirst, 1998 p. 2). Hirst argues that in countries such as Austria, the
Netherlands and Sweden, a combination of corporatism in economic

policy, together with a social policy organised around consensus and solidarity, allowed high levels of public provision and welfare to protect individuals from external risks. Adaptation to changed external conditions took place through policies of wage restraint, co-ordinated action by firms and labour market adjustment.

There are nevertheless constraints on welfare policy options. Increased mobility of capital and of highly skilled workers means that high taxation of capital and of higher incomes becomes more difficult. Welfare becomes funded increasingly from basic-rate income taxes, sales taxes, and other indirect taxation, and user charges become more common:

> This means that the public must both want such welfare services and be willing to pay for them. It implies both solidaristic values and appropriate political institutions that force decision-makers to respond to those values. Hence both attitudes and institutions become central, in the form of distinct national legacies that favour solidarism and public consumption ... The degree of international exposure *per se* is not the issue, rather it is the domestic political response to it. (Hirst, 1998 p. 3)

Hence, while the strong form of the globalization argument is unfounded, there is a more plausible position in which globalization is seen as one key external variable in a mix of internal and external pressures on the modern welfare state. The dilemma of globalization is that it raises the demand for social insurance – because of the need to offset new types of risk and economic change – but constrains the ability of governments to respond to that demand because of capital mobility and the sensitivity of firms to taxation levels and social regulation (Rodrik, 1997). Because of the (real or perceived) constraints imposed by globalization, as well as (real or perceived) voter resistance to higher taxation, governments consider themselves to be limited in their ability to manoeuvre in regard to levels of social expenditure and the means to pay for it. But nevertheless, national governments retain substantial autonomy with regard to economic and social policies, and many types of intervention remain open to governments (Garrett, 2000; Rodrik, 1997). Taxation and spending decisions by national governments are still mainly explained by traditional domestic policy variables such as government partisanship and the strength of organised labour (Garrett, 2000).

In the post-war era, the welfare state was identified closely with the project of nation building: 'the affirmation of liberal democracy against the twin perils of fascism and bolshevism' (Esping-Andersen, 1996, p. 2). Modern welfare states only achieved full development in the 'golden age' of the early post-war period 'when national economic boundaries were effectively controlled' (Scharpf, 2000 pp. 190–1). Hence national governments and unions could 'more or less ignore the exit options of capital owners, taxpayers and consumers' (ibid., p. 191). Under these conditions, national governments could not only use Keynesian demand management to achieve high economic growth and full employment, but also use employment and wage policy to achieve egalitarian and solidaristic social policy goals. This

> allowed the redistribution of primary incomes through cross-subsidisation in the private sector as well as secondary redistribution through public services and transfers financed through progressive taxation. Hence, 'solidaristic' wage policy could compress wage differentials between low-skill and high-skill groups with little regard for actual differences in labor productivity ... national health systems could offer medical care free of charge to everybody; and national systems of social assistance, unemployment and disability benefits and pensions could provide generous levels of non-wage incomes. (Scharpf, 2000, pp. 191–2)

These welfare states were designed to cater for a mass production – 'Fordist' – economy that has now largely disappeared, or is disappearing, from Europe. During the early post-war period, all the advanced democracies (regardless of regime type) were able to achieve their welfare-state goals without 'endangering the viability of their capitalist national economies'. However, from the 1970s, changes in the international environment increased the economic vulnerability of welfare states, and from this point, institutional differences between welfare state types or regimes begin to matter. In the 1970s and early 1980s, welfare states could respond to increased external pressures through a 'Keynesian concertation', in which demand management was linked to wage restraint through centralised corporatist bargaining – the paradigm case being Austria. But in the later 1980s and 1990s, the external environment changed more radically, as the internationalization of markets for goods, services and capital first equalled, then exceeded, the degree of international economic integration of the pre-1914 period (Scharpf, 2000).

This does *not* mean that countries are powerless to pursue welfare goals. The degree of welfare state rollback so far is modest. Levels of social expenditure in different countries are essentially stable. With the exception of the United Kingdom and New Zealand, changes have been marginal (Esping-Andersen, 1996). But states must pursue their welfare goals within constraints, which include some international economic constraints. Moreover, the set of policy options will differ across types of welfare state, with the greatest difficulties for those 'corporatist' states which had in the past relied on direct interventions into the operation of capital, product and labour markets (Scharpf 2000).

The impact of internationalisation will therefore be very different on different types of European welfare state. As private firms become more subject to international competition, they are less able to cross-subsidize between different lines of production, or between less productive and more productive jobs. Instead 'each product – and in the extreme, each job – must now earn its full costs of production plus an adequate rate of return on capital at internationally uniform prices' (Scharpf, 1999). This must inevitably put pressure on solidaristic wage policies and the minimum wage. So it is now much more difficult to try and achieve egalitarian welfare goals through intervention in private-sector employment relations; those welfare states that have in the past used this route must in the future rely more on the 'formal' welfare state and the tax system.

As we saw in Chapter 2, there has been no process of downward convergence across European welfare states, whether as a result of 'globalization' or of any other factors. Consequently, *relativities* between countries have been little changed – Scandinavian countries remain high-tax, high-expenditure; Anglo-Saxon countries remain low-tax and low-expenditure; with continental welfare states in the middle. National responses to pressures on their welfare states (whether internally or externally driven) will differ greatly one from another, because of differences in the level and structure of employment, in the level and structure of welfare spending, and in the institutional constraints and veto positions of different actors (Scharpf, 2000).

If it were the case that globalization fatally undermines welfare states, we would expect to find the strongest evidence with regard to those countries with the most extensive welfare systems. In fact, the more generous welfare states have successfully survived the economic pressures of the 1980s and 1990s, and indeed, there is evidence to suggest that the more generous welfare systems of some smaller European countries have assisted them positively in adapting to changed economic conditions. In Denmark, the welfare system supports flexibility and firm competitiveness, through the combination of low employment protection (allowing employers to adjust to changing conditions) with relatively high benefits and a universalist system. An excessive dependency burden is avoided through a combination of higher-than-average fertility rates, high participation ratio, low inequality and social exclusion, and growth in public-sector jobs. As a result, there is a high level of political will and political support (Hirst, 1998). Similarly, after experiencing something of a crisis in its welfare state in the early 1990s, Sweden's economy recovered and its welfare state survived.

Huber and Stephens (1998) look at the effect of internationalisation on the social democratic model of the welfare state, by examining the four countries in which arguably social democracy was most successful in achieving full employment and an extensive institutional welfare state: Austria, Norway, Finland and Sweden. They assess critically the 'commonplace view' that recent reversals in social democratic policy have been caused by the increasing internationalisation of the economy in general, and European economic integration in particular. In this view, policy options have been constricted or even eliminated; in particular generous welfare benefits become unaffordable, and increasing economic openness makes Keynesian demand management difficult if not impossible.

Against this, Huber and Stephens argue that the Golden Age social democratic model was predicated on an international regime in which trade barriers were low, but there were strong restrictions on capital flows. This combination of open trading and export dependence forced these small countries to develop economic and social policies that were compatible with competition in international markets. Since then, increasing global trade openness has had little impact – in particular, entitlements have not been cut.

Hence it is the supply-side measures, not demand management, that are the key to employment and growth in these small social democracies in the Golden Age. Many of these policies – such as low interest rates and state direction of credit – assume closed financial markets, and so financial internationalisation and deregulation undermined the important supply-side features of the Golden Age model. Another key element in the model was solidaristic wage policy; that is, wage restraint tied to centralised wage bargaining. The principle was equal pay for equal work across firms, regardless of profitability. In Norway and Sweden, as well as in Denmark, this policy was extended to actual 'wage compression', a reduction of wage differentials among workers of different skill levels. More recently, multinationalisation of capital, changes in occupational structure and changes in production techniques have weakened centralised bargaining, and hence wage restraint. Finally, in the three Nordic countries, serious mistakes in economic policy worsened the position (Huber and Stephens, 1998).

Hence, the social democratic model rests on some crucial institutional and social underpinnings, including strong and highly centralised unions, powerful social democratic parties, centralised employer organisations, and therefore highly centralised tripartite bargaining, as well as supply-side economic policies and the growth of external demand for exports. Given these structural characteristics, it is international financial liberalisation, and not the growth in trade, that has affected social democratic welfare states.

These and other examples provide compelling evidence against the reductionist view that there is one level of welfare expenditure compatible with high and rising living standards. Too much corporatism leads to immobilism and 'Eurosclerosis', while a strong state backing liberalised markets can lead to social exclusion and rising inequality. An ideal policy mix combines 'enough corporatism to win the commitment of the social partners in certain policy spheres and enough hierarchy to remove blockages and to unravel serious policy failures' (Hirst, 1998).

Many generous and extensive welfare states can survive, and indeed prosper, in a global era. There is little explanatory value in the notion of trying to relate welfare state development as a single variable to the degree of globalization or internationalisation. It is more useful to look at economic and social policies as part of an inter-related system, in which the various parts fit together (Atkinson, 1998a). It follows logically that policy options are between different 'packages', and these choices will be constrained strongly by history and by institutions. But there are nevertheless choices:

> It is not the case that all countries are driven by economic imperatives to follow a particular line. The attempt by bodies such as the IMF to impose a particular approach based on labour market flexibility and dismantling of social protection is not justified by appealing to economics. It involves a political judgement as well. (Atkinson, 1998a, p. 21)

Does Globalization Imply a European Welfare State?

The globalization argument is also used as one of the grounds for greater intervention by the European Union in social policy, and for the desirability, or even the necessity, of a European welfare state. The position taken is that globalization – increased trade, greater capital mobility and the deregulation of capital and financial markets – makes regulation by member state governments ineffective, and the independent maintenance of generous welfare states impossible. Therefore the only route towards avoiding competitive deregulation and the erosion of national welfare states is through re-regulation at the European level. But, as we have seen, despite the internationalisation of the economy since the 1970s, and the creation of a single European market and a common currency, welfare states in Europe have maintained their diversity; governments remain key actors in delivering welfare; and the more generous welfare states have survived and mostly prospered. There is no *logical* reason why a more extensive 'superstate' role in social policy at the European level is necessary, although market integration and globalization more generally imply closer co-operation between national governments in policy formulation and implementation.

A rather different argument links globalization to both the governance and the modernisation of welfare states. Giddens argues that the new mixed economy requires a 'modernised' welfare state. Existing welfare states grew out of wartime mobilisation, and formed a part of national state building:

> The modern state was forged in the crucible of war, and war or preparing for it influenced most aspects of state institutions. Citizenship rights and welfare programmes were mainly established as states sought to engage their populations and hold their support, a phenomenon that continued through the Cold War period. (Giddens, 1998, p. 71)

But globalization requires the state both to devolve power downward and to cede authority 'upward'. In the context of the EU, this means the construction of a political order that is neither a super-state nor only a free trade area. The 'fuzzy sovereignty' of the EU is not a symbol of its failure, in Giddens' view, but rather demonstrates that the EU is the 'prototype' of a new type of governance where the 'borders of current states are softening and becoming 'frontiers because of their ties to other regions and their involvement with transnational groupings of all kinds' (Giddens, 1998, p. 130). The current and future role of the EU in social policy will be considered in more detail in the next two chapters, and related citizenship issues in Chapter 8.

Nation states have lost some sovereignty, in the sense of a supreme, exclusive role. But there has been no general retreat, still less a demise of the state: 'States have remained a key locus of regulation and have thus far shown no sign of future dissolution' (Scholte, 2000). States survive but have lost their claims to exclusive, absolute rule, ushering in an era of complex and multi-layered governance. What has *not* changed is the bureaucratic nature of governance, in the sense that governance continues to involve organisations that are large, permanent, formal, impersonal and hierarchical. Hence, 'globalization is not dissolving the state and bureaucratism more generally any more than it is unravelling capitalism. Contemporary changes in governance are far more subtle and complex. If the trends ... pose a threat, it is not to the state and bureaucracy but to democracy. (Scholte, 2000)

If there is a threat, it is not to welfare *per se* but rather to democracy and the democratic control of welfare institutions. Supranational government, rather than a defence against globalizing trends, may turn out to be a partner to them in threatening citizen involvement and government accountability. The combination of globalizing trends together with the shift towards multi-level governance and the weakening of ties between voters, politicians, national bureaucracies and outcomes, is potentially very damaging to democracy and accountability. This issue includes, but goes beyond, the immediate question of the 'democratic deficit' in EU institutions.

Conclusions

The extreme version of the thesis, in which globalization is alleged to be in the process of destroying or undermining the welfare state, is clearly wrong, and is often muddle-headed in its portrayal both of the effects of increased international trade and international economic interdependency, and of the impacts of these trends on the welfare state. Even the more moderate version of the thesis probably exaggerates the impact of globalization. In particular, and continuing the theme of previous chapters, European welfare states remain very different, and there is no evidence of globalization enforcing a particular version of the welfare state on all members of the EU.

There is evidence of a levelling-out of welfare state expenditure, but no evidence of convergence of welfare states in terms of their levels of tax and spend. This suggests that political agency and social choice remain the key factors. By and large, countries have the welfare states that their populations choose, as mediated through the political and institutional mechanisms.

The death of the nation state has been much exaggerated, and national governments continue to be the primary agents responsible for delivering welfare to their citizens. But the constraints under which they act, and the policy universe in which they operate, have both been changed by globalization. The system of 'multi-level governance', which we shall look at in the next two chapters has in part been shaped by globalization. All this implies a greater role for the EU in social policy, but does *not* imply the creation of a European welfare state.

4

European Union Social Policy: Policy Development and Policy-making

The relationship between EU social policy and the social policy of the member states is complex. When the European Economic Community (EEC) was created in 1957, social policy was a minor consideration. Since then, the social dimension to 'Europe' has become increasingly important. Over this time period, the part played by national policies in the welfare of citizens has also expanded considerably. At the same time, the expansion of the EEC/EC/EU from six to fifteen members has meant an increase in the range of welfare states represented.

For much of the post-war period, there was no contradiction between an expanding role for European institutions and the strengthening of national states. In fact, as discussed further in Chapter 8, these two processes buttressed each other. More recently, the perception has grown of a conflict between greater European integration and the role of national states, particularly in terms of welfare.

Social policy was not a major stake in the early development of the EEC. The motor of the project was economic integration, and the social dimension was relevant mainly in terms either of the social consequences of economic integration actions or of the necessary social prerequisites (labour mobility, compatibility of benefits) to make the economic project work. More recently, social policy has become more significant, for three main reasons. First, because of the increasing volume of social legislation, not only in the form of directives and other actions by the Commission and Council, but also because of activities by the European Court of Justice. Second, because of the perceived political need by key political actors in the 1980s to stress the social as well as economic and business dimension of the European integration project in order to retain support from workers and citizens. Third, because the social field has in some cases become one of contestation between national and supranational interests.

The term 'European social policy' is ambiguous. A narrow definition would refer only to the social policy of the EU itself. A broader view would include both EU social policy and some (or perhaps all) aspects of the social policies of the member states. The interaction between these levels is complex. The phrase 'European welfare state' is even more fraught. Clearly, in a strict sense, a European welfare state does not exist. Europe is not a state, although it can to some degree be considered a polity. Moreover, European institutions have neither the competences nor the mechanisms for intervening in welfare in a comparable way to national governments. But at the same time European welfare *states* (plural) formulate and implement policy within a growing framework of supranational laws and institutions. Furthermore, the concept of a 'European social model' is used by politicians, journalists and academics, even though, as we have seen, it would be more accurate to talk in the plural here also. Inevitably, then, 'European social policy', like the word 'Europe' itself will continue to be ambiguous and to defy easy definition.

In this chapter and the next, I shall narrow the focus to concentrate specifically on the social policy of the EU itself. In this chapter, I look first at the development of social policy in the EU. My aim is to show how the development of social policy, and the content definition of the field, has been shaped by the broader process of economic and political integration in Europe. I therefore look first at the history of European social policy, and I go on to consider the role of European social policy today, using the 1994 White Paper as a reference point. From there, I discuss the process of how social policy is formulated in the EU, before drawing some conclusions.

From the Treaty of Rome to the Single European Act (1957–85)

The history of social policy in the European Union has been described as 'one of good intentions, high principles and little action' (Lange, 1993, p. 7). The motivation behind the original EEC Treaty in 1957 was overwhelmingly economic, with political overtones. Social aspects of the Treaty were directed mainly towards ensuring the achievement of the economic goals of the European Economic Community. The dominant philosophy of the Treaty was that welfare followed from economic growth, not from regulatory or redistributive public policy (Falkner, 1998). Hence the Treaty contained provisions relating to the free movement of workers (Articles 48–51); the right of establishment (Articles 52–58); freedom to provide services (Articles 59–66); improved working conditions and living standards (Article 117); close co-operation in the social field (Article 118); equal pay between men and women (Article 119); the right to paid holidays (Article 120); and the establishment of a European Social Fund (ESF) to improve employment opportunities and increase geographical and occupational mobility (Article 123–128) (Gold, 1993; Wise and Gibb, 1993; Falkner, 1998). The dominant orientation of the Treaty was, and is, neo-liberal and pro-market. The underlying philosophy is that higher living standards and better working conditions will result from the expansion of the market and the operation of market forces.

The role of social policy in the original Treaty of Rome was thus relatively minor. Indeed, in many ways, the Treaty of Rome was less concerned with social policy than either the 1951 Treaty of Paris, which established the European Coal and Steel Community (ECSC), or the Treaty establishing the European Atomic Energy Community (EAEC) in 1957. These latter treaties were concerned with the social impact of structural economic change, with living and working conditions of workers, and with health and protection issues for both workers and citizens. Moreover, the European Social Charter, precursor of the 1989 Community Charter of the Fundamental Social Rights of Workers, was established in 1961 by the Council of Europe, not the EEC (Hantrais, 2000, p. 2).

The social aspects of the Treaty were restricted to removing some barriers to labour mobility, and, at the insistence of the French, some harmonisation of social legislation across the EEC 6. In the French view, the lower social rights and social protection in the other countries would put France at a competitive disadvantage within a Common Market. France argued successfully for the inclusion of articles on equal pay and holiday pay (Hantrais, 2000; Falkner, 1998).

Overall, then, the EEC Treaty established the principle of a social role for the EEC, but a role that was both clearly limited and clearly secondary to the economic aims of integration. Member states were interested in a social dimension to the EEC, but 'the compromise that resulted from their failure to agree about objectives, and to set up mechanisms for achieving them, led it to what could be described as a modest, cautious and narrowly focused social policy' (Hantrais, 2000, p. 3).

Although Article 117 refers to the 'harmonisation' of social systems within the EEC, it is important to remember that the original six signatories – France, Germany, Italy, Belgium, the Netherlands and Luxembourg – all had broadly 'corporatist' social protection systems. Diversity of welfare systems would increase later with the expansion of the Community to include Anglo-Saxon and social-democratic welfare regimes in 1973 (UK, Republic of Ireland, Denmark); Mediterranean welfare systems in 1981 and 1986 (Greece, Spain, Portugal): more social democracy in 1996 (Austria, Finland, Sweden); and the possibility of transition countries and others after 2000. The question of harmonisation assumes a very different character when this range of diversity is involved.

In this early period, there was some action in the social policy field (Gold, 1993). The European Social Fund (ESF) was established from 1960, and the European Regional Development Fund contained 'social' as well as regional elements. However, by comparison with the budget for the Common Agricultural Policy, spending was tiny. Even by the end of the 1980s, ESF spending only amounted to about 7 per cent of the EC budget, compared with agriculture's 67 per cent (Wise and Gibb, 1993). There was mutual recognition of certain professions, measures to improve social security, and some action in the health and safety field. But after a series of clashes between the Commission and the member states, from the mid-1960s the Commission emphasised economic rather than social issues (Gold, 1993).

Uneven growth within the EEC and the effects of the Common Market itself led to a greater social awareness from the end of the 1960s. In 1974, the Council of Ministers adopted a resolution on a Social Action Programme, designed to achieve the three goals of full and better employment; an improvement in living and working conditions; and greater involvement of management and labour. The view presented of the Community's competence in the social policy field was a cautious one, foreshadowing the later use of the concept of subsidiarity. The principles of free movement of labour and equal competition between firms were stressed. The Social Action Programme itself comprised a 'spate of action in the areas of education and training, health and safety at work, workers' and women's rights and poverty, leading to the establishment of a number of European networks and observatories to stimulate action and monitor progress in the social field' (Hantrais, 2000, p. 5).

The first half of the 1980s was a period of mixed fortunes for EU social policy. There were some Directives on health and safety and on equal treatment, but there was deadlock in other areas, such as part-time work, temporary work, parental leave and working time. There were three main reasons for this lack of progress (Gold, 1993): the UK's opposition to initiatives which it felt would increase the costs of labour and create rigidities in the labour market; the political shift to the Right and the Centre-Right among member-state governments; and the increased concern over supposed 'competitive disadvantage', both between EEC countries and between the EEC as a whole and the rest of the world. The concept of 'subsidiarity' began to evolve, although with no clear legal meaning.

From the Single European Act to Maastricht (1985–92)

This was a crucial period for the European Union, both in social policy and more generally. The treaties that established the European Communities were subsequently amended in the 1985 Single European Act; the 1993 Treaty on European Union (the Maastricht Treaty); and in the 1997 Treaty of Amsterdam. By the mid-1980s, pressures for more social regulation had built up (Hantrais, 2000). These were aided by two specific political developments. In 1981, François Mitterand was elected President of France and put forward the idea of a European social space or social area. In 1985, Jacques Delors, a senior French politician became President of the Commission and began pursuing a more activist social policy at the European level.

Mitterand and Delors, together with Chancellor Helmut Kohl of Germany, were all committed to increasing the pace of European integration. As part of this process, they saw the need to deepen the 'social dimension' of Europe – that is, to give integration a more human face. In order to retain popular support for the European project, policies needed to be developed that would tackle some of the social costs of creating a single market in Europe and an integrated continental economy. The political danger for these men was that the European project would be seen as benefiting big business, bankers and politicians, while ignoring the needs of workers and citizens.

This more activist European social policy stressed the importance of employment problems, the need to develop the social dialogue (that is, corporatist relations between employers and unions), and co-operation and consultation over social protection (Hantrais, 2000; Wise and Gibb, 1993). Delors' own commitment to this new agenda was clear: 'The European social dimension is what allows competition to flourish between undertakings and individuals on a reasonable and fair basis ... Any attempt to give new depth to the Common Market which neglected this social dimension would be doomed to failure' (Delors, 1985 quoted in Hantrais, 2000). The 'action programme' presented by the Commission to the European Parliament in 1985 included creating a single internal market in the EC by the end of 1992; providing for social actions as well as economic policy in the Single European Act; a series of budgetary reforms (the 'Delors package') comprising changes to the Common Agricultural Policy, revisions to EC finances, better co-ordination of the Structural Funds, and a doubling of the Structural Funds budget; and a revival of the moribund 'social dialogue' between employers and unions (Gold, 1993). On the latter point, Delors was unsuccessful. At the Val Duchesse talks, named after the castle in Belgium where they took place, the employers' organisations refused to sign agreements that might become the basis for European legislation.

The Single European Act (SEA), signed by the twelve member states in 1986, was the first major revision of the EEC treaties. Its main purposes were economic – to secure the completion of the single European market and the free movement of goods, services, labour and capital within that single market. The SEA represented an important upward gear change in the pace of economic integration, after several years of much slower activity. Its consequences would be profound.

Social policy was not a major aspect of the SEA. But there were important extensions of the European Community's powers in social policy. The new Article 118a, amending Article 118 of the Treaty, allowed for decisions on health and safety of workers to be taken by qualified majority voting in the Council, and not only by unanimous agreement. Article 118b sought to develop the social dialogue at European level. A new section was added (Articles 130a–e) to strengthen 'cohesion' – that is, to promote economic development and reduce economic disparities – through better co-ordination of the Structural Funds. But overall, the social dimension to the SEA was minimal – the Act 'left the issue of the social space largely unresolved' (Hantrais, 2000) and the social aspects of the SEA were essentially a 'selective political spillover' linked closely to the market-making objectives of the Act (Falkner, 1998).

During the Belgian presidency in the second half of 1987, the idea of a social platform or social dimension to the SEM project was put forward. In 1988, Delors declared that a revival of social policy was needed, including a 'minimum platform of guaranteed social rights with a view to the implementation of the single European market of 1992' (quoted in Hantrais, 2000, p. 7). In December 1989, the heads of eleven out of the twelve member states, with the United Kingdom dissenting, signed the Community Charter of the Fundamental Social Rights of Workers, better known as the Social Charter. The Social Charter was not a legally binding document. It was a 'solemn declaration' which left decisions on implementation to the member states. The Social Charter referred to workers rather than citizens, and was concerned mainly with defining some basic minimum rights at work. As Hantrais (2000) points out, the frequent use of terms such as 'adequate', 'sufficient', 'appropriate', and 'satisfactory' meant that few substantive targets were identified.

The Social Charter was, however accompanied by a 'Social Action Programme' in which the Commission set out forty-seven initiatives for developing the social dimension of the SEM. These 47 initiatives comprised a mixture of updating existing measures, incorporation of some already in progress, revival of some deadlocked measures, and some genuine new proposals (Gold, 1993). The proposals reflected the principle of subsidiarity, so in some areas, no new initiatives were proposed, while in others non-binding Recommendations, Communications or Opinions were issued. The measures recommended in the Social Action Programme can usefully be divided into two types (Falkner, 1998). Type i measures relate directly to the completion of the internal market. They include, for example, initiatives on posted workers and European Works Councils. Type ii measures are only indirectly related to the SEM – for example, the proposals on working time and on written employment contracts. These proposals go beyond market-making to market-correcting initiatives. However, by the time of the Inter-Governmental Conference in December 1991, only two (relatively minor) measures had been adopted in Council – all the others had been blocked, mainly by the UK. The UK was the most visible opponent of much of the proposed social legislation. However, in practice, several other member states were often also reluctant, but were able to voice support to social initiatives, secure in the knowledge that the UK would use its veto.

At the June 1990 European Council meeting in Dublin, the controversial decision was taken, that, along with the forthcoming Inter-Governmental Conference (IGC) on economic and monetary union, there should be a similar forum on European *political* union. Hence, at the IGCs that opened in Rome in December 1990, although economic and monetary issues were the prime objective, negotiations on political union were held in parallel (Falkner, 1998). 'Political union' referred to a whole range of topics, from procedural reform to policy innovation, including social policy. At the Maastricht European Council in December 1991, it proved impossible to reach agreement among all twelve member states on the inclusion of the so-called 'Social Chapter' within the amended Treaty on European Union, as the United Kingdom was strongly opposed. A solution was found in the form of an opt-out for the UK from the social policy provisions of the Treaty. A separate 'Protocol on Social Policy' annexed to the Treaty allowed the other eleven members (and the fourteen members after 1995) without the UK to proceed in implementing their 'Agreement on Social Policy' using the institutions, procedures and mechanisms of the Treaty. The legal status of this device has been questioned (see Falkner, 1998, p. 79), but clearly it was a successful political accommodation to prevent deadlock. The Maastricht Treaty formally created the European Union, with Article 8 declaring boldly: 'Citizenship of the Union is hereby established. Every person holding the nationality of a Member State shall be a citizen of the Union.'

The Agreement on Social Policy set up arrangements for management and labour to enter into European-level collective agreements. In Article 2, it extended the principle of decisions by qualified majority voting to the areas of: health and safety at work, working conditions, information and consultation of workers, equality between men and women, and integration of persons excluded from the labour market. Other issues – social security and social protection of workers, protection of workers made redundant, representation, collective defence of workers and employers, conditions of employment for third-country nationals, and financial contributions for job promotion – remained subject to unanimous agreement.

The opt-out procedure for the UK raised practical as well as legal questions. How realistic was it to assume that the UK representatives would not influence (whether deliberately or not) the decisions of the other eleven member states when they were operating the 'Social Protocol' procedure? The UK would continue to be involved in social policy decisions taken outside the Protocol. What would be the position of collective agreements negotiated within the Protocol affecting multi-national firms with UK as well as other European workers? And so on. These questions became academic after the election of the New Labour government under Tony Blair in 1997.

Fulfilling a manifesto commitment, the new government announced that it was giving up the opt-out from the Social Chapter, thus paving the way for the Maastricht Social Agreement to be brought into the Amsterdam Treaty and bringing an end to these imponderables. During the 1990s, Directives were adopted on topics including European Works Councils, parental leave, atypical work, sex discrimination, and working time (Falkner, 1998; Hantrais, 2000).

The Maastricht Treaty emphasised the principle of subsidiarity: the Agreement on Social Policy empowered the Council to take social policy action 'by means of directives, minimum requirements for gradual implementation, having regard to the conditions and technical rules obtaining in each of the Member States'. A communication of October 1992 set out the principle of subsidiarity in more detail: the Union is empowered to act only when its aims can be better achieved at European rather than at national level, and the burden of proof is on the European institutions to show that action is necessary at that level, and also to show that binding instruments are necessary rather than support measures and framework directives.

Hence, by the mid-1990s, a more pragmatic and less legalistic approach to social policy had been adopted by the EU. The Social Protocol attached to the Maastricht Treaty does not mention harmonisation. The institutions of the EU had in effect accepted that there was a lack of commitment by member states to a top-down, legally enforced harmonisation:

> The bland tone of the Agreement on Social Policy and the fact that the Recommendation [on convergence of social protection] was not a binding legal document provide a further indication of the lack of commitment to a strongly interventionist social policy founded on the harmonisation of social protection systems. The Council appeared to be admitting that legislation on the harmonisation of social protection had not proved to be an effective instrument for achieving standardisation across the Union. (Hantrais, 1995, p. 26)

So after several years of increased activism in social policy, there was a move back to a more cautious and limited approach. In this, social policy was part of a broader pattern in the politics of the EU. The integrationist tide that had surged from 1985 reached its high water mark in the Maastricht Treaty of 1991. In the subsequent decade there would be a greater concern with issues of subsidiarity and the rights of member states. Moreover, the accountability, democracy and legitimacy of European institutions began to appear on the European agenda.

How should we interpret the Maastricht social policy provisions? One view is that the reforms at Maastricht were essentially a 'side-show' to the economic and monetary union (EMU) negotiations. This was not an example of a classic spillover, defined as increased integration in a second policy area functionally necessary to accomplish the integration goals of the first policy area. Rather, the social reforms were a by-product of maintaining momentum on integration and the development of economic and monetary union (Lange, 1993). The social dimension lags behind market integration because there are national systems of worker protection, and hence interest coalitions; because at the European level there is no link to broader-scale movements for workers' rights; and because, in the past support for state intervention came in part from the state and in part from sectors of capital – but there is no sign of this at the European level. Hence, 'any generalized effort to build a European social state or even a systematic attempt to harmonize European workforce regulation is unlikely' (Lange, 1993).

On the other hand, Falkner (1998) argues that this 'state-centric' explanation ignores the growing importance of European-level actors such as the European Commission and the social partners. More generally, the Maastricht outcomes were part of a long-term process of 'joint preference formation' on strengthening the Community's social policy role, involving all governments except the UK. Joint EC level preference formation had occurred since the late 1980s, so even governments with different economic interests came to Maastricht ready to strengthen the social dimension.

This latter argument is part of a general thesis that a corporatist policy community has emerged around European social policy. It provides a useful balance to state-centric explanations by including the actions of European-level organisations. However, the implication of continued and deepening policy activism by EU institutions is difficult to square with the post-Maastricht reality of reduced aims, rhetoric and activity in the field of social policy. As we shall see later, the Commission's goals as expressed in the White Paper on social policy are cautious, and couched in the market-friendly language of competitiveness. There is a genuine ambiguity at the heart of the Social Policy White Paper and other recent documents, reflecting the real conflict between the 'traditional' EC/EU agenda of increased social regulation and legal minima, and the desire to promote policies of economic efficiency and competitiveness.

Maastricht and After (1992–)

In retrospect, it is clear that Maastricht marked the end of the more rapid phase of social and political integration that began with the Delors presidency in 1985. The period since 1992 has been dominated by the strict convergence criteria agreed at Maastricht for the transition to economic and monetary union and the single currency, together with the 'Stability Pact' that committed participants to further fiscal austerity after the transition to the euro in 1999. Subsidiarity, co-ordination and recognition of diversity within the Union have replaced harmonisation and grand projects as the dominant terminology. The irony, of course, is that the policy path over this period – the transition to full economic and monetary union and the introduction of the single currency – will have radical and long-term effects, socially, economically and politically. At the same time, the EU of fifteen members is far more diverse than the European economic community created by the Treaty of Rome, and will become more so with further enlargement early in the twenty-first century.

Promoting employment, and tackling unemployment and social exclusion have became key issues on the social agenda in the mid- and late 1990s. While all member states agree on the prioritising of employment, their understanding both of the nature of the problem and of possible solutions differs strongly. By 1997, the Left or Centre-Left were in power in thirteen out of the fifteen member states. But the key ideological struggle was within the Left, as it sought in different ways to come to terms with the legacy of the conservative and monetarist hegemony of the 1980s and early 1990s. Tony Blair in Britain and Lionel Jospin in France were elected within a few weeks of each other, but represented very different positions along this spectrum (Pollack, 1999). At the meeting of socialist party leaders in Malmö, Sweden just before the European Council, Jospin attacked the monetarist and neo-liberal thrust of European integration: 'today, with high unemployment, low growth and increasing poverty, Europe can no longer be built on the backs of its citizens'. Jospin argued for a low rate for the euro against the dollar and the yen; for an 'economic government' to co-ordinate economic, taxation and wage policies;

and for an explicit EU commitment to growth and employment, including spending EU funds to stimulate job creation.

Blair, by contrast, represented a new, more market-orientated Centre-Left agenda. Like Jospin, Blair argued that employment should be at the centre of the EU agenda. But the solution was not old-style socialist intervention. European socialists must 'modernise or die' – a key Blairite domestic theme. Policies should emphasise flexible labour markets, retraining and welfare reform. With regard to the draft treaty, Blair indicated that he would accept an Employment Chapter and a Social Chapter, but only if these emphasised labour flexibility and avoided over-regulation of the labour market. He also rejected the suggestion that the EU be given additional funds to tackle unemployment.

Overall, 'on the issue of employment, the member states opted for Blair's version' (Pollack, 1999). Moreover, the story is essentially the same with regard to the other aspects of social policy. Britain agreed to end the opt-out, but argued against excessive regulation of the European economy and opposed any extension of qualified majority voting. The Amsterdam Treaty does include some moderate innovations in social policy, particularly the revised Article 141, which extends the principle of equal pay for equal work to 'work of comparable value', and extensions to powers regarding environmental protection, public health and consumer protection. But 'the Treaty of Amsterdam does not represent the triumph of a traditional socialist or social democratic ideal of regulated capitalism ... [It] was shaped largely by the new government, and the new governing philosophy, of Tony Blair' (Pollack, 1999). Moving beyond individuals and personalities, it is clear that the ideological shift away from policies of state intervention and *dirigisme* largely transcends traditional Left–Right distinctions. Modern governing parties in Europe, whatever their label, have, in their different ways, made their peace with the market.

At the start of the 2000s, as in earlier periods, the EU social policy story should be understood in terms of the broader economic and political context. The economic context comprised not only the successful launch of the euro in January 1999, with eleven of the fifteen member states participating, but also, and more generally, the fiscal orthodoxy found in most member-state governments (whatever the rhetoric) and embodied in the key institutional innovation at European level – the European Central Bank. The political context was how Left and Centre-Left governments across Europe would adapt to this economic and institutional legacy. While there were important differences between governments, touched on above, it is equally clear that no government was advocating a return to 1960s demand management and state direction of the economy.

At the institutional level, the key challenge was to anticipate the impact of enlargement early in the new millennium, mainly to the former communist countries of Central and Eastern Europe. The practical implications were (and are) immense. The political and administrative machinery of the European Union was designed almost half a century ago for six countries that were broadly similar in terms of their economic and social development. With a Union of fifteen countries, it already seems outdated. In the future it will have to be adapted further to cope with a larger and more diverse group of countries. As the report by experts (the so-called 'Three Wise Men') in October 1999 commented:

> there are now clear indications that the system is no longer working as it should in a Union of fifteen members. The question automatically arises whether the institutions, as initially conceived, will be able to serve efficiently a Union which may in the foreseeable future extend to 25–30 or even more participants. Since the fifties, successive treaties have introduced some adaptations of the institutional framework, but there has been no effort at comprehensive reform. This is a challenge we will sooner or later have to face. (von Weizsächer *et al.*, 1999)

The White Paper on European Social Policy

What is the role of European social policy today? A useful starting point in answering this question is the White Paper published by the European Commission in 1994, entitled *European Social Policy: A Way Forward for the Union* (European Commission, 1994). This followed an earlier Green Paper on social policy, and a White Paper on growth, competitiveness and employment. Although now more than six years old, the White Paper on European Social Policy still represents the most comprehensive recent attempt at setting out the EU role in social policy in a systematic way. It is therefore worth looking at the White Paper in a certain amount of detail.

The White Paper clearly bears the imprint of the post-Maastricht emphasis on subsidiarity and the pre-eminent role of the member states. The Preface states that 'Many of the challenges are for individual Member States to face, but the Union can and must play its role ... The Union cannot do everything and certainly should not seek to supplant the responsibilities at national, regional and local level.' Throughout the document, there is an emphasis on member states' actions, and the role of the EU in supporting or co-ordinating with them. The document recognises that total harmonisation of social policies is not an objective of the EU, although convergence over time through the fixing of common objectives is possible, and indeed 'vital'.

The White Paper begins by arguing that while jobs 'must continue to come top of the agenda', social policy involves more than just employment policy. It argues that, in a period of profound economic, social and technological change, the objective of the EU must be to 'preserve and develop the European social model'. This 'European social model' is defined mainly in terms of shared values, including democracy and individual rights, free collective bargaining, the market economy, equality of opportunity for all, and social welfare and solidarity. Furthermore, a concern with social and environmental goals does not necessarily conflict with the search for economic efficiency: 'the pursuit of high social standards should not be seen only as a cost but also as a key element in the competitive formula' (p. 10). Indeed, competitiveness and social progress are described as two sides of the same coin: 'the social environment is also an essential factor in determining economic growth. Progress cannot be founded simply on the basis of the competitiveness of economies, but also on the efficiency of the European society as a whole' (p. 12).

The White Paper lists the instruments of policy action as: legislation and collective agreements; financial support and incentives; mobilisation and co-operation; and information and analysis. In the view of the Commission, there is no longer a need for 'a wide-ranging programme of new legislative proposals', because of the 'solid base' of European social legislation already achieved (p. 13). Financial support will continue to be mainly through the Structural Funds. Mobilisation and co-operation refer to support for networks, exchanges of experience and cross-national actions. Finally, the European Commission is identified as having an important role not only in disseminating information, but also through its function of commissioning research.

The White Paper then discusses specific EU social policies. These can be grouped under five headings (those used below are not precisely the headings used in the document):

(i)   jobs, skills and working conditions;
(ii)   labour mobility;
(iii) equal opportunities;
(iv)   social protection and social inclusion; and
(v)   public health.

The first category is given the most weight. On jobs, the EU role is seen mainly in terms of supporting member state policies through co-operation, research, information and the promotion of social dialogue. The language and the general approach are very much within the framework of a pro-market competitiveness agenda. In terms of skills, again there is an emphasis on supporting member state activity, but this is complemented by a direct role for the Union via the European Social Fund, which should 'increasingly make a carefully targeted contribution to the development of a skilled, adaptable and mobile workforce. The development of human resources is a fundamental component of the Union's strategy for growth, competitiveness and employment' (p. 26).

Better working conditions for employees – or, as the White Paper puts it, 'legislating for higher labour standards and employee rights' – is described as an important part of the social achievements of the EU. The White Paper argues that the priorities for the future comprise: completing the existing social action programme; consolidating the 'good base' of labour standards; and promoting health and safety at work. The outstanding business for completing the existing social action programme at that stage comprised proposals on information and consultation of employees; on 'posting' of workers (that is, minimum standards for workers working temporarily in another member state); atypical work (part-time and temporary work); and the working-time directive.

As far as labour standards in general are concerned, the White Paper concedes that there is no consensus among member states and others about whether there should be any further raising of standards. While some argue that excessively high labour standards have a negative impact on the competitiveness of firms in particular regions or countries, there are others who argue that high labour standards are an 'integral part of the competitive formula' (p. 31). The Commission's view is that consolidating and implementing the existing body of law will be 'at least as important' as any new proposals (p. 32). Finally, the commission sets out a series of further measures on health and safety at work.

On free mobility of labour, there are no substantive proposals, and a recognition that the issue of social security and labour mobility will be approached through effective co-ordination of national systems and not through any top-down harmonisation.

Under the heading of 'equal opportunities', can be grouped together a series of sections on the integration of immigrants, actions to combat racism and xenophobia, and measures (mainly work-based) to promote equality of opportunity between men and women.

The fourth category is social security and social inclusion. In the White Paper, the Commission argues that there needs to be a move away from passive income maintenance towards more active labour market measures. The European Social Model should be maintained, but also needs to be adapted. The diversity of social protection systems is recognised, and hence member states should foster convergence of social protection policies by having fixed common objectives. Rising social protection expenditure is clearly identified as a problem for member states.

Social inclusion or social integration is seen primarily as a responsibility for Member States, but with some complementary EU support, for example, in terms of spreading best practice and supporting innovation. The EU's research programme and spending programmes such as the Community Initiatives have a role here. Finally, a role for EU activity in the public health field is identified, with specific programmes on cancer, on health promotion, and on prevention of drug dependence.

What are we to make of the White Paper? First, the Commission, in this document, takes as a central idea the notion of a 'European Social Model'. But as we have seen in Chapters 2 and 3, while there are undoubtedly some pressures towards convergence of social policy across European countries, there is certainly no *single* European Social Model. We saw earlier that there are at least three or four broad types of 'social model' within Europe: Anglo-Saxon, corporatist, social-democratic and Mediterranean. Many analysts would argue that even this type of classification is too simplistic, and in reality the diversity of welfare systems cannot be reduced to four models. Enlargement to Central and Eastern Europe in the near future will increase that diversity.

So when the Commission talks about a European Social Model, it cannot be referring to an actual existing state of affairs. The term 'European Social Model' must therefore indicate either an ideal type or a distinct set of values, or some combination of the two. The

European social model is sometimes referred to in terms of shared values that distinguish European from non-European societies. There are, however, a number of problems with defining the European Social Model in terms of values. First, by emphasising supposed 'shared values', the historical development of welfare states as the outcomes of political, and in some cases industrial, struggles between competing classes is glossed over (Esping-Andersen, 1990; Baldwin, 1991). Second, the emphasis on values, and implicitly a shared moral agenda, implies a process of state-building and identity creation at the European level in the twenty-first century, paralleling the role of social policies in helping to define nation states and national identities in the twentieth century. But this raises a whole set of political, constitutional and practical issues. The analogy with national state building and national welfare states is misconceived. The 'policy space' in the social field is simply not there. More fundamentally, the analysis raises key issues about whether a European super-state and a European identity are desirable or acceptable to European citizens – an issue to which I shall return in Chapter 8.

In general, there is a muddled and generally defensive air to the White Paper. It was written shortly after the ratification of the Maastricht Treaty, and hence at the very moment when the trend towards ever-greater integration had turned. As a result, there are two important themes running through this document. First, the spirit of subsidiarity is everywhere. There are countless references to the rights, responsibilities and actions of member states, and the role of the EU is generally portrayed in terms of co-ordination, information dissemination, and occasional tidying up. This is a far cry from the high politics of grand European integration in earlier periods. The second recurring theme – or perhaps strain would be a better word – is the tension between the expansion of the social agenda, and in particular the maintenance and enhancement of high social standards throughout Europe on the one hand, and the competitive and deregulatory economic agenda on the other. There is an uneasy and often unconvincing defence of the traditional social agenda of high social standards, particularly those associated with the Rhineland corporatists and the Scandinavian social democrats.

One is aware throughout of the need to square the social agenda in this document with the competitiveness agenda of the earlier White Paper on *Growth, Competitiveness and Employment* (Com (93) 700). In the Growth White Paper, the causes of Europe's unemployment problem are seen to be excessive spending and inappropriate macro-economic policies:

The current levels of public expenditure, particularly in the social field, have become unsustainable and have used up resources which could have been channelled into productive investment ... the constant rise in the labour costs – affecting both its wage and non-wage components and caused, at least in part, by excessively rigid regulation – has hindered job creation. (European Commission, 1993a, p. 41)

the main explanation for the poor unemployment performance of the Community over the past two decades is to be found in the constraints that unresolved distributional conflicts and insufficient structural adjustment placed on macroeconomic policies. (European Commission, 1993a, p. 43)

The solutions promoted in the Growth White Paper include anti-inflationary policies, flexible labour markets, macroeconomic stability and controlled public finances. The macroeconomic framework should support market forces rather than constrain them 'as has often happened in the recent past' (European Commission, 1993a, p. 49). The first medium-term objective should be the stability of monetary policy, with an inflation target of between 2 per cent and 3 per cent. It is argued that once inflationary expectations are stabilised and the prospects of lower budget deficits established, interest rates can come down.

In the Growth White Paper, the Commission states that all member states are agreed that European labour markets are not working efficiently. It identifies specific problems such as a lack of flexibility, particularly with regard to the organisation of working time, pay and mobility, as well as problems of skills mismatch. This rigidity causes high labour costs and means that firms adjust to changes in demand by shedding labour or replacing it with capital:

Social protection schemes have – in part at least – had a negative impact on employment in that they have, in the main, tended to protect people already in work, making their situation more secure and consolidating certain advantages. They have in effect proved to be an obstacle to the recruitment of jobseekers or of new entrants to the labour market. (European Commission, 1993a, p. 146)

Other relevant factors include 'the high level of non-wage costs, particularly in the form of statutory levies and charges, and insufficient motivation to work due to inappropriate social protection systems and employment services' (European Commission, 1993a,

p. 146). There is also, according to the Commission, widespread agreement among member states about possible solutions – 'the introduction of greater flexibility in the organisation of work and the distribution of working time, reduced labour costs, a higher level of skills and pro-active labour policies'. However, member states also want to maintain social protection systems. The Commission's own view is that improvement in Europe's employment performance will require greater flexibility in the labour market, comprising reduced labour costs, particularly for unskilled and semi-skilled workers, investment in education and training by business and governments, and a shift to active labour market measures in the design of policy.

Hence, throughout the White Paper on social policy, there is a generally unsatisfactory attempt to present the competitiveness agenda of increased market forces, labour flexibility and reduced entitlements as if there was no conflict between this and a defence and enhancement of the 'European Social Model'. So when the authors of the social policy White Paper write that 'the pursuit of high social standards should ... be seen ... as a key element in the competitive formula' (p. 10), it is not at all clear what this means. Similarly, it is not clear what is meant by 'the social environment is also an essential factor in determining economic growth. Progress cannot be founded simply on the basis of the competitiveness of economies, but also on the efficiency of the European society as a whole' (p. 12). The first sentence is at least a hypothesis, although no evidence is given either way. But what is meant by 'the efficiency of the European society as a whole'?

Fourth, the specific issues examined in the White Paper, while familiar to any student of the history of the social policy of the EU and its predecessors, make up an eclectic list when considered against any first-principles definition of social policy. There is little or nothing on health care, social care, family policy, education or housing, while there is rather a lot on labour market issues and working conditions.

Developments since the White Paper

Since the 1994 White Paper there has not been a comprehensive statement on the EU's overall approach to social policy, but it is clear that there has been no major change from the approach outlined in the White Paper. In 1996, the member states agreed to add an

Employment Chapter to what became the Amsterdam Treaty. As Pollack (1999) shows, the Amsterdam Treaty represented a victory for the pro-market centre-left policies associated with the British prime minister, Tony Blair, rather than the more traditional Left interventionist policies of the French prime minister Lionel Jospin:

> The Employment Chapter agreed to in Amsterdam and incorporated into the Treaty (Articles 125–130 [109n–109s] formally makes 'a high level of employment' an EU objective and provides for coordination and monitoring of national employment policies, and the creation of an advisory committee on employment. However, at the summit Blair and Kohl joined together to rule out any harmonization in the area of employment policy, and to block any major new EU spending on employment programs, which are restricted to pilot projects of limited scope and duration. In short, the new treaty provisions place employment clearly on the EU agenda ... yet the approach is voluntaristic and falls short of granting the Union any significant regulatory or redistributive capacity.' (Pollack, 1999)

The Commission's Communication on the Social Action Programme of April 1998 (COM (98) 259) sets out a 'blueprint for European social policy covering the years 1998–2000'. It defines three main headings: jobs, skills and mobility; the changing world of work; and an inclusive society. Few specific details are given, however.

In 1999, a new Commission was appointed, following the Jacques Santer debacle and the resignation of all twenty Commissioners. As part of the process of appointing the new Commissioners, they were required to give statements to, and respond to questions from, the European Parliament. An examination of the statements made by the new Commissioner for Employment and Social Affairs, Ms Diamantopoulou, shows that her approach to defining the role of the EU in social policy is very close to that set out earlier in the Social Policy White Paper.

In her statement, the Commissioner wished to emphasise her attachment to the 'European Social Model' and the 'values' associated with it, identified as democracy, justice, participation, social dialogue, and the mechanisms that underpin social solidarity and social cohesion. She argues that the model needs to be reformed to adapt to changing conditions, but the aim of reform should be to reinforce, and not to reduce, solidarity. Furthermore, echoing the arguments of the 1994 White Paper, she maintains that social policy and social solidarity are not burdens on society, but rather they 'should be key factors in improving productivity'. Consequently, social reforms – such as social cohesion, gender equality, worker involvement and corporate social responsibility – contribute to optimising economic performance. She goes on to argue (without quoting any evidence) that 'the European Social Model is now recognised as both a productive factor in economic performance and as a mark of a cohesive society'.

The questions by the European Parliament and the responses from the incoming Commissioner cover the following subjects:

- reducing unemployment;
- social dumping;
- the European Social Model;
- occupational health and safety;
- demographic change;
- equal opportunities and discrimination;
- social exclusion;
- social dialogue and collective bargaining;
- reconciling family and working life;
- the environmental dimension; and
- EU enlargement.

From this list, it is clear that the general content definition of the EU social policy field has not changed significantly in more than six years since the 1994 White Paper.

The role of the European Union in social policy today is far greater than that envisaged at the time of the 1957 Treaty. There has been a steady expansion in the scope, role and objectives of EU social policy. But at the same time, EU social policy continues to bear the imprint of the specific circumstances that attended its creation in the 1950s. These include a focus on a specific set of issues, mainly linked to the labour market, and an ambiguity about whether social policy is an important policy area in its own right or should be considered mainly as an adjunct or facilitator for economic integration.

Social Policy-making in the European Union

How is social policy made in the European Union? 'Policy-making' normally implies a *state* that both formulates and implements policy.

However, the European Union is not a state, and yet it clearly has the capacity to formulate, implement and evaluate policy. How, then, should we understand policy-making, and specifically the making of social policy within the EU? This takes us to a continuing debate about the nature and political economy of the European Union. Among analysts, there has long been a debate between 'intergovernmentalists' and 'neo-functionalists'. For intergovernmentalists, the politics and policy of the EU is best understood as the interaction of sovereign nation states, which are considered as 'hard billiard balls'. Member states are the key actors (Rhodes and Mazey, 1995, p. 8). Intergovernmentalism draws on the theory of 'realism' in international relations. While early versions tended to treat the national state as a single, coherent actor, later versions ('liberal intergovernmentalism') allowed for greater complexity in the definition of 'national interests'. At the centre of this analysis are the 'grand bargains' or quasi-constitutional reforms of the EU treaties. EU structure is acceptable to national governments only in so far as it strengthens their control over domestic affairs (Falkner, 1998).

The main alternative paradigm is neo-functionalism. Here it is argued that public and private actors form incremental, transnational linkages, so that supranational institutions develop incrementally (Rhodes and Mazey, 1995, p. 8). For the neo-functionalist, 'spillover' is a key concept: integration means moving from one decision or sector to another. In an early formulation, Haas (1964, quoted in Falkner, 1998) referred to 'policies made in carrying out an initial task and grant of power can be made real only if the task is expanded'. Falkner (1998) classifies several different types of spillover. *Functional* spillover refers to the fact that 'due to the interdependence between sectors or issues in modern economies it is impossible to treat them in isolation (action in one area begets action in another one): a classic example is the implementation of the common market necessitating accompanying measures (e.g. in social policy) which were not anticipated by the founding fathers of the EC' (Falkner, 1998, p. 8). *Political* spillover refers to shifts in political expectations or loyalties. *Geographical* spillover occurs because more states want to join the integration process. *Cultural* spillover occurs when the loyalties of elites shift toward the supranational level.

In other words, should we understand the European Union to be purely a collection of treaties and a set of bargaining outcomes reached by independent and irreducible nation states? Or should we treat it as a state in the making, with social policy both an outcome of this process and an input into further rounds of political and economic integration, and hence state-making? Like many theoretical debates in academe, this discussion has veered towards the obscure much of the time. Equally, like many academic 'theories', it is not always clear what, if anything, is generated in the way of falsifiable hypotheses, nor what would count as a definitive burden of proof. Nevertheless, the analytic difference between treating the EU as, on the one hand, an international organisation, a relationship between states; and, on the other, treating it, however imperfectly and ambiguously, as an emerging polity, a 'quasi-state', is a crucial one. It bears directly on the analysis of how to interpret and understand European social policy, and even more fundamentally, on the debate about the future of the EU and the desirability and feasibility of a Federal Europe. A brief excursion through the literature will therefore be helpful.

In the 1970s, closer European integration, especially in the social and political spheres, seemed utopian. Early functionalist theories such as that of Haas (1964) seemed obsolete, and 'realist' intergovernmentalism appeared more germane. But with the renewed impetus to integration in the 1980s, 'grand theory' re-emerged (Caporaso and Keeler, 1995). A range of authors argued that the development of the European Community could not be understood solely in terms of the international and particularly economic forces that obtained, important though these were. Also relevant was the purposive activity of the European Commission, of business groups, and of mobilised government elites (Sandholtz and Zysman, 1989).

Probably the dominant view at the time of writing (2001) is to see the EU as a unique example of 'multi-level governance'. The European Union is a set of institutions as well as a market and a free-trade area (Caporaso and Keeler, 1995). It is a complex of norms, rules, procedures and understandings and it is a mistake to think in terms of a 'fixed pie' over which the EU institutions and the member states battle (Marks, 1992). Rather, there is a system of multi-level governance in which the national, the supranational, the regional and the local levels are all involved. The outcome of the continuing process of European integration is therefore open-ended and uncertain, and it is unlikely that a 'tidy polity' will emerge. In this view, the outcome should not be understood as a point on a continuum from a loose confederation of strong member states to a federal European state; rather there is a complex, fluid situation and a multi-layered polity (Marks, 1992).

Similarly, and with specific reference to the social policy of the EU, Pierson and Leibfried (1995) argue that the EU has the 'characteristics of a supranational entity' – bureaucratic competencies, unified judicial control, significant capacities to develop and modify policies' (p. 1). It is more than an international organisation – it is the central, albeit weak, level of an 'emergent multi-tiered system of governance'. Pierson and Leibfried (1995) acknowledge that the institutions of the EU are designed precisely to inhibit decisive action and to give the member states the greatest say. But, they argue, for a wide range of policy activity, including social policy, it cannot be reduced simply to bargaining among autonomous states. They suggest that there are four main reasons why policy is not solely under the control of member states: the autonomous actions of EU organisations; the impact of previous policy commitments; the scope and overlap of issues (that is, spillover); and the actions of non-state actors.

The various institutions of the EU are able to act autonomously in different ways. The main power of the European Commission is that of agenda setting. The Commission is able to manage the complex and fragmented system of policy development, and to negotiate the labyrinth of regulatory policy making. The European Court of Justice (ECJ) has unexpectedly proven to be a major influence on the extension of EU social policy-making. The nineteenth-century USA has been described as a 'state of courts and parties' (Skowronek, 1982). That is, the courts and the political parties were the key institutions that bound together a disparate continental society into an emerging *national* state. Pierson and Leibfried (1995) describe the EU as a 'state of courts and technocrats'. The ECJ 'constitutionalises' European policy and has involved itself in a more extensive judicial review process than most national counterparts. It has fewer impediments to action than other EU institutions. Policy activism is possible through the use of simple majority rules – 'legal instruments, rather than spending or taxing powers are dominant at the EU level' (Pierson and Leibfried, 1995). Much integration happens through low-profile accumulation of legal decisions.

Second, there are the cumulative effects of treaty commitments. Revisions to treaties are difficult because of the requirement of unanimity. Essentially, there is a ratchet effect, in which incremental changes accumulate over time. Third, there is 'issue density', meaning both the spillover effect and the fact that, while member state governments can scrutinise (and veto) proposals in the treaty revisions, policy-making continues incrementally between treaty revisions and inter-governmental conferences. Both the Commission and the ECJ are able to take advantage of this to extend their authority. Finally, also relevant is the role of non-state actors: cross-national social actors, pressure groups, and lobbyists of various kinds (Pierson and Leibfried, 1995).

Furthermore, it is a mistake to assume that 'multi-level' means a zero-sum game. There will be conflict between the levels of government, but the outcomes can be positive (Marks, 1992; Pierson and Leibfried, 1995). However, few commentators envisage any large-scale pre-emption of the existing predominance of the nation state in welfare. A great deal of the policy 'space' is already occupied by the national state – in contrast to the situation in the nineteenth-century USA. The central components of the national welfare states – education, health care, and retirement security – will remain under national control. The EU has limited resources; national programmes pre-empt administrative and fiscal as well as policy spaces. The EU must implement policy via the national bureaucracies. EU expenditure is 1 per cent of European GDP, and less than 4 per cent of the spending of the central governments of the member states. Furthermore, given the diminished role of national governments in other policy areas – for example, macroeconomic policy – they will be reluctant to cede power in this area to the EU. Consequently, EU initiatives are likely to be 'most evident around the edges of these national cores, in policy domains that are unoccupied or that the integration process renders particularly fragile' (Pierson and Leibfried, 1995, p. 33).

Much of the research on the EU policy-making process is dominated by a pluralist approach, with a focus on groups, organised interests, strategies and influence. The EU has been described as an example of 'limited pluralism' (Rhodes and Mazey, 1995) in which some groups are more influential than others. The degree of pluralism varies by sector, being relatively limited in the sectors of 'high politics' (security, foreign policy, EU institutional reform) and greater in sectoral policy-making. Rhodes and Mazey (1995) conclude that the EU is neither a sovereign state nor an international organisation. The Maastricht Treaty was only one step on a longer road of piecemeal integration. As the European Community became the European Union, there was more talk of the EU as a 'European polity' and a 'system of governance'.

Although many areas of domestic public policy have been 'Europeanised', the EU has yet to develop a stable set of policy-making institutions and procedures (Mazey and Richardson, 1995). EU policy-making is centred on the Commission and an ever-closer relationship with a 'complex melange' of policy actors. The European policy style emphasises bargaining, coalition building and consensus. Greater integration has promoted greater interest-group activity and increased lobbying. These authors argue that although 'institutionalisation' is happening – the system is becoming more stable – this is not a corporatist-style 'concertation'. There is an 'absence of anything resembling a balance of class or sectoral interests at the European level' (Mazey and Richardson, 1995, p. 343). Mazey and Richardson conclude that in the unstable, multi-dimensional system of EU governance, the Commission is likely to remain the key actor, and they characterise the Commission as an 'adolescent and promiscuous bureaucracy'.

Others, however, stress corporatism rather than pluralism. In her study of EU social policy-making in the 1990s, Falkner argues that the procedural innovations of the Maastricht Treaty – the extension of Community competence and the participation of the social partners in the policy process – have led to a 'corporatist policy community' being set up: 'corporatist patterns of policy-making and even the specific features of interest representation which were often found to accompany them ... still play a role in contemporary European governance' (Falkner, 1998, p. 187). But Falkner too espouses the concept of 'multi-level network governance' – 'From this perspective, the EU itself appears to be a multi-network system' (ibid., p. 188).

This 'New Governance' perspective, in which the EU is seen as more than an international organisation, but less than a state, has to a large extent become the current orthodoxy (Hix, 1998). The European Union is *sui generis*, a unique set of multi-level, non-hierarchical and regulatory institutions, involving a mix of state and non-state bodies. The development of the EU does not involve a 're-run' of national state formation. The EU's key function is the regulation of social and political risk, and not the redistribution of resources. Policy-making in the EU is complex, involving co-operation between different levels. Policy networks involving private interest groups and scientific and technical expertise are important. Informal processes and informal agreements often precede formal (Council of Ministers) policy-making, with a network of EU and national agencies administering the outcome. It is 'governance without government' (Rosenau and Czempiel, 1992).

Against this view, Hix (1998) argues that while the EU is not a state in the classical sense, it is nevertheless a 'political system': there are formal rules for decision-making; EU policies have enormous *indirect* redistributional impact; and there is a politics of the EU involving the mobilisation of citizens, private groups and others. Moreover, EU politics are becoming normalised – they are not only about integration, but also about traditional Left–Right concerns: unemployment, inflation, justice and so on. This leads him to suggest an alternative view: politics and government in the EU are not that different from elsewhere. The EU is not like a traditional European state – but it is a quasi-federal 'regulatory state', like the USA before the 1930s. As the European Union becomes more important, European citizens are becoming more sceptical, and hence there is increased importance attached to the question of 'how it can work better'. Public opinion judges governance at the European level on the same criteria as at the national level.

This has profound implications for the legitimacy and accountability of the European Union, to which we shall return later. In most democracies, regulatory agencies are connected to majoritarian institutions – but this is not so in the EU. Democracy implies government *by* as well as *for* the people, meaning control over inputs, and the ability to choose between competing elites and rival agendas. The 'standard version' of the democratic deficit argument focuses on the issue of the power of the European Parliament *vis-à-vis* the Council and the Commission. But this is naïve because European elections are fought on national and not European issues. An expansion of parliamentary power in these conditions might reduce rather than enhance the legitimacy of the EU (Hix, 1998).

What have we learned from this diversion through the thickets of theory building? First, that the EU is difficult to characterise as a system of governance. It is clearly more than an international organisation, yet equally clearly it is not a state. It is not the top tier of a federal system of European government – though there are political actors that would like it so to be. Second, part of the difficulty of classification is because the object is a moving target. Treaty revisions and incremental policy-making by the EU institutions are changing continually both the process and the substance. In much writing about EU policy-making there is a teleological, and even Whiggish, element. Closer union, and further integration, are identified with 'progress', and difficulties that arise are treated as technical problems to be 'solved' on the road to progress. Third, the concept of 'multi-level governance' has wide backing. It offers a way out of the increasingly sterile debate between the positions of inter-governmentalism and neo-functionalism. But what does it in fact mean? *Descriptively*, it is hard to challenge: governance in the EU involves a combination of national, regional, local and supranational agencies, which act sometimes in concert, sometimes in conflict. Policy-making involves building coalitions and consensus across a range of actors, developing policy networks, setting the agenda, and incorporating potential enemies. But what does this concept generate *analytically* or *predictively*?

It may be thought that this is a rather abstruse academic debate, of no relevance to the real world. But we need to try to understand exactly what the EU is, if we are to make any headway in considering the future of European social policy. In the next chapter I consider the pressures for and against a stronger European role in social policy, and assess how the EU's role with regard to welfare is likely to develop in the future.

Conclusions

European social policy began as a relatively minor component of European integration among six European countries with broadly similar social systems. In the years since then, the European Union has become far more diverse, and national welfare systems have themselves expanded greatly. The potential scope of European social policy, and the complexities of harmonising, or even co-ordinating across fifteen member states have grown considerably.

Nevertheless, European social policy at the start of the twenty-first century retains much of its early focus on issues such as employment, health and safety, equal opportunities, labour mobility, and other aspects of the labour market. More recently, issues such as the need to reconcile high levels of social protection and social standards with the needs of a productive economy, and the limits of the European role *vis-à-vis* those of member states and sub-national governments have become more prominent.

5

European Union Social Policy Today and Tomorrow

Introduction

The general argument in this chapter is that a European welfare state does not exist at the time of writing, and is unlikely to be brought into existence in the future. Nevertheless, there is a real and important sense in which we can talk about the social policy of the European Union as something distinct from, although necessarily closely interacting with, the social policies of individual member states. The tension between these two statements is not a peculiarity of social policy itself, but rather is a dramatic demonstration of the ambiguity and potential conflict that lies at the heart of the European integration project itself. The scope for substantial expansion of the European Union's social policy-making capacities is very limited, and it is extremely unlikely that anything that could be called a European welfare state will come into existence in the first few decades of the twenty-first century. Nevertheless, the Union and the member-state governments will have to deal with the social consequences of continuing and deepening economic integration, as well as enlargement. This interaction between the economic and the social aspects of integration will then be explored in Chapter 6.

In this chapter I first analyse the form and content of European social policy in terms of the traditional governmental functions of taxation, spending and regulation. I then consider the institutional capacity of the European Union for an expanded European role in welfare, and conclude that this capacity is already stretched by the EU's current role, particularly with regard to principles of legitimacy and accountability. From here I go on to consider, first, the general arguments for and against transnational social policy, and finally the specific likelihood of a European welfare state emerging.

The nature of European social policy

In Chapter 4, we looked at how European Union social policy has developed from its limited origins in the 1957 Treaty of Rome to the present-day much more extensive range of interventions, and at the process of social policy formulation within the EU. What about the nature of EU social policy in 2001 – which issues are addressed, which mechanisms used, and what role do the different European institutions play?

First, in terms of *content*, EU social policy action has been concentrated on a specific sub-set of the potential social policy field. As shown both in statements of policy and actions undertaken, EU social policy has mainly been about:

- regulating the labour market;
- regulating conditions at work;
- establishing equal opportunities in the work sphere;
- occupational health and safety;
- labour mobility;
- social protection;
- and, to a limited extent, social inclusion.

More recently, action has been extended into areas that at the national level would normally be considered to be at the margins of social policy, such as urban policy and environmental protection.

The scope of EU social policy is thus very restricted in comparison with the range of social policies implemented at national, and in some cases sub-national, levels within the member states. Within member states, the politics of social welfare is centrally concerned with issues such as health care, education and housing, which are at best peripheral to the EU agenda.

Why has European Union social policy been focused on these specific areas? Several factors are relevant. First, to some degree, the EU's policy sphere reflects a 'continental' view of social policy, where the term itself carries a strong implication of labour market regulation, and, more generally, the relationship between different social groups. This can be contrasted with the traditional British, or Anglo-Saxon, content definition of social policy, as being mainly about the collective provision of public services. Second, EU policy activism is often in areas where the overlap between economic and social policy is strongest – that is, where the potential for policy spillover is greatest. Thus to some extent the sphere of activity of EU social policy confirms the predictions of functionalist spillover theory. Third, in other central areas of social policy, there seems to be relatively little scope for European intervention, as both the mechanism and the rationale for policy intervention are based more clearly at national level. In the terminology of Leibfried and Pierson (1994), the policy space is already occupied. Fourth, given these *structural* reasons for the focus of European social policy, *institutional* factors will then tend to intensify and deepen the process. That is, once competence and activity are established in particular policy areas, the process will tend to be self-sustaining. In these areas where the EU has established some kind of legitimacy, the ECJ will give rulings and the Commission will act as a policy entrepreneur, deepening its influence in existing areas of activity and widening out to adjacent policy areas. In other areas where legitimacy is more problematic, these processes are less likely to develop.

The *form* of intervention at EU level is similarly idiosyncratic in comparison with social policy intervention at national level. Government intervention in the social field usually comprises some combination of regulation, fiscal policy and direct provision. At the European level, direct provision of services is absent, and hence social policy intervention at the European level is mainly through the two mechanisms of taxing/spending and regulation.

Taxing and Spending: the EU budget

On the revenue side, the EU is barred explicitly from borrowing to fund expenditure; the Community's own Budget must always balance. The choice of a tax base for revenue raising will have some distributive consequences between member states, between sectors, and between households. Since 1970, the so-called 'own resources' system has been used. The EU's income is raised from a combination of customs duties, agricultural levies, and a share of national VAT receipts, calculated on a hypothetical 'harmonised' tax base. Since 1988, a fourth resource has been added, related to the GNP of each member state. At the same time, the VAT base was capped. The total of 'own resources' which finance the EU budget are capped as a percentage of total EU GNP – the ceiling was set at 1.20 per cent in 1994, rising to 1.27 per cent in 1999 and thereafter.

To the time of writing, then, the main choice for financing the EU budget has been VAT. Strictly speaking, this has not been equivalent to providing the Community with its own tax base. This is because, first, there are differences between the 'harmonised' and actual tax bases in each country; and second, that there is no evidence that changes in the rate at which the EU 'calls up' VAT contributions from the member states in fact affects the rate of VAT levied. These two factors weaken the principle of accountability in revenue raising, and Smith (1992) argues that there is no merit in continuing the 'pretence' that member states' contributions do in fact relate to VAT. The VAT base can be objected to on distributional as well as accountability grounds. Countries with a high share of investment or public consumption will have a lower VAT base relative to GNP, and hence the use of a VAT base is probably regressive (Smith, 1992). To this extent, moving to a greater reliance on the GNP resource is a step forward on distributional grounds.

In the year 2000, the budget of the European Union was 93.3 billion euro, representing about 1.11 per cent of European GDP. On the expenditure side, agricultural policy remains the major component, although its share has fallen considerably. The proportion of the Community budget going to the Common Agricultural Policy (CAP) peaked at 68 per cent in 1985, and fell to below 44.5 per cent in 2000. The CAP is a sectoral rather than a redistributive policy, and given its weight in the overall EU budget, is the main reason why the budget's overall effect is regressive (Begg and Mayes, 1991). The next largest component of the EU budget is structural and cohesion policy, with spending at 35.2 per cent of the total in the year 2000.

The contributions of the different member states to the financing of the EU and the relationship between individual member states' contributions and receipts raises sensitive political issues. The Commission makes available information only reluctantly on the net contributions of the member states to the EU budget. The Commission and most member states have always rejected the '*juste retour*' principle, in which contributions and receipts for each country must balance exactly, seeing this as a recipe for fragmentation.

Nevertheless, calculations of net contributions can be made. For 1990, Smith (1992) shows that Ireland and Greece benefited most, as to a lesser degree did Portugal, Spain, Denmark and the Netherlands. The largest contributors (on a percentage of GDP basis) were Luxembourg, Belgium, the UK, Germany and France. More recent figures released by Michelle Schreyer, the European Commissioner for budgets, show that, in 1999, the largest net recipients, expressed as a proportion of GNP, were Greece (3.2 per cent of GNP), Portugal (2.79 per cent), Ireland (2.50 per cent) and Spain (1.31 per cent). In volume terms, the largest recipients of EU expenditure were Spain, France, Germany, Italy and the UK. The largest net contributors were the Netherlands (0.57 per cent), Luxembourg (0.55 per cent), Germany (0.49 per cent), Sweden (0.47 per cent) and Austria (0.38 per cent).

However, such calculations are based only on the formal incidence of expenditures and revenues. Effective incidence will differ considerably (Smith, 1992). First, the location of expenditures or revenues may not be a particularly good guide to where the benefits or burdens in fact fall (the so-called Rotterdam effect). Second, transfer payments and payments for real resources are taken together, whereas from the point of view of the member-state government, the latter, but not the former, have an opportunity cost. Third, and more fundamentally, the above calculations measure only the first-round effects, whereas Community measures will have wider effects: Customs duties raise the price of internal substitutes; intervention buying raises prices throughout the Community, and so on.

Expenditure on the structural funds doubled in real terms between 1987 and 1993, but this still left expenditure at less than half of 1 per cent of European GDP, and representing less than 6 per cent of the welfare gain estimated to accrue to the community from the completion of the single market (Kleinman and Piachaud, 1993, p. 11). Under the 'Delors II' package, expenditure on the funds (including the new Cohesion Fund, agreed at Maastricht) rose from 18.6 billion ECU in 1992 to 29.3 billion ECU in 1997, at 1992 prices. The share of the budget going to the Structural Funds increased from one-sixth in 1988 to more than one-third in 2000. Structural Funds expenditure (including the Cohesion Fund) amounted to 32.7 billion euro in 2000, but this is projected to decline somewhat to 29.7 billion euro in 2006.

The Structural Funds comprise: the European Regional Development Fund, which funds investment, particularly linked to creation or maintenance of jobs, infrastructure projects, education and training, research and development and environmental projects; the European Social Fund, which helps long-term and young unemployed, those excluded from work, and promotes equal opportunities; and specific funds linked to agriculture and fisheries (the European Agricultural Guidance and Guarantee Fund, and the Financial Instrument for Fisheries Guidance).

In the 1994–9 period, for the first time, all these funding programmes were co-ordinated in a series of multi-annual programmes, geared to the following six objectives:

- Objective 1: Regions seriously lagging the EU average (less than 75% regional GDP).
- Objective 2: Help to regions or areas seriously affected by industrial decline.
- Objective 3 (non-spatial): Help to the long-term unemployed, youth and the socially excluded.
- Objective 4 (non-spatial): Help to those affected by changes in industry and production.
- Objective 5a: Modernisation of the agricultural and fisheries sector.
- Objective 5b: Development of rural areas.
- Objective 6: Help to areas with very low population density.

In addition, there are a number of specific programmes known as Community Initiatives.

From 2000, the number of Objectives was simplified to three:

- Objective 1: Assistance to the most deprived areas.
- Objective 2: Assistance to areas facing industrial decline, rural areas, urban areas and areas facing decline in the fishing industry.
- Objective 3: Assistance to education, training and employment.

Similarly the number of Community Initiatives will be reduced from thirteen to three. In the 1990s, 51 per cent of the EU population was covered by Objectives 1 and 2 – the aim is to reduce this to between 35 per cent and 40 per cent, although there will be transitional protection for those affected.

Expenditure on the Structural Funds goes mainly on physical infrastructure and human capital. The basic principle is to enhance the ability of regions – both peripheral regions and older industrial areas – to compete in the single market. The notion of cohesion is nowhere defined: 'It is largely a politically determined condition which relates to the acceptability of existing disparities and the efforts being made to change them.' (Begg and Mayes, 1991, p. 65). The rationale for structural funds expenditure is a mixture of promoting adaptation and compensating losers. Expenditure is directed towards the productive capacity (human or physical) of particular areas, to enable them either to overcome backwardness or peripherality, or to withstand the strains of industrial restructuring. The Delors Report on Economic and Monetary Union states:

> The principal objective of regional policies should not be to subsidize incomes and simply offset inequalities in standards of living, but to help to equalize production conditions through investment programmes in such areas as physical infrastructure, communications, transportation and education so that large scale movements of labour do not become the major adjustment factor.'
> (quoted in Tsoukalis, 1993, p. 246)

However, in practice, such expenditures also contain purely compensatory or redistributive elements as well. The implicit rationale is that an enlarged market and a monetary union supposedly bring welfare gains – and part of these gains can be used to compensate losers. But, in practice, the fact that more than half the expenditure of the EU goes on the CAP, coupled with the regressive effects of the VAT base, mean that it is likely that the overall fiscal effect of the EU budget is regressive, despite the goals of Structural Funds expenditure.

Second, in the context of the macroeconomic policies espoused by the member states and the Commission, it is not clear whether structural policies are intended to reduce the overall level of unemployment; or to redistribute its geographical incidence; or simply to ameliorate conditions for those for whom there are no jobs. That is, current macroeconomic orthodoxy rules out demand-side reflation as a solution to unemployment. Is structural fund expenditure designed to operate on the supply-side by raising productive capacity? If so, in what circumstances is it likely to work? Or is the aim to raise effective demand locally, at the expense of reduced activity elsewhere in the Community? Or should it be treated, in effect, as consumption rather than production expenditure? The lack of clear answers to these questions is only in part a consequence of the lack of clear thinking about the goals of particular sorts of public policies. It also reflects the genuine mixture of 'economic' and 'social' goals of such policies at member state as well as at EU level, and hence the limitations of trying to separate these two aspects of policy rigidly.

Structural Funds expenditure is often explained by commentators as a 'side payment' needed to maintain progress in the core EC/EU task of increasing economic integration. Increases in Structural Fund expenditure can then be explained through a mixture of 'intergovernmentalism' – those member states that gain most from integration compensating those likely to gain least in order to maintain their support, and 'neofunctionalism' – the Commission acts to expand its functions, powers and influence. The 1988 reforms of the Structural Funds aimed at greater efficiency, rationality and additionality. The reforms involved a change in emphasis from projects to programmes, more explicit priorities, greater co-ordination and an increased role for regional (and local) authorities. Further reforms in 1999 simplified the numbers of priorities, with the goal of modernising the Funds, improving their effectiveness and better targeting the regions in need.

Prior to 1988, the Structural Funds had been a straightforward device for financial transfers between member states, but after the 1988 reforms the situation became more complicated. These reforms led to a strengthening of the Commission's role and increased institution building among regional and local governments (Marks, 1992; Hooghe and Keating, 1994; Pollack, 1995). The expansion of regional policy to the point where Structural Funds expenditure represents about a third of the total EU budget cannot be explained either as a straightforward outcome of Commission policy, nor simply as an interstate transfer, but rather should be understood as the contested outcome of a number of political and economic factors (Hooghe and Keating, 1994). Structural Funds policy does not reflect just bargaining interests of member states, but can be seen as an example of the emerging practice of 'multilevel governance'.

However, member states still dominate the budgetary process as a whole. It is difficult, if not impossible, for the Structural Funds to legitimise a more redistributive role without a greater sense of European identity – 'European-ness' – among the general public. Similarly, the notion of a 'Europe of the Regions' in which the nation state withers away is unrealistic (Marks, 1992; Hooghe and Keating, 1994). The Funds remain small-scale; national governments retain a high degree of influence; regional input is fragmented and variable; and spillovers to other policy fields are limited.

Enlargement poses additional problems for structural and cohesion policy and the principle of redistribution between growing and lagging regions. The Commission's second report on economic and social cohesion makes clear that in a Union of twenty-seven countries, about a third of the expanded population would live in 'cohesion countries' with a per capita GDP of less than 90 per cent of the EU average. While the population would grow by a third with enlargement, GDP would increase by only 5 per cent. As a result, there would be a greater disparity between rich and poor in the EU and the emergence of three categories of member state: rich, intermediate and poor, according to a speech to the European Parliament on 31st January 2001 by the regional policy commissioner, Michel Barnier.

But in any case, Structural Funds policy remains a blunt instrument for achieving redistribution goals. Targeting is imprecise as to areas of greatest need, for a variety of reasons, including the variables chosen to determine eligibility, the lack of uniform comparable data across the EU, and the inappropriateness of the spatial scale used (McAleavy and de Rynck, 1997). This is a general feature of any area-based attempt to tackle poverty. For example, in England in 1997, two-thirds of all unemployed people lived *outside* the forty-four districts officially described as 'most deprived' (Smith, 1999). More importantly, even if these technical difficulties can be overcome, there remains a key distinction between redistribution across areas and redistribution across households. Redistribution on a *household* basis would take the EU into uncharted waters and constitute an invasion of the 'policy space' of national governments:

> [policy] tends to be inefficient because of the difficulty of targeting for redistribution communities containing a mix of rich and poor people. If our concern is with inequality among individuals, redistribution should be aimed at individuals, not regions. But this is precisely what Member States do not want the Community to do. (Majone, 1993)

It is therefore unlikely that the Structural Funds can be seen as the basis for a more comprehensive system of budget-based redistribution. They remain small-scale; their focus is spatial and not individual; and the limits to the expansion of this policy are likely already to have been reached. There remains then a key fault-line between pressures for a more redistributive EU budgetary policy, and the fiscal and political implications of this. A greater role in redistribution implies either a larger budget with no change in accountability – thereby aggravating the democratic deficit; or a larger budget with strengthened political accountability to European citizens – implying a major step towards a Federal Europe.

Views on the benefits or otherwise of the Structural Funds differ sharply. For Hooghe (1998) they epitomise the positive values of a European model of 'regulated capitalism', distinct from the Anglo-Saxon model of neo-liberalism. The 1988 Reform is described as the 'bedrock' of the anti-neo-liberal programme. In contrast, Blanchard (1998) argues that

> It is true that much of the money spent at this point on Structural Funds is wasted. But this, I believe, is largely possible because voters have not caught up to it. If, as I hope, the European budget becomes subject to sharper voter scrutiny, the political economy of European integration will force transfers to remain limited in scope and size: the generosity of the French for the Portuguese or the Greeks is surely much smaller than that of the Parisians for their less fortunate compatriots.

At heart, the Structural Funds remain a fudge between an inter-governmental system of side-payment transfers to promote collective action, and an embryonic system of regional aid and redistribution within a single political unit. The ambiguity of the Structural Funds as a mechanism reflects a deeper ambiguity about the nature of the EU as a political system.

The European Union's Regulatory Role

As we have seen, the EU's direct role as a taxer and spender is relatively small. To the extent that the European Union can be considered a 'state' it is mostly a regulatory state. It does not have a role in direct provision, and its taxing and spending role is minor in comparison to that of the national states. It is through regulation in various forms that the EU mainly has an impact on citizens and businesses in Europe.

Social policy is no different in this respect. The expanding social policy role of the EU has been achieved mainly through an increase in social regulation (although the Structural Funds have grown in both absolute and relative terms). Social policy in the EU is made through a complex institutional framework, involving the main institutions of the EU (the Council of Ministers, the European Commission, the European Parliament and the European Court of Justice), various tripartite committees, regulatory authorities and various platforms for social dialogue (Cram, 1993). Within this complex arrangement, the most important organisations have been, and continue to be, the European Commission and the European Court of Justice (ECJ), although the influence of the European Parliament is increasing.

The *European Commission* has an active interest in expanding the scope of EU social policy, and hence its own importance. In the absence of an expansionary budget, the chosen instrument is therefore regulatory policy (Cram, 1993); EU social policy remains limited. But the Commission, by using regulatory rather than expenditure policies, increasingly sets standards to which the member states must adhere. The unpopular task of tax-collecting is left to the member-state governments, while the costs of EU regulatory policies fall mainly on employers.

Because regulatory policy is relatively costless to the regulator, the regulator can increase its area of competence without spending more. However, there is a balance: member states have the last word. The Commission has shown itself to be an 'adept strategist', a 'purposeful opportunist' (Cram, 1993). The Commission is not a government, but it is charged with providing the dynamic for further integration. In the early stages of the EEC, it took a broad view of its role in social policy. This was curtailed in the 1960s, and since then, the Commission has been more circumspect. It utilises the skills and advantages of a bureaucracy, promoting marginal, incremental change. Day by day, through drafting regulations, Eurocrats construct a public policy formulation for further envisaged integration. Hence, non-binding 'soft' law creates preconditions for further action. The Commission's research funding role is crucial in expanding the agenda. Having commissioned relevant research, it is able to act at politically opportune moments. For example, the Social Action Programme was drawn up before the Social Charter was signed.

The Commission expands the frontiers of the possible, continually preparing for new opportunities. It builds on declarations; it institutes social programmes, observatories and research projects. Although much of what happens is symbolic politics only, this may have a catalytic effect. Euro-rhetoric and EU 'soft' law can create its own dynamic, leading to expansion in policy activity. The Commission remains the key actor among European institutions in social policy-making (Mazey and Richardson, 1995). The absence of a clearly identifiable government allows the Commission to play a major initiation role.

The European Court of Justice plays an increasingly important role in the development of European social policy. Leibfried and Pierson (1995) categorise three processes in the advancement of the social policy of the EU: positive, activist reform in which social policy initiatives arise from the centre (Commission, Council, ECJ);

'negative' reform in which the ECJ imposes market compatibility; and indirect pressures.

They summarise actions under the first category as being 'rather feeble' (p. 45), involving high aspirations and modest results. European integration has eroded national welfare state sovereignty, but mainly through other mechanisms. There are many barriers to a more activist social policy at the European level: the EU institutions are designed in a way to frustrate rather than initiate reforms; member states protect welfare state prerogatives; the lack of financial resources; conflicts between member states; and not least the very divergent and deeply institutionalised national welfare states. This changed somewhat during the 1990s with the extension of qualified majority voting for some social legislation.

However, the second mechanism – the impact of enforcement of 'market compatibility' requirements, particularly by the ECJ – has been more influential. There has been a gradual, incremental expansion of EU regulation and ECJ decisions on social policy. For a long period, this 'low politics' was ignored by commentators apart from specialised welfare lawyers. The ECJ has now made more than 300 decisions on social policy co-ordination. As a proportion of all judgements concerned with core common market topics, decisions on social policy rose from 6.3 per cent of ECJ decisions in 1968 to 22.8 per cent in 1992. By 1992, only competition policy was a larger category.

Competence and activity by EU institutions expands without reference to the substantive importance of the underlying issue. So intra-European migration is relatively small and decreasing. But it provides a 'critical mass' for generating ever-increasing litigation in the ECJ. This increased activism at European level has an impact on national welfare systems, as member states seek to retain control over entitlements. Thus there are moves to replace transfers with direct services and, more generally, pressures for Bismarck-type (contributory) rather than Beveridgean benefits. There is still some distance to go to a 'fully federalised' system – that is, one in which there is full access to the welfare state for anyone moving across an EU border. But the ECJ has adopted a wide definition of 'employment' and, in addition, uses the 'free movement of services' as an 'entering wedge' in which EU citizens are deemed free to consume services in any member state. Leibfried and Pierson (1995) conclude that there has been a partial abridgement of member-state sovereignty over social policy to encourage worker, and consumer, sovereignty.

Hence member states cannot limit social benefits to their own citizens, even though citizen-making has been crucial in state-building, especially in France and Germany. They cannot insist that benefits are consumed within their own territory; and they must accept that other states have a say in adjudications. Member states have naturally sought to resist this, but the ECJ has been insistent. Leibfried and Pierson (1995) conclude that the formal ground of 'co-ordination' has become a catalyst for an 'incremental, rights-based homogenization of social policy'. This does not amount to supranationalism, but it implies more than just harmonization – rather it is 'a marketplace of co-ordination, with the ECJ acting as market police, enforcing the boundaries of national autonomy' (ibid., p. 65).

At the start of the 2000s, the Commission and the ECJ are clearly the key institutions in the development and formulation of European social policy. During the 1990s, the powers of the European Parliament have slowly strengthened, and it is possible that the Parliament will play a greater role in social policy in the future. Direct elections from 1979 increased the symbolic importance of the European Parliament, and the debate about the democratic deficit in the late 1980s and 1990s demonstrated at least the potential for the Parliament to play a greater role. The powers of the European Parliament in EU decision-making were strengthened in both the Maastricht and (especially) the Amsterdam Treaties, so that by the end of the 1990s decision-making in many areas was shared effectively between the Commission and the Parliament.

The crisis in the EU following the publication of the independent report into fraud and mismanagement in March 1999 increased the visibility and the influence of the European Parliament – rather to its own surprise. It was the actions of the European Parliament that triggered the chain of events leading to the resignation of the entire twenty-person Santer Commission. Moreover, the Parliament exercised its powers in subjecting the proposed new Commission under Romano Prodi to a far more exhaustive examination than previously before confirming the new appointments.

The Parliament has some way to go before it shakes off its own image as expensive, inefficient, potentially corrupt and largely irrelevant. Turnout in the 1999 European elections fell below 50 per cent, further weakening the legitimacy of the institution. However, as the *Financial Times* put it on 16 September 1999, 'there are some grounds for thinking the Strasbourg assembly has grown up over the last nine months'. More than half of the members of the Parliament at the time of writing are new entrants elected for the first time in June 1999. According to the *Financial Times,*

> the evidence [from the parliamentary hearings into the new Commission] ... suggests that a new and more serious breed of legislator has been attracted to the European Parliament ... A new sense of discipline was evident in the way MEPs responded to Mr. Prodi's remarks. Speeches were generally kept within the strict time limits allowed, and were to the point ... Several MEPs said the Parliament must also reform itself, and accept greater accountability on pay and expenses ... The Parliament will follow the activities of the new commissioners with unparalleled intensity. If any put a step wrong, Mr. Prodi will come under intense pressure to remove them.

Social Policy and Institutional Capacity

European Union institutions formulate and implement social policy – even though there is no European government and the EU is not a state. This raises two types of issues of institutional capacity. One type of issue relates to the competence and ability of the institutions to formulate, implement and evaluate policy on behalf of hundreds of millions of citizens. The other type relates to the legitimacy and accountability of the EU institutions in so doing. The key institutions at the time of writing are the European Commission and the European Court of Justice. Neither institution is democratic, nor were they ever intended to be. The analogy of the ECJ with the Supreme Court is highly imperfect, as the Supreme Court functions in the context of a fully democratic federal system, with a powerful federal government and bureaucracy, political parties organised on a continental scale, and a complex system of checks and balances. Not only do these not exist in Europe, it is difficult to imagine them doing so in our lifetimes. But the ECJ, as we have seen, already makes law for Europeans, particularly in the social sphere.

The Commission is the body that most closely resembles, in principle at least, the kind of rational-bureaucratic government mechanism with which citizens are most familiar in their national states. However, it is neither an elected government nor a disinterested bureaucracy. Its reputation, not only in terms of accountability, but also in terms of competence, has suffered greatly from the corruption and nepotism scandals of the late 1990s. This has also rebounded on attitudes towards European integration more generally:

> The debacle of the European Commission under Jacques Santer has both confirmed and reinforced a widespread perception that an overprivileged and unaccountable elite has misused the growing power of Brussels – that mismanagement, nepotism and even fraud have been rife. That perception has, in turn, taken a dreadful toll of idealism about Europe. (Siedentop, 2000, p. 144)

The forced resignation of Santer and the other Commissioners in 1999 represented the moment in which the everyday politics of European nation states finally collided with the secret garden of the European Commission. The unparalleled events of March 1999 demonstrated the institutional weaknesses, lack of accountability and sheer inefficiency of the existing policy system of the EU. Following the devastating report of the Committee of Independent Experts into fraud, mismanagement and nepotism in the European Commission, the entire twenty-person Commission resigned. The report accused the commission of losing control of the 19 000-strong administration in Brussels and ignoring mismanagement. They accused the commissioners of irregularities in managing humanitarian aid, tourism, vocational training and other EU programmes. The report famously concluded:

> The studies carried out by the Committee have too often revealed a growing reluctance among the members of the hierarchy to acknowledge their responsibility. It is becoming difficult to find anyone who has even the slightest sense of responsibility. (Committee of Independent Experts, 1999, p. 144)

The House of Commons' Public Accounts Committee, following the report of the Committee of Independent Experts, found that in the Commission there was a lack of clarity about who was accountable to whom and for what, and a cultural emphasis on devising policy without regard to effective management (House of Commons Committee of Public Accounts, 1999). As the PAC report makes clear, the most worrying aspect is not the more lurid examples of corruption and cronyism, but the basic lack of effectiveness and institutional capacity in delivering programmes and providing accountability for public money. The culture within the Commission puts emphasis 'on policy development at the expense of efficient and effective management of policy implementation' (para. 9f).

Policies were adopted without identifying the benefits to be gained from them, or the costs and staffing implications. Bureaucrats were more concerned with drafting complex regulations than determining objectives and evaluating outcomes. As a result there is a myriad of small schemes 'requiring inordinate administration that undermines the purpose of the project and achieves poor value for money' (para. 9g). For example, the Commission is responsible for at least 1500 individual Structural Funds programmes.

The Committee of Independent Experts criticised the Commission for inadequate supervision of projects at the most senior level (para. 23) and told the PAC that 'there was no culture of management or financial control within the Commission' (para. 35). Performance measurement within the Commission appears to be decades behind good governmental practice elsewhere. Dismissal of incompetent staff rarely occurred (para. 54), while whistle-blowers were protected inadequately (paras 64 and 65).

These institutional weaknesses also partly explain subsequent abuses: for example, in the employment of temporary staff. Incredibly, in some areas, the Commission still measured the success of policies by the amounts spent rather than by what was achieved (para. 45). The former budget and personnel commissioner, Erkki Liikanen, one of a small number of Commissioners who were reappointed, echoed these criticisms by the PAC. Liikanen told MEPs in the parliamentary hearings that reform would be difficult, and stressed that he had found EU institutions had a culture that resisted criticism: 'We have not been able to change it all, and I am sure this new commission will not be able to change it all.'

In addition, the Public Accounts Committee concluded that effective management was hampered by outdated staffing codes, which 'fail to ensure the appointment and promotion of staff on merit'. The suggestion was even made that the Commission's appointment procedures need reform along the lines of the Northcote Trevelyan reforms in the British civil service – reforms that took place in the middle of the *nineteenth* century! It also found that financial reporting, audit and follow-up arrangements were inadequate, and that arrangements for combating fraud had not been effective.

In response to the scandal and the resignations, the new commission, led by Romano Prodi, promised extensive institutional reform, under the leadership of Vice-President of the Commission, Neil

Kinnock. In the preface to the Consultation Document, 'Reforming the Commission', Kinnock writes that the objective of the Reform Strategy is 'to make changes which will ensure that efficiency, accountability, transparency, responsibility and service are applied as working conventions everywhere in this unique multinational public administration' (Kinnock, 2000, p. iii). However, the commitment to radical reform is somewhat undermined by the following paragraph which refers to 'ever-increasing obligations', 'outdated' (not inefficient) systems and 'fragmented' (rather than non-existent) responsibility. Kinnock writes, 'the staff of the Commission has performed well in difficult circumstances'.

Radical change in the Commission seems unlikely. The Public Accounts Committee of the House of Commons, reporting in July 1999, found that:

> in spite of the call for changes we are concerned that there was no real belief or will to make them happen. Everyone spoke of the difficulty and complexity of making changes. To move an inch was seen to take so much effort that there was an acceptance that to achieve marginal change was a triumph and all that could be expected. (Public Accounts Committee, 1999)

Certainly, Paul van Buitenen, the Commission official whose whistle-blowing started the whole process in train, and who subsequently lost his job because of it, remains sceptical about the reform proposals. While Kinnock argues that the present conventions and regulations of the Commission are obstacles to its proper working, van Buitenen argues that it is not the form of the regulations, but the willingness of the Commission to use the proper procedures that is the problem: 'this implies that the introduction of a new set of practices, conventions and regulations, however necessary this may seem, would not automatically solve the problems which led to the resignation of the previous Commission' (van Buitenen, 2000, p. 238). As of January 2000, van Buitenen concludes that nothing has changed, and moreover: 'a proper reform process has to be studied, prepared and implemented carefully. The present proposals do not seem to follow this path ... The reform plans of Mr. Kinnock read like a management course manual and seem to have as their principal objective, the selling of the reform to the press and the public' (van Buitenen, 2000, p. 260).

The immediate issue, then, for the Commission, and for the EU institutions as a whole, is not the specific challenge of EU enlargement, which will necessarily mean a reform of the institutional structure, nor the major question of whether the EU needs a written constitution. Rather, it is the more prosaic but crucial question as to whether the Commission and the other institutions have the institutional capacity and legitimate authority to continue with their current functions in acting on behalf of European citizens.

In summary, there are serious deficiencies in the institutional capacity of the European institutions to take on functions that might comprise the foundations of a European welfare state. Nevertheless, the European Commission and the ECJ, and to a much lesser extent the European Parliament, already discharge some of those functions, raising important questions about accountability, legitimacy and citizenship.

How Likely Is a European welfare state?

How might a European social policy develop in the future? Will the EU surrender competence to the member states through an ever-stricter interpretation of the subsidiarity criteria? Alternatively, will the process of integration continue and deepen, embracing political and social integration as well as economic, and lead ultimately to the construction of a European welfare state? Or will there be more of the same – a continuing, complex and messy set of overlapping roles and actions at member-state and European levels? Of these three options, the last one is by far the most likely. In order to understand why, it is useful to set out the pressures for and against a greater transnational role in social policy.

Pressures for a stronger European role in welfare come from a number of sources. First, there are the spillovers or externalities associated with economic integration – 'problems connected to the completion of the internal market encourage the EC to invade the domain of social policy' (Leibfried and Pierson, 1994, pp. 37–8). While in principle one can make a tidy separation between 'market issues' and 'social issues', in practice, this is not possible. Economic and market activity is embedded in a dense network of social and political institutions. Furthermore, the strict separation between different stages of economic integration – free trade area, single market, full economic union – is not possible in practice (Kleinman and Piachaud, 1993).

Second, the threat of social dumping is sometimes advanced as a reason for a European social policy. However, as we saw in Chapter 3, this argument is unconvincing.

Third, many aspects of national (social) regulation equate to non-tariff barriers to trade. Member states will not be allowed to offer minimum unemployment or pension benefits to their own citizens without extending these to other EU citizens who have also worked in the country. This is likely to mean more tightly contribution-based programmes, and to remove a significant range of policies for combating low incomes from member states. Similarly, the single market and the euro are leading to a narrowing in the range of indirect tax rates across the EU (Leibfried and Pierson, 1994).

Fourth, the Maastricht Treaty grants all member-state nationals something called 'European citizenship'. At the time of writing, this means relatively little (see Chapter 8). But it is at least conceivable that in the future there will be pressures to define a European *social* citizenship more substantively. European integration is highlighting 'the contrast between the greatly expanded role of Brussels and the still very weak links between individual Europeans and the EC' (Leibfried and Pierson, 1994, p. 42).

However, offsetting these pressures for a stronger European role in social policy are a number of important obstacles to the development of any European welfare state (this section draws closely on Leibfried and Pierson, 1994). First, there is the fragmentation of political institutions in the European Union. EU institutions are designed specifically to inhibit bold initiatives. Despite some reforms, such as the introduction of qualified majority voting, it remains easier to block than to initiate policies. The expansion of the EU to fifteen members, with further enlargement in the future, together with the reluctance of national governments to surrender veto powers and voting strength, further exacerbates the collective action problem.

Second, there is the absence of social-democratic 'power resources'. In the power resources model of national welfare state development, emphasis is placed on the role of social-democratic forces – Left parties and strong unions – in overcoming opposition to the establish-ment of welfare policies. But the political power of organised labour has declined at the national level, and has not established itself transnationally or at the European level. Indeed, the reinvigoration of European integration was associated precisely with the emergence in many member states of an anti-social-democratic consensus in economic policy. In contrast with the history of the welfare state nationally, the key institutional and political factors are absent at the European level.

Third, there is the heterogeneity of the EU. There are widely different levels of economic development across the Union, much more than the regional variations in the USA, for example. Hourly wage rates in manufacturing in the mid-1990s varied from US $16.30 in Germany to US $3.00 in Portugal. Poverty rates, defined as households with incomes below 50 per cent of average EU personal income ranged from 2.7 per cent in Belgium to 68.6 per cent in Portugal. Cultural as well as economic heterogeneity is important. The history of the development of national welfare systems in Europe shows that strong perceptions of common citizenship and underlying social homogeneity are important. These conditions are almost entirely lacking at the EU level. The sense of European citizenship is very poorly defined. As Vobruba (1994) puts it 'the politically staged decline of the importance of borders is not paralleled by a simultaneously developing feeling of community on the European level' (Vobruba, 1994, p. 7).

Fourth, we have to take into account the 'pre-emptive' role of national welfare states. This means more than just the diversity of types of welfare state in Europe: much of the 'space' for social policy is already occupied. Welfare state development was part of national state-building. Core components of the welfare state will remain national, leaving only the fringes to European initiatives. In addition, the EU lacks the capacity to introduce extensive policies without turning to national bureaucracies to implement them.

We can therefore conclude that the scope for a European welfare state is limited. In particular, the prospects for extensive social policy on either the corporatist or social-democratic model at the European level is almost non-existent. A European social or welfare state in the full sense will not arise. There will continue to be intervention in social matters at the European level, but this will be mainly through regulation, not fiscal policy, and still less through direct provision of services: 'Fiscal realities reinforce the juridification bias inherent in EC institutions. Because of revenue constraints, rule-making rather than monetary transfers seems certain to be the preponderant path of social policy development' (Leibfried and Pierson, 1994, pp. 46–7).

Hence there is no possibility of a Northern-European-type welfare state being transferred to the European level. There is no prospect of replicating the type of social-democratic or corporatist welfare states found in Scandinavia or Northern Europe – the 'Stockholm fallacy'. But the EU will continue to have a social role. True federalisation will not happen in the medium term, but it will not be possible to keep social issues off the agenda. Social policy is a 'stepchild' of European integration. Much of the pace in European social policy has been forced in areas such as consumer protection, ecology, equal opportunities, health protection and industrial safety, which are at the margin of traditional social policy. For a European social state to exist, social citizenship rights would need to be 'constitutionalised' – that is, social rights would need to be incorporated into European administrative law. A stronger European political union would require a strengthening and clarification of the concept of European citizenship.

Leibfried and Pierson's (1994) analysis leads them to three hypotheses about the future development of a European welfare state. First, that social intervention will be via regulatory or Court-centred action, not via transfers and service provision in the typical way of national welfare states. Second, that social initiatives are most likely where there is the support, or at least the acquiescence, of the business sector. Third, that further action will be not be in the core areas of national welfare states (pensions, health care, education) but on the periphery, where space for initiative is available.

While agreeing that the development of a supranational counterpart to the Swedish-style welfare state is highly unlikely, Room (1994, 1995) finds more scope for an expanded EU social role. He argues that both 'Stockholm social democrats' and 'Brussels neo-functionalists' ignore non-governmental actors, such as the church, NGOs, and regional and local governments. Social rights do not necessarily and uniquely derive from trade union action. Social policy is more than just a technical concomitant of completing the single market. The Commission, as a major sponsor of research in this area, steers the research agenda and the policy debate towards a technical view of social policy and an agenda of convergence, in which political, as opposed to technical, choices are played down. But supposedly technical issues involve political choices. For example, the choice of a poverty line is not just a technical matter but has large political stakes. In fact, poverty has risen up the political agenda in some member states in part precisely because of (Commission-funded) research on the subject.

So, while the 'mainstream' view of a European welfare state – from either a Stockholm or a Brussels perspective – leads to a bleak conclusion, in Room's view this ignores some of the most interesting developments around the margins of social policy. Room gives the example of the EC poverty programme, under which national organisations bid for funds. This apparently technical exercise – to identify best practice in the EC and to publicise it more widely – was a political experience for the projects involved. EC funding became 'a pool of resources for their own local struggle' (Room, 1994, p. 28).

This is one example of a more general process in the governance of the EU. The competitive struggle for EU structural funds creates an infrastructure of organisations and practices that are focused on the European level, although they also involve networking and coalition-building at national and subnational level also (Goldsmith, 1993; Hooghe and Keating, 1994; John, 1994). The component parts of this infrastructure then become actors in the maintenance, development and expansion of a European social policy agenda. This process does not establish anything like a European welfare state, but equally it comprises something rather more than a set of inter-governmental relationships, with the Commission acting merely as guardian of the treaties. A form of supranational political infrastructure is being created.

My own view is that Leibfried and Pierson's conclusions are broadly correct: the prospect of any kind of comprehensive European welfare state – let alone a maximalist, fully de-commodified version – in the foreseeable future is very small. But social issues will remain on the agenda, and indeed, will increase in importance. While the core welfare issues remain at the national level, they are increasingly affected by European action. Second, as argued by Room, and accepted by Leibfried and Pierson, there is considerable scope and 'space' for action at the margin of traditional social policy, in either its continental (labour market) or Anglo-Saxon (service delivery) sense. Third, all EU action, via structural funds, directives and recommendations or in other ways, helps to build up an infrastructure of organisations, networks and practices which itself then becomes a player in the subsequent development of social policy. The real question then is whether this relationship must develop inevitably in a clientelist direction, or whether a more progressive outcome is possible.

Fourth, the extensive and continuing changes in the operation of labour markets, operating at a European scale – the persistence of mass unemployment, the shift to part-time working, greater female participation, downward pressures on wage rates and the social wage, and so on – have profound consequences for social protection systems. These impacts are felt cross-nationally, suggesting at the very least some level of European involvement in policy response.

Fifth, and perhaps most important, the issue of a European welfare state is closely connected with the big issue of what kind of Europe citizens want, essentially, there are three options: a minimal EU role, based around the subsidiarity principle; constitutional fixes, with action requiring majority approval, and hence a bias towards blocking rather than activity; or a (possibly utopian) federal constitution, approved by citizens (Weale, 1994, 1995). At the time of writing, there is considerable ambiguity among both elites and populations, between all three of these options, reflecting ambiguity about the scope, extent and goals of European integration more generally.

Conclusions: Where Are We Now?

The broad conclusion is that we are not going to see a European welfare state in the immediate future, nor even in the middle term:

> National social policy is ever more strongly determined by the European level. But this is neither a unidirectional nor a one-dimensional development ... A 'European welfare state' as an independent 'regime' structuring the life chances of the European citizen is not on the horizon. European social policy rather follows market integration and functionally depends on it. (Leibfried, 2000, p. 45)

At the start of the 2000s, European social policy is fragmented, and concentrated on a few specific issues, particularly those linked with economic integration and with the labour market. This state of play reflects the unique nature of the European Union, embodying multi-level governance and a continually shifting policy agenda. It also reflects the institutional opportunism of key policy actors such as the Commission and the ECJ who have successfully used the regulatory agenda as a basis for action. Expenditure-based policy is relatively minor in comparison. Hence, in the terminology of political scientists and European analysts, there are clearly elements both of inter-governmentalism and of neo-functionalism in European social policy.

The current institutional arrangements raise serious questions about the legitimacy, accountability, capacity and competence of those EU institutions, particularly the Commission and the ECJ, which are expanding, or attempting to expand, the social policy agenda. These questions cannot be divorced from the more general ones about the future direction of the EU institutions, and of the European Union itself. There is considerable pressure on the EU institutions at present, both from internal causes such as their perceived problems, and from external causes, particularly the clear need to reform arrangements if enlargement and a Union of twenty-five to thirty states is to come about. In many ways it seems obvious that the EU needs institutional reform, to create more 'normal' institutions, a clearer relationship between the citizens of the Union and what is being done on their behalf, and a stronger chain of democratic accountability, representation and politics. But any move away from the complex, messy and frustrating system in place at the time of writing means a move towards a more straightforwardly federal system, in which the EU becomes a government, if not a state. It is not clear that either the member states, or European citizens, wish to make this move – at least not at this time. This issue is discussed further in Chapter 8.

What has this got to do with social policy? These are the 'big questions' about the EU and European federalism, and surely have more to do with economic policy and political will? But in fact social policy is deeply implicated in this continuing discussion. First, because, as I shall discuss in the next chapter, the continuing process of *economic* integration in Europe has major *social* consequences.

Second, because social issues have strong impacts on citizens, and a key part of the future agenda for the EU is to build the link between the EU and the individual citizen. The report of the 'Three Wise Men' on the institutional implications of enlargement (von Weizsächer *et al.*, 1999) emphasised this:

> In the course of its work the group has discussed the necessity of more simplicity and clarity in the governance of European affairs, more transparency, flexibility and accountability in the way the institutions work. The fact that most Europeans do not understand the working of our institutions must surely be a problem govern-ments should consider ... We must find ways of connecting or reconnecting to the people: why and how the institutions work and to whom they are accountable must be demystified.

European integration is a *political* goal and a *political* ambition. From the mid-1950s to the end of the 1980s, European integrationists pursued this political goal by economic means. Creating first a free trade area, then an economic community, and later a single market in Europe would not only make future wars within Europe impossible, they believed, but would also strengthen support for integration by creating tangible benefits for nations and citizens. Over these thirty-five years, this was a remarkably successful strategy. But by the early 1990s, the strategy had run its course. Creating a single currency took the integration project beyond the purely economic and into the area of the political and the constitutional. At the same time, the collapse of communism in Central and Eastern Europe changed the political agenda radically in Europe, and even the definition of 'Europe' itself. If European integration is to proceed further in the future, it will have to do so as part of a more overtly political process, and one in which the social policy agenda around which most national politics revolve – jobs, health, schools, quality of life – will form a large component. Welfare is not therefore a secondary issue, to which attention will turn when the great constitutional and economic issues have been decided; it will be a key part of the political debate in Europe, just as it is on the national political stages.

Third, social policy and the welfare state have historically been a key part of nation-building in European countries. European social policy – and even more the concept of a European welfare state – imply an equivalent to nation-building at the supranational level. But what is this equivalent? And is it something to which European citizens wish to give their assent?

Finally, in studying European social policy, it is important to maintain a pragmatic and empirical approach. In much of the relevant literature, there is a strong teleological, or even Whiggish, overtone. It is assumed that the reader shares the basic prejudice that more social policy is better than less, and that European social policy must be superior to that of any particular member state. But social policies have costs as well as benefits. Citizens within each nation will decide collectively how much and what sort of welfare they want. Moreover, there is no a priori reason to assume that much – or perhaps any – social intervention need be at the European level. Crucially, it will depend not only on individual choices but also more generally on the degree, nature and extent of economic and political integration (Kleinman and Piachaud, 1993).

6

One Money, One Muddle:
Social Policy and the Euro

In this chapter, I shall look at the impact of economic integration in Europe on social issues and on the development of a European social policy. I then go on to examine the social consequences of the most important recent step in the integration process – the creation of the single currency, the euro. From here I consider the question of whether a European social policy implies a much larger European Union budget and hence whether the future of social Europe is necessarily federal.

Integration: Economic, Social and Political

European economic integration creates both new possibilities for prosperity as well as new (and sometimes reinforced) axes of disadvantage and inequality. In the development of the European Union and its predecessors, economic, social and political factors have been closely interwoven. As we shall see, there are both theoretical and practical objections to trying to insulate the economic on the one hand from the social and the political on the other.

It is incorrect to portray the European Community as a purely economic or commercial project to which explicitly political or social dimensions have only recently been appended. A more realistic assessment of the integration process in Europe is that political integration has always been the desired goal, with economic integration and the creation of a prosperous European economy as the key means of achieving this political goal. Political ideas for European integration have existed since the seventeenth century, if not earlier. But in the post-Second World War period, two factors in particular stimulated developments (Panic, 1996). First, there was the threat of communism – not only the external threat from the Soviet Union and its allies, but also the internal threat posed to capitalist democracy in Western Europe by the strength of domestic communist parties. Second, the reconstruction of Western Europe after the Second World War demonstrated the interdependent nature of the major European economies, and hence the need for economic co-operation.

Political and social goals were an important part of the strategy of the founding fathers of the European Economic Community (EEC), and political and social factors have been crucial in shaping the development of what was always foreseen as an 'ever closer union'. Functionalism was a key part of the strategy – economic integration would be used as the key driver of political integration. It was a strategy that was, in general, successful in the first three decades after the Treaty of Rome. The Single European Act of 1985, the Single European market (SEM) programme it gave rise to, and the signing of the Maastricht Treaty in 1991 can be seen as the high point of this strategy. From then on, economic integration and economic prosperity remained a necessary, but no longer a sufficient, condition for political integration. Further political integration would require, in addition to a single market and a single currency with their attendant 'spillovers', a more substantial social, political and cultural basis among citizens as well as among elites.

Voter assent to further integration measures could no longer be taken for granted. This was first demonstrated by the ratification process of the Maastricht Treaty, in which there was initial rejection of the Treaty by Denmark and only a very narrow popular assent in France. Over the course of the 1990s, support for membership of the European Union fell by 20 percentage points (see Chapter 8). By December 2000, a majority of people in Sweden, the United Kingdom, Denmark and Finland were opposed to the euro, while in Germany opinion was almost equally divided, with 47 per cent in favour and 44 per cent against (European Commission, 2001).

In many ways, this shift represents the 'normalisation' of the EU as a tier of government – citizen attitudes to the EU are now based more on a consideration of the benefits and costs to themselves, rather than seen as a judgement of the institutions *per se*. A crucial factor in this 'normalisation' was, of course, the fall of the Berlin Wall in 1989, and the subsequent ending of the Cold War. The nature of the European Union, an institution forged at the height of the Cold War, and the meaning of the EU for its citizens would of necessity change with the ending of the bipolar world. The model of integration that obtained from the mid-1950s to the late 1980s, based on a technocratic rationale and delivered by elites with, at best, tacit assent by citizens, would no longer suffice.

This development raises key issues about the nature of citizenship, the reality of 'European citizenship' which the Maastricht Treaty bestowed, and the relationship between citizenship and welfare, which I examine in more detail in Chapter 8. First, however, we must look at what effects the dominant project of economic integration, proceeding through the creation of a free trade area, the establishment of a single market, and the institution of a single currency, has had on social outcomes and social policy in the Community.

The Community's self-declared economic and social role is both wide-ranging and vague. According to Article 3 of the Maastricht Treaty, (the 1992 Treaty on European Union)

> The Community shall have as its task ... to promote throughout the Community a harmonious and balanced development of economic activities, sustainable and non-inflationary growth respecting the environment, a high degree of convergence of economic performance, a high level of employment and of social protection, the raising of the standard of living and quality of life, and economic and social cohesion and solidarity among Member States.

As the EEC6 has grown into the EU15, internal political relationships have become more complex. The six original EEC countries were a relatively homogeneous group compared with the diversity that now exists in the European Union in terms of economic circumstances, living standards, and social policy arrangements. This has made the distributional, social and constitutional issues associated with a single market and monetary union much more acute than would have been the case with a group of countries whose economic structures and social arrangements were more similar.

As we saw in the previous two chapters, there has always been some kind of social dimension, or social policy wing to the European integration project. The social policy that emerged from the discussions leading up to the signing of the Treaty of Rome, which set up the EEC in 1957, was initially modest and limited. But subsequently the extent of European Social Policy has been enlarged progressively.

Second, a tidy separation between economic and social aspects of European integration cannot be sustained intellectually. Even in purely economic terms, the textbook distinctions between customs union, common market and monetary union are difficult to maintain in the case of modern nation states characterised by mixed economies and the pervasive influence of public policy. In practice, it is useful to think about the economic and social aspects of integration together rather than separately. Discussing 'social' consequences in isolation from economic issues can be misleading. It reinforces the belief that 'economic' processes alone create a pot of wealth, while 'social' issues relate only to the issue of how this given pot is to be divided.

European economic integration should be placed in a context of wider developments. These include the transition to a more integrated global market, with free flows of capital internationally and a new international division of labour; a political shift among OECD and other governments towards market-orientated policies, emphasising economic development and market-based solutions; and a reduced role for the state, reflecting not just the shift to market ideology on the part of elites, but also arguably a reduced faith in government activism and tax-and-spend solutions on the part of voters.

Understanding Economic Integration

Standard neo-classical trade theory predicts that the creation of a customs union or free trade area yields gains from trade to both trading partners. Each country or region can specialise in the sectors in which it has comparative advantage, and this holds true even if one partner has an absolute advantage in all sectors. In each country or region, resources are allocated more efficiently as capital and labour move to the sector in which they can be employed more efficiently.

If this is extended to a common market or economic union, then further gains become available from factor mobility. In countries with an abundance of capital and relative lack of labour, wages will be relatively high, attracting labour migrants from countries with a large labour supply and low capital endowment. Capital will flow in the opposite direction. Hence, free markets and the signals given to economic agents via the price system act over time both to maximise economic welfare, subject to the underlying resource constraints, and to produce a convergence in living standards between the trading partners. There is a linear progression from customs union to common market to monetary union. Each stage is portrayed as more complex, but definitely preferable to the previous stage (Tsoukalis, 1993).

However, this simplified economic analysis ignores some key factors. First, there is no sense here of dynamic relationships, of any inequalities of power, nor indeed of history of any kind. How one region or country got to be 'capital-endowed' and another 'labour-endowed' is not part of the story. Second, even within the terms of the model, market forces may not be sufficient to lead to equilibrium and convergence. In practice, factor mobility – particularly labour migration – is far from perfect. Third, the theory does not take account of the heterogeneity of labour nor the complementarity between particular forms of capital and labour. It is not at all clear in a modern economic system that capital is necessarily attracted to regions or countries of relatively cheap but low quality – whether it is or not will depend on a host of other factors, such as the location of markets and the level of transport costs. Putting it another way, any inward flow of physical capital may be exceeded by the outward flow of human capital represented as the migration of the more highly skilled and entrepreneurial workers.

Economic integration in Europe involves modern mixed economies in which government intervention is extensive and pervasive. Eliminating barriers to trade is not simply a question of negotiating away tariffs and quotas, because there are a whole range of *indirect* government interventions – industrial policy, education and training policies, transport policy and so on. which have a similar effect to direct tariffs and quotas (O'Donnell, 1992). Hence creating a genuine common market among such countries is tantamount to creating an economic and monetary union (O'Donnell, 1992; Tsoukalis, 1993). Moreover, an economic and monetary union normally implies a government whose political jurisdiction coincides with the economic jurisdiction of the monetary union. Hence the 'economic' or 'trade' issue of establishing a common market cannot be separated from the 'political' issues of federalism and sovereignty.

In reality, then, there is no clear separation between the different 'stages' of economic integration – Customs union, common market, monetary union – nor is there anything historically or logically inevitable about the supposed progress towards greater integration. Ironically, the arguments of both federalists and anti-federalists often ignore this. So federalists assume or imply that full union is where the system inevitably is headed, while anti-federalists argue that a common market can be set up without the need for any wider economic, political or social frameworks.

The official European Commission view, while acknowledging other theoretical positions, has largely reflected an optimistic reading of economic integration. The Commission's estimate of the impact of the single market on economic welfare argued that the single market would bring gains for both macro and micro reasons – the macro gains from the more efficient resource allocation, micro gains from the exploitation of economies of scale as well as a more competitive environment leading to prices being closer to production costs (Emerson, 1989; European Commission, 1988). Similarly, with regard to a single currency, the EU view in general reflects economic orthodoxy and belief in markets. A single currency and central bank will not only reduce transactions costs and exchange rate uncertainty, but also by making anti-inflationary policies 'credible' will promote virtue through changed behaviour by governments who will no longer run 'excessive' deficits and by labour who will no longer make 'uncompetitive' pay claims' (Emerson and Huhne, 1991).

Essentially, then, there are two linked arguments in the EU's advocacy of closer integration – one about economic growth and welfare gains, and the other about convergence towards an equilibrium position. First, it is argued that integration – a single market, and then a single currency –will raise economic welfare across the whole community. Second, integration will lead to convergence between regions. Some regions and areas in decline will need assistance in the transition period – both to enable them to undertake the necessary structural changes (adjustment) and to maintain incomes or living standards (compensation). However, these are secondary and transitional issues. The EU, and particularly the Commission, take the view that their role is to assist transition, a process that involves short-term problems. Bliss (1990) summarised the EC's strategy as one of trying to make the short-term shorter, while Emerson (1990, p. 54) described one of the goals of the Structural Funds as being to raise the quality of public economic infrastructure and the level of human capital 'to the point that the regions in question are no longer disqualified on these scores from progressing to a high level of economic development'.

Hence there is an implicit political contract between the EU and the weaker regions: accept the full force of European integration and competition, and in exchange the EU offers to 'raise the level of basic economic resource endowment (other than its natural features) to usual Community standards' (Emerson, 1990, p. 54).

By contrast, many regional and development economists have often stressed divergence rather than convergence as the fate of less developed regions or countries within a single market or monetary union, and the importance of processes of circular and cumulative causation. In this view, successful places get on to a virtuous upward spiral in which the successful performance of their export sector leads to higher productivity growth and hence higher output; this higher output then feeds back into higher productivity growth, and hence a new round of output growth, and so on. The key aspect is the positive relationship between productivity growth and output growth. The faster the growth in output, the faster the increase in labour productivity. Conversely, backward regions are locked into a downward spiral of low productivity and slow growth (Kaldor, 1970; Dixon and Thirlwall, 1975; Armstrong and Taylor, 1985).

The growth rate of a region or a country is also constrained by its 'balance of payments' position (Thirlwall, 1980; Armstrong and Taylor, 1985, p. 74). If imports exceed exports, then one of four things can happen:

(i)   if there is an inflow of transfer payments this can help to pay for the exports, and hence maintain living standards;
(ii)   if the area has its own currency there can be a devaluation, thus boosting exports and reducing imports;
(iii)   labour mobility may increase; and
(iv)   if none of the above is possible, a reduction in imports will come about through a fall in output. This will lead to a fall in employment and possibly therefore an increase in out-migration of labour.

In the case of regions, (i) is possible but (ii) is not (regions do not have their own currencies). In the case of independent countries (ii) is possible but (i) is not. Labour mobility in Europe is generally low – for example 3 per cent of Americans change their region of residence annually, but only 0.6 per cent of Italians and 1.1 per cent of Britons and Germans (OECD, 1990 quoted in Eichengreen, 1998a). Economists are divided on whether rates of labour mobility will increase after European Monetary Union (EMU) – Eichengreen (1998a) thinks this is possible, while Bean *et al.* (1998) and Obstfeld and Peri (1998) consider it unlikely.

In a Europe with monetary union and a single currency (ii) is no longer possible for individual countries and (i) is very weak. This is the position at the time of writing in 'Euroland', which has a single currency, but, unlike monetary unions everywhere else, no federal or central system of automatic or discretionary fiscal transfers; and instead only relatively small transfers via the EU Structural Funds.

This has obvious implications for declining regions and slower-growth economies within a European single market and/or monetary union.

What happens when these boundaries disappear – that is, when countries come together in an economic union, will depend on a number of factors, particularly the extent of economies of scale and the level of transport costs. It is not the case that a reduction in transport costs (or a removal of tariff barriers) will *necessarily* lead to a concentration of production in the 'cheap labour' periphery. Imagine a hypothetical example of two countries (Krugman and Venables, 1990). One has high production costs (core) and one has low production costs (periphery). With the lowering of trade barriers, if transport costs are high, production will take place in both locations, each serving the local market. If transport costs are very low, production will be concentrated in the periphery, taking advantage of the cheaper production costs there to serve both markets. But there will be a range of medium transport costs over which production will in fact be concentrated in the core rather than the periphery. This is because 'in the medium transport case, costs are low enough to make it worthwhile to concentrate production, but still high enough that access to markets outweighs production costs as a determinant of location.' (Krugman, 1991, p. 97).

Hence the impact of economic integration on the location of activity is a *contingent* process. A variety of factors will influence both the location of economic activity and the gains and losses to individuals from changed patterns of trade. The above theoretical framework allows us to understand a puzzle first raised in Chapter 3 – namely how and why it is possible for two mutually contradictory fears to be expressed about the single market and monetary union. The first fear is that integration will lead to the export of jobs from the core to the periphery of Europe in search of lower wage rates (so-called 'social dumping'); while the second is that it will lead to greater economic concentration in the core, and hence the further relative decline of the lagging regions. But, as we saw in Chapter 3, the evidence for the existence of social dumping is weak.

The second fear – that production will be concentrated in the European core – relates to the strength of agglomeration effects. However, agglomeration economies operate mainly at the level of cities or city-regions, rather than nation states. Hence, while such fears are unlikely to be realised at the national or even regional level, the existence of agglomeration economies and cumulative causation processes may lead to greater *intra*-country inequality in a free trading and monetary union EU. That is, convergence – increased economic equality – at national or regional level is quite compatible with increased economic *inequality* at the household or individual level.

Winners and Losers from the Single Market

The pattern of gainers and losers from economic integration cannot easily be predicted. Over many years, the European Commission has held the view that economic integration – both the completion of the single market and the adoption of economic and monetary union – is desirable for distributional as well as growth reasons. The optimists' case for the completion of the single market was that economic welfare will be increased through a combination of cost reductions from scale economies, improved efficiency from more competitive markets, the fuller play of comparative advantage, and innovations in products and processes (Emerson, 1989). These 'static' gains from the completion of the Single Market were estimated by the Commission itself in the 'Cecchini Report' to 4.3–6.4 per cent of European GDP (Cecchini *et al.*, 1988). If so-called 'dynamic' gains from the increased return to capital, and hence greater capital accumulation are included, the gains might be as high as 15.4 per cent of GDP (Baldwin, 1992). Cheshire (1999) comments, 'The omission from the Cecchini Report of any discussion of the spatial impacts may have reflected the fact that the Directorate of the Commission responsible for the study – Economic and Financial Affairs – had no explicit remit for regional issues; or it may have been a matter of political convenience' (Cheshire, 1999, p. 845).

The Commission refused any attempt at forecasting the distribution by country or region of the gains to economic welfare (of the order of 7 per cent of European GDP, it argued). It predicted confidently: 'neither economic theory nor relevant economic history can point to any clear-cut pattern of likely distributional advantage or disadvantage'. (Emerson, 1989). The analytic framework of this report was a mainstream neo-classical 'gains from trade' model. Nevertheless, despite seeking to avoid discussion of the distributive issue, the report makes it clear that the economic gains calculated are based on the assumption that 'micro and macroeconomic policies would ensure that the resources released as costs are reduced are

effectively re-employed productively. This concerns labour in particular.' (Emerson, 1989). Clearly, then, if such resources are not
productively re-employed (that is, if European unemployment were
to rise as in fact it has done), there are distributional as well as overall
economic welfare consequences.

What is the evidence as to whether national and regional inequalities have narrowed or widened in the EU? Between 1960 and 1973, a
period of relatively strong growth, there was some convergence of
national and regional incomes, while between 1974 and 1986, with
lower growth, the trend was one of slight divergence (O'Donnell,
1992). Between 1958 and 1972 there was a narrowing of regional
disparities in France, Germany and Italy, while disparities between
member states were halved. This occurred from a combination of
higher growth rates in the poorer countries, and a fall in internal
variance because of the movement of population from agricultural to
industrial areas (Nevin, 1990). Similarly, an index of per capita
income disparity for the EC12 fell sharply in the 1950s and 1960s,
but hardly changed between 1970 and 1990. However, the composition of the disparity changed: inter-country disparities fell, while the
intra-country regional component remained almost the same (Cingolani, 1993). There was convergence at both country and regional level
in GDP per head in the 1960s and up to the mid-1970s. Since then
there has been some convergence at country level, but inter-regional
differences have widened (Collier, 1994).

A similar story is found in Dignan (1995). In the period to 1974,
there was a consistent reduction in GDP per capita disparities
between countries in the EC12 and, with the exception of the UK,
between the regions of the EC12. From 1974 to the mid-1980s, there
was little convergence. Since the mid-1980s, convergence has re-
emerged, although not as strongly as in the earlier period. However,
the convergence seen both in the 1950s/1960s and in the 1970s/1980s
derived from faster GDP growth in the lagging countries. Hence,
while this has been convergence between peripheral countries and the
EC core, regional relativities *within* countries have diverged, supporting theories of cumulative causation and spatially polarising forces
(Dignan, 1995). So, in the 1980s, Ireland and Spain gained on the EU
average in terms of GDP per head; for Portugal there was no change;
and Greece in fact lost ground. But several of the least favoured
regions (Galicia, Asturias, northern England, Mezzogiorno and
Wallonia) failed to keep pace with their respective member states
(Begg and Mayes, 1993).

Moreover, regional disparities are greater for *unemployment* than for *GDP per head*, and arguably this measure gives a clearer indication of disadvantage and inequality: 'Per capital income measurements for a region can be close to the Community average but can hide large intraregional disparities; regional unemployment rates give a clearer indication of welfare differences within and between regions' (Collier, 1994, p. 146).

Regional unemployment disparities widened in the first half of the 1980s, although this trend was reversed in the second half of the decade (Collier, 1994). A similar pattern is shown if we look at the change in unemployment in the 1980s according to the EU's own definition of areas in need of assistance. The fall in unemployment between 1986 and 1991 was less in the Objective 1 areas than in the unassisted areas: from 15 per cent to 14 per cent in Objective 1 areas against a fall from 9 per cent to 7.5 per cent in the unassisted areas. In the Objective 2 areas, however, the fall in terms of percentage points was more than twice as great, from 13 per cent to 9.5 per cent (European Commission, 1993b).

Cheshire (1999) provides a summary of the many studies that have been undertaken of the spatial impact of the SEM. These are all *ex ante* studies, it being generally accepted that the effects of the SEM will take time to work through, and so *ex post* studies are not yet available. Cheshire identifies three broad approaches: the first set starts from measures of the sectoral impact of the SEM; the second group approaches the problem from the basis of pure economic theory; and the third group uses aggregate data to estimate the longer-term spatial impacts of integration and/or predict the likely effects of the SEM. Despite these wide variations in methodologies,

> One may summarise the conclusions of the studies that have been identified in the following way, therefore. The great, almost overwhelming majority of them identify European integration in general, and the SEM in particular, as differently benefiting 'core' or central regions of Europe compared to peripheral ones ... the greatest potential gains are concentrated in the core of Europe which, over time, has been becoming more broadly defined. (Cheshire, 1999, p. 850)

We can identify a consistent story emerging from these various studies. At the national level, the Ricardian prediction that free trade ultimately benefits all parties is largely confirmed, at least at the macro scale and in the long term. But this optimistic scenario can coexist with increased disparity and growing inequality at a finer grain level of analysis – inequalities between regions, between communities and between households.

The 'grain' of the analysis is therefore important in understanding the relationship between economic integration and the growth of inequality and social exclusion. This has important consequences for the appropriate social policy response, the balance between action at national and EU levels, and the type of policy that is most appropriate. If the problem is defined in traditional terms of lagging regions or lagging nations, then policies of inter-state transfers and infrastructural spending, such as the early ERDF and the post-Maastricht Cohesion Fund are appropriate. However, if (as appears to be the case) persistent social and economic inequalities are associated more with endogenous variables such as educational and skills levels, and the level of entrepreneurship, the rationale for redistribution at *regional* level rather than at a smaller scale becomes weaker. And if we move one stage further, to considering inequalities and redistribution at the *individual* or *household* levels, the use of regional policy becomes extremely inefficient. However, to move from inter-state transfers or even Union-wide regional policy towards a system of household-level redistribution implies a fully Federal system and hence has enormous political and social implications.

The Social Consequences of EMU

Economic and monetary union in Europe is unique: 'there is no reason why currency domains need to be coterminous with sovereign states. Yet the one to one correspondence between countries and currencies is one of the most robust regularities of monetary economics. If Emu proceeds in Europe ahead of political union it will be an unprecedented event' (Goodhart, 1997). Within a monetary union, the ability of governments to respond to economic distress or social inequalities is severely curtailed. Manipulation of the exchange rate (devaluation) is no longer possible; monetary policy is the responsibility of the independent European Central Bank; and the requirements of the Maastricht convergence criteria and the Stability Pact restrict the use of fiscal policy (taxing and spending) within debt and budget deficit guidelines. Moreover, there is no federal government whose own taxing and spending would act to stabilise the effect of economic shocks, and there is no federal social security or federal unemployment benefit system: 'the EMU is constructed on a model that has no equivalent anywhere in the world, and that has prompted anxieties about the consequences that the chosen approach will have' (European Social Observatory, *EMU*, No. 2, December 1997)

In the absence of exchange rate, monetary and fiscal responses to external shocks, the only mechanisms remaining are labour mobility and wage flexibility. Putting it more bluntly, if the economic position of a country or region deteriorates, its workers must either accept lower wages or move elsewhere. If they do neither, unemployment will rise. Optimists about EMU believe that within EMU, rigidities in European labour markets will reduce. Wages will become more flexible and the level of labour mobility will increase. Pessimists come in two varieties. The first kind (mainly some economists and business commentators) believe that this simply will not happen, and continuing rigidities will make EMU unworkable. The second group (mainly social policy commentators and some politicians) believe that increased flexibility *will* happen – wages will fall and workers will have to move across national borders, leading to further downward pressure on wage levels, reduced social protection and growing inequalities.

Which is more likely? Labour mobility in Europe remains low. Migration has a path-dependent character – barriers that have discouraged mobility in the past will also do so in the future. However, behaviour may change: 'once there no longer remains the option of exchange rate changes to facilitate adjustment, workers and unions will recognise the need to substitute greater labor market flexibility' (Eichengreen, 1998a, p. 5). Steps towards greater wage flexibility have been taken, and the Schengen agreement to remove border controls and the portability of pensions will give some modest boost to incentives to move, and to create expatriate networks. Furthermore the 'homogenising influence of the media and the spread of English-language skills should loosen the hold of cultural specificity' (Eichengreen, 1998a, p. 6) – not a proposition to gladden the heart of proponents of European exceptionalism.

More generally, EMU is likely to increase pressures for labour market reform: 'In simple terms, once a country has lost the "easy option" of devaluation, it has no alternative but to tackle unemployment through supply-side measures' (Bean *et al.*, 1998, p. 85). Furthermore, EMU may also lead to a shift in collective bargaining from the national to the European level. The best unemployment performance in the OECD has been in countries with either very decentralised wage bargaining structures, such as the USA, or very centralised ones, such as Scandinavia. With EMU, centralised bargaining at national level becomes equivalent to decentralised bargaining at the continental level, and hence less beneficial to employment performance. Differences in productivity across European countries make it unlikely that centralised wage bargains will be optimal, and so Bean *et al.* (1998) conclude that economic integration 'should spur labour market reforms in the direction of more decentralised systems of wage determination' (p. 86) and indeed recent evidence suggests that the SEM has already led to greater decentralisation in wage bargaining.

Some commentators and politicians argue that monetary union will lead inevitably to a federal Europe in which a much larger Federal European government engages in both redistribution and stabilisation policies. They argue that the loss of sovereignty over macro-economic policies by member-state governments will render individual countries and regions more vulnerable to asymmetric economic shocks. In order to avoid the severe social consequences of adjustment to this, Federal policies of redistribution and stabilisation will be required. Note that this argument can be deployed both by federalists – who advocate a European government – and by anti-federalists, who fear it.

The more general point is that the existence or not of a monetary union and single currency is not just a technical question of the most appropriate economic policy, but it also raises fundamental issues of social identity and political citizenship. There is a large literature on so-called 'optimal currency areas'. On most criteria, the European Union is not an optimal currency area. But – so what? All nation states, apart from the smallest, have separate currencies, yet it is highly unlikely they are all 'optimal currency areas' (Goodhart, 1996). Currency union is a function of political cohesion, evidenced by, for example, the actions taken by successor states to the break-up of the Soviet Union and Yugoslavia, who quickly established their own currencies.

Single currency and political identity are closely bound up with one another. In a mature currency union in a cohesive federal country or in a unitary state, the blame for adverse economic shocks falls on proximate events, not on the fact of currency union. This is clear in the case of the USA:

When oil prices fell, Texans ... did not blame their plight on their fixed dollar. (Goodhart, 1996)

the drive for Emu [is] designed to shield Europe from the instability of international financial markets, much as Arizona or New Hampshire have been shielded from the Asian financial crisis and felt only the mildest repercussions of the collapse of the Asian currencies by virtue of their participation in an integrated and stable monetary zone, namely, the United States of America. (Eichengreen, 1998b, pp. 4–5)

Exactly the reverse is likely to obtain in the first few years of a monetary union in Europe, although this is partly a 'chicken-and-egg' problem, that is, it is the 'taken-for-granted' nature of monetary union in the USA or Canada that inhibits secessionist responses.

As part of the Maastricht Treaty, member states agreed that those wishing to join the single currency had to meet certain criteria – the 'Maastricht convergence criteria'. These are the economic and financial requirements that member states must meet before being able to join. While the Maastricht Treaty talked in general terms about growth, cohesion and employment, the specific details of the requirements and timetable for EMU embodied a strict deflationary regime. The concept of economic and monetary union enshrined in the Treaty reflected the economically conservative views of the central bankers who made up the bulk of the Committee for the study of Economic and Monetary Union under Delors' chairmanship, which reported in April 1989. Great stress was placed on the necessity of 'convergence' of the national economies of the member states, with convergence defined as conformity to the norms of orthodox monetary policy: low inflation, low government borrowing and low government debt as well as low interest rates and a period of stable exchange rates leading up to the EMU.

In this concept of convergence, there was no room for elements of the real economy such as unemployment, poverty or inequality. There is no commitment from the member states, for example, to a target rate of unemployment, or even a band (narrow or wide) within which different countries might 'float'. Quantitative estimates of the levels of poverty or inequality that might be deemed to be unacceptable to a European Union are entirely absent. This contrasts strongly with the detailed specification of the monetary and fiscal convergence criteria. The fiscal convergence criteria set were strict: public deficits should be below 3 per cent of GDP, and public debt should be below 60 per cent of GDP. It was clear at the time that these targets, if strictly adhered to, could not be achieved by some member states within the time scale set down, nor indeed for many years afterwards. In practice, a certain amount of 'fudging' the rules allowed eleven countries to sign up to the single currency in January 1999. The Maastricht criteria themselves are a product of the specific political circumstances surrounding the negotiations. In particular, they followed from the desire of the French government to see a newly-unified Germany securely bound into the framework of a new Europe, coupled with the insistence of the German government on obtaining no less a degree of fiscal and monetary rectitude in a European EMU than it had been used to enjoying domestically. The final compromise was 'essentially based on a French timetable and German conditions' (Tsoukalis, 1993, p. 217).

As well as the convergence criteria, the member states, at the insistence of Germany, also agreed to a 'Stability Pact' which will govern the fiscal policies of member states within the economic and monetary union. This was in response to fears that fiscal profligacy by some member states within EMU would lead to higher interest rates and higher inflation throughout Euroland. The Stability Pact limits budget deficits to 3 per cent of GDP (as in the pre-EMU convergence criteria). If this limit is breached, and the country is not in recession (defined as GDP falling by 0.75 per cent), fines of between 0.2 per cent and 0.5 per cent of GDP will be levied by the EU financial authorities. The Pact also suggests limiting budget deficits to 1 per cent of GDP in the long term (Baimbridge *et al.*, 2000, p. 237).

Some have argued for expanding the Maastricht criteria to include convergence in real variables; for example, unemployment, productivity and growth (Arestis and Sawyer, 1996). Arestis and Sawyer argue that a single currency is acceptable only if there are no adverse impacts on employment, output and inequality across the EU. While this sounds reasonable, in practice it is difficult to see how such conditions could be met in practice. If regional convergence criteria involving real variables such as unemployment and productivity were invoked, most existing unitary and federal states would fail the test.

More important than the specific criteria is the fact that the supranational level of decision-making, the agreements reached, and the new institutions proposed, reflect a deflationary and orthodox economic stance. This supports and reinforces the consensus among the national governments of the member states about the limitations of state intervention, the need for financial orthodoxy, and the importance of reassuring financial markets about the current and future good conduct of governments. The pursuit of the convergence criteria and the Stability Pact gave an institutional, treaty-based additional strength to the deflationary orthodox consensus among European central bankers and politicians in the 1990s. While the 1990s European recession led to greater rhetoric about the need for recovery, and action to reduce unemployment, there was neither the political will nor the institutional machinery to introduce a European recovery programme.

In this, European policy-makers were in line with the shift in attitudes and behaviour of economic policy-makers at member-state level. Since the 1970s/1980s, there has been a retreat from post-war Keynesianism and from the commitment of governments to maintaining full employment. In its place has come, to a greater or lesser degree in different countries, the prioritising of market forces, economic deregulation and so-called supply-side policies. Inflation rather than unemployment is the key policy target, and step by step the acceptance of permanently high levels of unemployment has come to be seen as an inevitable, even a desirable, part of modern European society. While economic neo-liberalism was accepted far more explicitly and enthusiastically in Mrs Thatcher's Britain than anywhere else, these ideas 'were gradually adopted by other European leaders, although with a mixture of anticipation and embarrassment characteristic of young virgins' (Tsoukalis, 1993, pp. 51–2). The acceptance of more market-orientated policies in France after 1983 and the failure of 'Keynesianism in one country' was a turning point in view of France's subsequent central role in the relaunching of the European integration process.

Does a European Social Policy Imply a Larger Budget?

In a monetary union, the partners give up their autonomy over key aspects of economic policy – particularly monetary policy and the exchange rate. This loss of autonomy restricts the ability of countries (or regions) to adopt appropriate policy responses to external shocks. In existing federations, as well as in unitary states, a key role is played by central public finance in both redistributing income and in protecting more vulnerable regions against external shocks. It has been estimated that, in existing federations, central public finance reduces the income differentials between regions by between 30 per cent and 40 per cent (MacDougall, 1977). These transfers mainly take the form of automatic stabilisers – for example, increased payments of unemployment benefit to the region suffering from the external shock, or relatively higher taxation receipts from the more prosperous regions. But there can also be grants-in-aid either from central to local level (as in Britain) or directly between regions (as in Germany).

The debate over the need for some kind of fiscal federalism to accompany monetary union has swung from one extreme to the other since the mid-1970s (Eichengreen, 1998a). The MacDougall Committee (1977) argued that a similar federal system of stabilising public finance would be desirable in the European Community, and that the size of the EC budget should therefore be expanded to at least 5 per cent of European GDP, with expenditure and revenue having a progressive distributional incidence (Smith, 1992, pp. 111–12; Melitz and Vori, 1992). Ten years later, the Padoa–Schippoa Report (1987) distanced itself from the prefederalist programme of the MacDougall Committee, emphasising the principle of subsidiarity. Since then, according to Melitz and Vori (1992), the pendulum has swung back towards the earlier MacDougall position. For example, Sachs and Sala-i-Martin (1989) in an influential study, warned of the dangers of the EC moving towards monetary union without an equivalent to the US federal budget which in their estimate absorbs 35 per cent to 40 per cent of regional shocks.

Subsequent studies revised these estimates downwards. Moreover, these later studies often drew a distinction between the stabilisation and redistribution aspects of central public finance (Goodhart and Smith, 1992; von Hagen, 1992; Melitz and Vori, 1992; Bayoumi and Masson, 1995). Stabilisation policy refers to action taken to reduce the impact on particular regions of asymmetric, exogenous shocks, such as a rise in energy prices. For example, Goodhart and Smith (1992, p. 1) argue that payment of unemployment benefit for a limited period after unemployment would be stabilising without implying sustained redistribution. Von Hagen argued that in the USA there was much less automatic stabilisation (strictly defined) than MacDougall assumed; much of the USA fiscal system is redistributive rather than stabilising. Goodhart and Smith (1992) disagree with some of the technical aspects of von Hagen's work, and reworking the data, find that there is a worthwhile element of stabilisation within the system. However, they find the distinction between the two effects useful. Eichengreen (1998a), summarising this work, concludes that 'the emerging consensus appears to be that the original Sala-i-Martin and Sachs estimates should be regarded as upper bounds' (1998a, p. 13).

Several studies in the 1990s looked explicitly at the feasibility of setting up a relatively small 'insurance fund' at a European level to ensure greater stabilisation in the face of exogenous shocks. Much of this literature suggests, either implicitly or explicitly, that the stabilisation function is necessary while the redistribution aspect is contentious, or even harmful. For example, van der Ploeg (1991) acknowledges the stabilising advantages of a European Federal Transfer Scheme (EFTS) but criticises the redistributive implications. The problem with an EFTS is that 'unemployed individuals are then even less likely to pack their bags and find a job elsewhere in Europe and individual governments are less likely to pursue a rigorous and effective unemployment policy'. But even at national level, the unemployed are less likely to migrate than other groups. The idea that free mobility at the continental level will act to equalize unemployment rates and produce a tidy equilibrium outcome is scarcely credible. Van der Ploeg admits that most of the objections to an EFTS, based around moral hazard and adverse selection arguments, could also be deployed against national unemployment insurance schemes.

The stabilisation function carried out by the member states of the European Union, at national level, offsets roughly the same share of local income shocks as does fiscal federalism in the USA (Eichengreen, 1998a). The implication is that there is no need for a European, supranational system of stabilisation as long as the automatic stabilisers of the member states are allowed to operate. However, if the Maastricht convergence criteria and the requirements of the Stability Pact prevent these national stabilisers from operating adequately, then political demands for more activism at the European federal level will grow. The strict requirements of economic orthodoxy embodied in EMU may therefore spill over into greater political pressures for a federal European state. Eichengreen (1998a) also points out that, while one rationale for the fiscal restrictions of Maastricht is to encourage policy co-ordination, the effect of the Excessive Deficit Procedure and the Stability Pact, by limiting the flexibility of national fiscal policies, may be to impede rather than encourage policy co-ordination.

Economists also worry about the moral hazard implications of federal stabilisation and inter-regional transfers. Melitz (1994) argues that any unemployment-based co-insurance programme would have to have strong safeguards to prevent countries from following risky macroeconomic strategies, supported by the knowledge that high unemployment will lead to budgetary transfers from their EU partners. Obstfeld and Peri (1998) argue that, in existing currency unions 'transfers tend to be quite persistent and sometimes respond to shocks with lags. Indeed, through various mechanisms, transfer programmes intended to provide social insurance may lengthen the adjustment process and, in extreme cases, induce regional dependence on fiscal inflows' (p. 209). Hence, they argue, the sharp distinction between redistribution and stabilisation functions of fiscal transfers 'while conceptually valid, is overdrawn in practice'.

Governments' room to manoeuvre in EMU has been curtailed not just because of the necessary reduction in their monetary and exchange-rate powers, but also, of course, through the member states' agreement to self-denying ordinances through the Maastricht convergence criteria and the Stability Pact. However, Eichengreen (1998b) is relatively sanguine that member states will retain sufficient stabilisation powers. While the Stability Pact will be an effective constraint at the beginning of EMU, if member states succeed, as intended, in reducing their deficits further over time and moving their budgets into balance, they will then have more fiscal room for manoeuvre. This, according to Eichengreen, will give them the capacity to cope with all but the most severe recessions – and there are exceptions within the Stability Pact for exceptionally severe recessions. Together with a slow but steady rise in labour mobility and increased wage flexibility, EMU will become easier over time. However, Eichengreen sees a danger if the requirements of the Stability Pact are enforced too strongly. With restricted capacity to operate national fiscal stabilisers, depressed nations and regions will demand more subsidies from the European Union, leading to pressures for greater EU budgetary powers. This will run up against the distinct scepticism towards political integration, not just in Britain and Denmark, but also in Germany (Eichengreen, 1998b).

Obstfeld and Peri (1998) discuss the likely response of member states with a single currency to macroeconomic shocks. Comparing European countries with the USA shows that in Europe there is less reliance on labour migration, and more on inter-regional transfer payments as a means of coping with shocks, and the speed of regional adjustment appears to be slower. If EMU aims at the same level of social and economic cohesion that obtains in member states at present, there will be considerable pressure to set up a transfer union, that is, to extend the existing mechanisms of income redistribution. Obstfeld and Peri, like many economists, view the possibility of a European transfer union – that is, a tax-and-spend European federal state – 'with alarm' (p. 246), and suggest ways of avoiding this outcome, including relaxing the Stability Pact soon after EMU starts, and limiting the EU's total borrowing power.

The Future is Federal?

> EMU is an entirely novel experiment in full monetary unification among major political powers without full political unification or an overarching fiscal authority. (Obstfeld and Peri, 1998, p. 243)

> The debate on Emu, and the EU more generally, is not helped by using the term 'federal' as an absolute term. The choice for Europe is not between a federation and a non-federation, but rather the appropriate degree of federalism. (Currie, 1998)

In comparison with any existing currency union, European EMU is extremely atypical, to say the least, in that there is only a minimal role for central public finance. Although most current monetary unions were set up before stabilising mechanisms were in place, at the time these unions were set up, rural–urban migration carried much of the burden of adjustment (Melitz and Vori, 1992). This adjustment mechanism will not be available in the European EMU:

> The Community is now proposing to move to full monetary union without even establishing those fiscal changes regarded by Mac-Dougall as a necessary precondition in the 'pre-federal integration' period, in which Community finance might play some part in stabilisation and growth policy, let alone the 'small Community public sector' which they saw as providing the 'necessary public finance underpinning for a monetary union'. (Goodhart and Smith, 1992, Appendix, p. 2)

Is it really possible for an entity that is neither a unitary nor a Federal state to maintain a common currency? Should not political integration precede economic integration (Buiter *et al.*, 1999)? The strategy adopted by European leaders has been the opposite –

assuming a fast track to EMU would bring political union in its train. EMU and even the SEM imply a federal Europe. But the full range of central institutions that are necessary to any real Federal arrangement are not yet in place nor even proposed:

> I sympathize with the position of those (like Margaret Thatcher) who, faced with the loss of sovereignty, wish to get off the European Monetary Union train altogether. I also sympathise with those who seek integration under the jurisdiction of some kind of federal constitution with a federal budget very much larger than that of the Community budget. What I find totally baffling is the position of those who are aiming for economic and monetary union without the creation of new political institutions (apart from a new central bank) and who raise their hands in horror at the words 'federal' or 'federalism'. (Godley, 1992, p. 19)

This combination of economic union in the absence of political integration is unprecedented. In the debate about European integration, the issue of federalism has been fudged. This has happened for understandable and powerful political reasons. Indeed, one could argue that Maastricht was an optimal outcome politically in that it avoided a formal break into a two-tier or 'variable geometry' Europe. But socially the consequences may be devastating. In place is a deflationary macroeconomic consensus, enshrined at European level by the Maastricht convergence criteria and the provisions of the Stability Pact. Also in place are the powerful economic forces unleashed by the integration process, leading to restructuring of industries, firms, communities, cities and regions throughout Europe, and bringing in their train immense social costs alongside great social benefits and opportunities for some.

The external value of the euro against major global currencies fell considerably after the launch of the single currency. But at the time of writing (February 2001), the general economic outlook for the countries of Euroland is positive. The Euroland economy recovered in the second half of 1999, and grew strongly in the first half of 2000. Growth in both Western Europe as a whole and in Euroland was estimated at 3.3 per cent for 2000, and forecast to be 3 per cent in 2001 and 2.75 per cent in 2002 (PricewaterhouseCoopers, *European Economic Outlook*, January 2001). At the same time, distrust and doubt about the single currency project is growing. Scandinavia and the UK remain very sceptical, and even in Germany only a small majority in December 2001 supported the single currency of which they were already a member.

What is *not* in place is any institutional arrangement for giving citizens a degree of social protection in the widest sense against economic forces at the continental level analogous to that they currently receive at the national level. National governments are losing some of their ability to intervene in markets, to resist market forces for social ends. But these powers are not being reconstituted at the federal level. This raises questions about welfare and citizenship, which I shall look at in Chapter 8.

European integration at the time of writing is in a contradictory and untenable position. Some might call this position 'pre-federal', but this would be misleading, suggesting as it does a preliminary and temporary phase along an agreed path. One explanation is to see the present arrangements as reflecting unreconciled political differences, and the consequences of an excessive belief in the ability of market forces and deregulation to solve underlying political and social difficulties. Others would categorise this phase as a necessary stage in the modernisation of both European economies and European politics to accommodate the realities of a more Globalized world. A further version is to argue that the seeming ambiguity and contingency is not a transition stage but is the very nature of a new form of multi-tiered European governance. So it is argued that New Governance, far from being a failure, is in fact better adapted than more linear or hierarchical systems to cope with a world of shared authority.

How do we assess this? The traditional textbook separation between a Customs union, single market and monetary union is of limited explanatory value when dealing with a group of modern mixed economies, such as the fifteen EU countries, characterised by complex economic structures and high degrees of state intervention (Tsoukalis, 1993). Partly as a consequence of this, the elements of political, social and economic integration are closely interwoven, and have been so since the signing of the Treaty of Rome in 1958. A more useful distinction might be made between positive and negative modes of integration. Leibfried (1993) makes just such a distinction between the negative mode, which concentrates on removing obstacles to the operation of free markets, and the more ambitious positive mode, which requires a more activist programme by the state and reliance on a developed executive and parliament. The consolidation of the USA as a federal state at the end of the nineteenth and beginning of the twentieth century is an example of the former, and as such conforms to Marshall's sequencing of citizenship rights: first civil, then political, and finally social. But such a sequence is not inevitable. Unification in Germany in the nineteenth century, an example of positive integration, involved the extension of social citizenship to the working class under Bismarck, preceding political citizenship (universal suffrage) by four decades (Leibfried, 1993, p. 136).

Taking this further, we might identify two types of political and economic integration – the 'Jeffersonian' and the 'Bismarckian' (Kay and Posner, 1989). Jeffersonian integration is a relatively slow process that would allow 'a greater degree of pluralism and diversity' as well as 'a process of social Darwinism to spread "best practice" throughout the Union'. Bismarckian integration refers to 'the imposition fairly early in the process, of a strong central authority on the component parts' (Kay and Posner, 1989, p. 55). Currie, discussing tax harmonisation, uses a similar metaphor:

> Even if convergence of tax rates were required, it could take two forms. One is top-down, a Bismarckian or Napoleonic process of central decision-making, laying down what national governments should or should not do. The other is a Jeffersonian process of market pressure, where national governments respond to market pressures in setting tax rates. (Currie, 1998)

A race to the bottom is not inevitable, because a high tax/high investment regime may be superior to a low tax/low investment one.

Despite the similarities in their analytical categories, Leibfried comes to very different conclusions from Kay and Posner. For Leibfried, the continental social scientist, Europe is engaged on the narrower path of negative integration, which limits the social gains from the process severely:

> The citizenship on which a unifying Europe might come to rest seems primarily an economic or civil notion, secondarily a political one, and only lastly a social one ... This pattern repeats British and American precedents and is not anchored well either in German or in Scandinavian history. Unity in such a restrictive frame would turn into a unity of 'possessive individualism', a unity of market only. It will not be the unity of an enlightened 'Social Europe' synthesising its traditions of democracy and solidarity, of civil and social rights, and building on its traditions of merging the citizen and the social state. (Leibfried, 1993, p. 150)

This development is not inevitable: a top-down 'Europeanisation' of poverty policy is possible; for example, based on a common formula. But the political and juridical basis for such a European standardisation does not at the time of writing exist (Leibfried, 1993, pp. 148–9).

For Kay and Posner, the British liberal economists, the 'present continental urge' towards integration is Bismarckian. This is not only harmful, but is based on a misunderstanding of the relative importance of market and state in the process of integration:

> The process of economic integration in Europe is both inevitable and desirable and is one which is bound to undermine the capacity of any country to pursue independent economic policies. But integration cannot be imposed: the actions of the Commission and the Council of Ministers can help it – a bit – or hinder it – a bit – but that is all. (Kay and Posner, 1989, p. 66)

In this approach, greater faith is placed on the abilities of markets, particularly factor markets, to reach efficient solutions. Inequalities in regions should be dealt with by removing labour market 'rigidities' rather than by regional policy or other legislated transfers.

Conclusions

Currently, the EU is an embryonic federal system with no federal institutions, apart from a central bank that is politically unaccountable. There is no democratic and accountable system of control over the existing EU institutions. The cliché 'democratic deficit' is far too mild a term to describe this astonishing absence at the centre of the integration process. Most importantly, there is no federal fiscal role of any size to offset the deflationary framework of the convergence criteria and the regional shocks that will ensue from EMU. Instead there is at the European level only a fragmentary and limited system of redistribution via the structural and cohesion funds; while at the national level, the convergence criteria and the Stability Pact limit the choices of national governments.

For three decades, integrationists pursued a strategy of using economic integration as the motor of the political project of European unity. Over this period, in general, the strategy was successful. But this cycle has now run its course, and the current stage of economic integration – the creation of a single currency – not only generates social consequences requiring social policy interventions, but also poses fundamental questions of citizenship, identity and democracy. I shall look at some of these questions in Chapter 8. But first, we must consider the most pressing economic and social issue in Europe: unemployment and social exclusion.

7

Europe Isn't Working: Jobs, Unemployment and Social Exclusion

Introduction

Promoting employment and reducing Europe's high level of unemployment have now become the most important social issue in the European Union. The Commission's 1999 Review of the EU economy stated that 'persistently high unemployment and a low employment rate remain key problems in the EU', and it refers to the EU's 'dismal' labour market performance through much of the last three decades of the twentieth century. Allan Larsson, the Director General for Employment and Social Affairs at the Commission, has spoken about a 'new approach' to labour market policies, orientated strongly towards active labour market policies and a preventative approach. This reflects a Europe-wide shift in social policy 'from welfare to work' (Larsson, 2000, p. 2). Despite the rhetoric, however, unemployment has not become the number one *economic* issue, which remains price stability and prudent public finances.

It is often argued that social policies in general, and the extent and generosity of European welfare states in particular, have contributed to Europe's poor jobs record and persistent high unemployment. A common criticism is that welfare state institutions and policies were created in earlier decades for a very different type of economy and society, and no longer map well on to patterns of work, family and leisure at the start of the twenty-first century.

European welfare states, mainly conceived and developed at a time of full employment and steady economic growth, have been affected seriously by a series of economic and demographic changes: the return of mass and persistent unemployment; the restructuring of production and the shift from a production to a service-based economy; demographic changes, particularly population ageing and

161

the decline of traditional marriage and family-building; and increased female participation rates and growing polarisation between two-earner and no-earner households. But it is further argued by some that welfare policies not only fail to respond to the needs of individuals and households in a modern economy and society; policies actively worsen the situation for Europeans by inhibiting job creation and raising unemployment. Moreover, it is argued that high unemployment in Europe is a major source of social exclusion – tackling social exclusion will require, above all, policies that transfer individuals from welfare to work.

In this chapter, I first look at the evidence on employment and unemployment in Europe, and the causes of Europe's poor performance on jobs and joblessness. Next, I look at the growth of 'new poverty' and social exclusion, and at the relationship between poverty and exclusion on the one hand, and the labour market on the other. Then, I look at the role of European level policies on unemployment and exclusion.

Employment and Unemployment in the European Union

In the period 1975–2000, employment in Europe grew in eighteen out of the twenty-five years, with job growth being particularly strong between 1985 and 1990, when there was a net gain of 10 million jobs. But these were offset by three periods of heavy job losses in 1975, 1981–3 and 1992–4, each following a macroeconomic 'shock' – oil price rises in the first two cases and monetary crisis in the early 1990s. Overall, between 1975 and 2000 there was job growth in the EU15 of 17 million, but job losses of 9 million, giving a net increase of only 8 million (Larsson, 2000).

A key indicator of the jobs performance of the economy is the *employment rate*. This refers to the proportion of the working-age population that is employed. Employment in the EU grew to 151 million jobs in 1998, an employment rate of 61 per cent, with unemployment in 1998 around 10 per cent. However, the European employment rate is well below those in both the USA and Japan.

Europe's job creation record since the mid-1970s has been much inferior to both the USA and Japan. The employment rate in the EU15 in 1976 was just above that of the USA, and only a few percentage points below that of Japan. Since then, EU employment rates have fallen from just under 65 per cent to only just over 60 per cent. Meanwhile, in the USA, the employment rate has grown to 75 per cent. Employment rates have increased, albeit less spectacularly, in Japan to a similar rate of 75 per cent. In the USA, total employment in 1998 was almost two-thirds higher than in 1970, while in the eleven countries with a single currency (Euroland) employment had expanded by less than 10 per cent. Private sector job growth in Euroland was virtually non-existent. If Europe had a similar employment rate as the USA, there would be 35 million more people employed (Larsson, 2000, p. 5).

There is no evidence that jobs are created or destroyed faster in North America than in Europe – but workers circulate more quickly through the existing jobs. In the USA, regional mobility is much higher than in major European economies such as the UK, Germany, France, Italy and Spain – although regional mobility is high in Sweden and Norway, where it has been a deliberate feature of labour market policy (Nickell, 1997).

GDP per capita is lower in Europe than in the USA. However, this is because of the lower employment rate, not because of lower levels of productivity in Europe, measuring productivity in terms of GDP per hour worked. Measured in this way, productivity in the main countries of Northern Europe (Belgium, France, West Germany, the Netherlands and Norway) is higher than in the USA, despite GDP per capita being lower (Nickell and Layard, 1998).

The difference in employment rates between Europe and the USA is not constant across different types of worker. Rather, it is concentrated among workers who might be classed as more peripheral to the labour market, while employment rates for prime-age males show little difference. Employment rates of men aged 25–54 are very similar across the EU and the USA. In the EU, the employment level is around 85 per cent, in the USA, around 88 per cent (Larsson, 2000, p. 7). However, among women, there is a large gap in employment rates, with around 50 per cent of women aged 15–64 in Europe in employment, compared with almost 68 per cent in the USA.

In a parallel fashion, differences *between* European countries in employment rates turn out to be concentrated among particular groups. The relatively low aggregate employment rate in Europe appears to be a particular problem among inactive prime-age women and older people: 'Indeed, these groups account for most of the cross-country variations in aggregate employment rates, while prime-age males have rather similar employment rates in most countries' (European Commission, 1999b, p. 132). Among those aged 25–54, the proportion of people in employment is almost exactly the same in the UK, France and Germany. The difference in the employment rate between the UK on the one hand and the continental economies on the other, is mainly related to higher youth unemployment, and lower employment among older workers (Atkinson, 2000).

The key job creation difference between Europe and the USA lies in the service sector. Employment rates in agriculture and manufacturing are similar; but in services there is a gap of 14 percentage points. Employment growth in services has been significantly and systematically lower in the EU than in the USA (European Commission, 1999b). If Europe had the same employment rate in the service sector as the USA, there would be an additional 30 million jobs in Europe (Larsson, 2000, p. 6).

The sectors growing fastest in Europe are business services; health and social work; hotels and restaurants; education; and retail trade. These are all sectors where the gap between European and American employment rates are largest. In the first three sectors, the proportion of skilled and unskilled jobs is similar in both the USA and Europe; that is, the USA appears to be creating jobs across the occupational structure. But overall, the USA employs more low-skilled people than does Europe – 20 per cent of the working-age population in the USA; 13 per cent in the EU. Europe has thus generated far fewer low-paying jobs than has the USA, especially in services. But it remains contentious whether a wider dispersion of wages would raise employment rates (European Commission, 1999b, p. 143). The Commission's regular studies of *Employment in Europe*, argue that there is no evidence that wider wage dispersion is related to higher employment rates, either in services or in the economy as a whole. But writers such as Siebert (1997) argue that the fact that wage differentiation has grown in the USA and the UK while remaining unchanged in continental Europe is significant, reflecting the inflexible nature of the labour market institutions in most of Europe. According to these writers, this rigidity is a major cause of high European unemployment. I shall discuss possible causes of Europe's high unemployment below.

One of the major changes in labour markets, not just in Europe, but throughout the OECD, has been an increase in part-time working. The OECD (1999b) points out that part-time working is very heterogeneous. Part-timers get lower earnings per hour worked and receive lower levels of training than full-timers; they are also less likely to be in stable jobs. But compared with other types of 'non-standard work' (for example, temporary and shift work) part-time employment is viewed relatively favourably by many employees, both part-time and full-time. Moreover, attitudes are most favourable in those places where part-time working is most strongly developed. A European Commission study in 1995 showed that across eleven EU countries, 31 per cent of part-time workers would prefer to be in full-time work, with 12 per cent of full-timers preferring part-time (OECD, 1999b). The percentage of part-timers wishing to work full-time (and hence by implication, unhappy to be working part-time) ranged from 41 per cent in France; 43 per cent in Italy; and 62 per cent in Portugal, to 15 per cent in Germany; 14 per cent in Denmark; and 8 per cent in the Netherlands.

The other side of the coin of Europe's poor jobs performance is persistently high unemployment. In the mid-1970s, Europe had lower unemployment than the USA. Since then, the unemployment position has deteriorated steadily, rising from just over 4 per cent in 1976 to well over 10 per cent in the mid-1990s. In the USA, unemployment did not fall below European levels until 1984. But since then unemployment has fallen from a peak of nearly 10 per cent to less than 5 per cent in 2000.

Not only is European unemployment high; also, importantly, is European *long-term* unemployment. In 1998, half of the unemployed people in Europe had been out of work for a year or more. Unemployment rates are particularly high among the young, and to some extent among women, with young people typically having unemployment rates two to three times higher than adults. Not surprisingly, low-skilled workers fare worst. Although the supply of low-educated workers has fallen, demand for them has fallen further. In almost every EU (and indeed OECD) country unemployment rates are higher among the less educated (Nickell and Layard, 1998). The regional dispersion of unemployment is significantly worse in the Euro area – the eleven countries that joined the single currency in 1999 – compared with the USA, and in most Euro-area countries the regional dispersion has worsened with the rise in unemployment generally (European Commission, 1999b, p. 132).

It therefore seems clear that the bulk of Europe's current unemployment problem has structural rather than cyclical causes. The European Commission's own research suggests that between three-quarters and four-fifths of unemployment is of a non-cyclical, and hence structural nature (European Commission, 1999b).

If we look at *non*-employment rates rather than *un*employment rates, the picture is much more consistent across the OECD than the position for unemployment: 'The US, Canada and Australia have non-employment rates similar to those in Europe. Only Japan and Sweden have low non-employment rates by OECD standards' (Balls, 1994). Moreover, non-employment rates rose everywhere in the 1980s. But this still does not undercut the argument that the bulk of the European jobs problem is structural. Slow growth might explain the rise in unemployment in Europe in the first half of the 1990s as the ERM transmitted high interest rates and deflation from Germany across the Continent. But non-employment remained high in the 1980s during strong economic growth (Balls, 1994) and unemployment and non-employment remain high in Europe despite five years of growth in the late 1990s.

Moreover, non-employment and unemployment are not inter-changeable. An unemployed person is much more unhappy, *ceteris paribus*, than a person who is out of the labour force; hence, one should not combine the categories. But differences in definitions and practice mean that some individuals recorded as unemployed in one country would be recorded as out of the labour force in another.

Variations across European Countries

Increasing employment and reducing unemployment has been identi-fied as a European priority by European institutions. To some extent, one can describe and analyse the 'European labour market' and contrast this with the situation in the USA, as set out briefly above. But equally, it soon becomes apparent that there are important differences, both across regions within the EU, and across member states, and indeed these differences are as important as the similarities between European countries. Although there has been some conver-gence in GDP per head across EU regions since the early mid-1980s, this process had not occurred with regard to employment rates – in fact, there has been slight divergence in employment rates over this period. Regional differences in employment rates within most mem-ber states have remained the same, suggesting that the causes are structural, and that regional policies – both at member state and EU level – have been more successful in correcting disparities in GDP per head than in getting balanced job creation (European Commission, 1999a). Furthermore, as well as differences in the operation of labour markets, there are key differences at national level in the relationships between unemployment, poverty and social exclusion (see below).

All European countries are moving towards becoming service economies, but this transition is particularly difficult for Germany, France and Italy. In these countries it is especially difficult to create service jobs. For example, in starting up a new business, it takes two procedures in Denmark, five in the UK, and six in the USA. But it takes ten in Germany and sixteen in France (Larsson, 2000, p. 13). In these three countries (Germany, France and Italy), there is also a low level of female labour-market participation, and it is likely that these phenomena are linked. In these three countries, the overall employment rate was lower in the late 1990s than in the mid-1980s (European Commission, 1999a). High growth in services is found in Austria, the UK and the Netherlands.

There is no evidence of convergence in regional employment rates across the EU, and indeed in the 1990s it appears that disparities have widened (European Commission, 1999a). In 1998 the employment rate averaged 61 per cent but this ranged from over 80 per cent in one Finnish and three English regions, to less than 40 per cent in Calabria and Sicilia. Most of the regions with the highest employment rates were in the UK, while regions with the lowest rates were in southern parts of Spain and Italy. 'Regions' here refer to the official European Common 'NUTS 2' classification, roughly equivalent to groups of English counties. Growth between 1985 and 1990 benefited regions where employment was already high, rather than where it was low. In the recession of the early 1990s, regional disparities narrowed, but in the recovery after 1994 they widened slightly.

Hence disparities have in general widened, or at least remained constant – the regional pattern of employment rates has not changed much since the 1980s, supporting the view that there are structural problems of job creation. The link between Structural Fund (SF) support and job creation appears to be weak. Widening disparities were particularly marked in Italy, Portugal and to some extent Spain – all countries that get substantial SF support. Moreover, the relative position of those areas targeted for help via the Commission's Structural Funds has worsened in comparison with the rest of Europe. In the poorest regions in Europe (the Objective 1 regions) average unemployment fell during 1986–91 from 15 per cent to 14 per cent, whereas in the unassisted regions it fell from 9 per cent to 7.5 per cent (European Commission, 1993b).

This is not to say that SF support is ineffective – there has been convergence in GDP per head, but this has not been translated into employment (European Commission, 1999a). This finding is consistent with a characterisation of European labour markets as favouring insiders rather than outsiders, and hence being associated with real wage growth (or at least maintenance of real wages) rather than job creation.

As we saw above, variations across European countries in employment rates largely reflect differences in the employment rates of women, and younger and older men. This variation may be at least partly a result of cultural factors, and in particular the participation rate of married women. Nickell (1997) calculates the proportion of 'potential' labour hours actually worked, by combining measures of the employment rate with data on the number of hours actually worked per year (assuming a 40-hour week over fifty-two weeks). This shows that in Japan, Portugal and the USA, about two-thirds of potential hours are worked, while in Spain and Belgium, this falls to 40 per cent (no estimate was made of the informal economy). Employment rates are lower in assisted regions, particularly in Objective 1 areas. Between 1986 and 1991, there was everywhere – assisted and unassisted areas – a greater increase in employment than a decrease in unemployment, hence an increase in labour force participation. This suggests that there may be convergence going on in labour participation rates, as more women seek work (European Commission, 1993b)

Employment rates differ greatly across the member states. In Denmark, the UK, Sweden and Austria, rates are above 70 per cent, while in Italy and Spain they are just over 50 per cent (Larsson, 2000). In Austria, Denmark, Greece, Portugal and the Netherlands, employment rates for male workers are higher than in the USA. These are countries with very different labour market regimes, yet they all have high employment for men in this core group. At the very least, this suggests that the relationship between 'welfare regime' and jobs performance is not that simple. However, only two countries – Denmark and Sweden – have a similar level of female employment to the USA. The EU's 'under-employment' is mainly concentrated in four big member states – Germany, France, Italy and Spain – whose working-age population approaches that of the USA (nearly 160 million and 175 million, respectively). These four countries together have an employment rate of 58 per cent compared with 74 per cent for the USA.

The relationship between employment growth and job quality also differs across countries. Even where countries have similar rates of employment growth, the relative expansion of different sectors changes the mix of skills required (European Commission, 1999a). In the Netherlands and Belgium, there has been a disproportionate increase in high-skilled, non-manual jobs, while in the Republic of Ireland and Denmark, job growth has been more evenly distributed. This might reflect different patterns of consumer demand, or it might reflect varying obstacles across the EU to creating low-skilled jobs. Some countries are simply quicker at adapting to change. Where growth sectors are expanding faster, there will be better overall employment performance (for example, the Netherlands relative to Belgium) (European Commission, 1999a).

There is an enormous variation in the unemployment performance of countries in Europe. Taking first a broader definition of OECD Europe over the period 1983–96, unemployment averaged 1.8 per cent in Switzerland and 19.7 per cent in Spain (Nickell, 1997). Of the population of OECD Europe, 30 per cent live in countries with an average lower unemployment rate than in the USA. The lowest unemployment rates were in countries not normally associated with labour market flexibility: Austria, Germany, Norway, Portugal, Sweden and Switzerland (Nickell, 1997). More recent evidence, confined to EU members only, suggests a somewhat different list, with Austria, Portugal, Denmark, the Republic of Ireland, the Netherlands and the United Kingdom identified as countries which either have 'relatively low structural unemployment rates or have managed to reduce them significantly' (European Commission, 1999b, p. 130). But the substantive point remains true. With the exception of the UK, these are not countries identified as having particularly flexible labour markets, and they cover the range of types of 'welfare state regime'. Poor performers in terms of high structural unemployment are the four major economies of Germany, France, Italy and Spain.

Why Is European Unemployment So High?

A range of suspects can be identified to explain why European unemployment is so high. One view targets the 'European Social Model' itself. It is argued that Europe's labour market institutions, its social regulations and its generous social protection arrangements are to blame. Labour market rigidity means that European economies and labour markets do not adapt, or do not adapt quickly enough, to changes in demand. Generous social protection raises the 'reservation wage' – the minimum that job seekers are looking for from employment, and hence extends the period of unemployment. Government regulations, bureaucracy and high taxes on employers make it difficult for existing firms to create new jobs, and for new firms to be created.

For example, Siebert (1997) argues that institutional changes since the mid-1970s are the central reason for Europe's poor labour market performance, and explain the differences in employment and unemployment between Europe and the USA. In labour-market institutions, Siebert includes the minimum wage, unemployment benefit, social security and welfare payments, and formal wage-bargaining rules. Changes to these in the 1970s – increased duration of benefits, easier access to unemployment benefit, more generous entitlements, and a rise in the minimum wage – have raised the reservation wage. This means that the unemployed have less incentive to search for and to accept work at low market wages. Insiders are less prepared to take into account the unemployment costs of wage increases, as the burden is shifted to taxpayers. The wage floor moves up, the earnings distribution is truncated from below, and low-skilled workers are priced out.

According to Siebert (1997) the UK and the Netherlands have 'overhauled' their labour market institutions, leading to falls in unemployment in these countries. In the Netherlands, where there has been wage restraint, reductions in benefits and more stringent tests, there was strong employment growth of 1.8 per cent per year between 1985 and 1996. In the UK, Thatcherite reforms reduced union power, abolished wages councils and made unemployment benefit both more restrictive and less generous. Employment increased only slightly, but this was a better performance than in the rest of Europe. At the opposite end of the scale are the welfare states of the 'French–Mediterranean' group, where there has been no improvement in the functioning of the labour market, of which France is the 'exemplar'. However, what Siebert does not acknowledge is that the Netherlands and the UK remain very different types of welfare state, and that the welfare state in the Netherlands remains relatively generous. Siebert's conclusion is that the effects of Globalization and technology require flexibility, but this is prevented in Europe by institutional conditions.

In complete contrast to this *microeconomic* explanation of rising unemployment, are explanations based on *macroeconomic* conditions. Michie and Wilkinson (1994) contrast the reflationary policies practised by Japan and the USA in the early 1990s with Europe's dogged insistence on the anti-inflationary policies of the Maastrict Treaty. Increases in European unemployment have been associated with de-industrialisation, with 5.5 million manufacturing jobs lost in the EC12 during 1976–86, 40 per cent of them in Britain. Balance of payments constraints mean that shifts between sectors have an impact not just on relative shares, but also on absolute levels of output and employment. They conclude that European unemployment is largely the result of restrictive macroeconomic policies, and the distribution of unemployment between member states largely a function of the failure to develop balance of payment adjustment mechanisms. They foresee the danger that the 'EC will follow Britain in a drift towards poverty, low wage and poor employment conditions for a large and growing section of its workforce' (Michie and Wilkinson, 1994, p. 25).

Explaining unemployment remains an area of controversy and debate. Nevertheless, there is probably a consensus among most economists around a mainstream explanation that includes both the impact on European economies of exogenous shocks (macroeconomic causes) and the poor response of European labour markets to those shocks (microeconomic causes). Hence, Europe's persistent unemployment results from the interaction of external shocks, which raise unemployment temporarily, with the characteristics of labour market institutions and product market regulations, which slow adjustment and hence turn temporary into long-term unemployment:

> temporary shocks may lead to persistent unemployment when there are mechanisms at work that tend to translate actual unemployment over time into increases in non-cyclical structural unemployment. The strength of these propagation mechanisms will depend on specific labour market institutions and product market regulations, which are likely to differ significantly across countries. (European Commission, 1999b, p. 128)

These external macroeconomic shocks include: the productivity slowdown associated with the rise in commodity and oil prices in the 1970s; the sharp increase in real interest rates in the 1980s; and the more recent shifts in labour demand away from less skilled labour, whether due to technological change or the impact of changes in world trade. Labour market institutions alone cannot be held responsible, as there is no evidence that such institutions and arrangements have become more rigid since the 1980s: 'In fact, if anything, over the past decade, institutional arrangements in Europe appear to have become more employment-friendly from an overall point of view' (European Commission, 1999b, p. 134). It is the combination of factors that is responsible. Macroeconomic shocks could in principle have led to wage 'adjustments' (that is, falls in real wages of European workers) without any rise in unemployment beyond the most temporary. But labour market institutions prevent this adjustment taking place – workers and governments resist the fall in real wages. Real wages for those in work – 'insiders' – are maintained, but at the cost of a growing number of 'outsiders' – a section of the workforce becomes long-term unemployed, and increasingly separated from the labour market. The share of wages in national income in Europe remained roughly constant in the last decades of the twentieth century, there has been little rise in employment and a sharp rise in unemployment, and average real wages have risen. Hence, those in work have appropriated the benefits of rising real GDP (Ormerod, 1998).

So rising European unemployment is caused by a combination of external shocks and internal labour market arrangements. But how significant are these labour market institutions? One view is that Europe's greater regulation and rigidity goes a considerable way to explaining the differences in unemployment between the USA and Europe. Both continents have experienced similar demand shocks and shifts in demand for labour, particularly less skilled labour. In the USA, flexible labour markets, regional mobility and perhaps some effects of large-scale immigration have meant that the outcome of these trends has been stagnation in average wages and a fall in real wages for less skilled workers. In continental Europe, on the other hand, wages and working conditions have generally been maintained, but the price has been paid in the form of persistent high unemployment.

In other words, in Europe, insiders have maintained their position to the detriment of outsiders, whereas in the USA, more of the pain has fallen on insiders – those already in work. In the USA and the UK, wage rate dispersion has increased – the difference between the wage rates of skilled versus unskilled workers has grown – while in most continental countries this has not happened: 'Falling demand for unskilled labour had different effects on wages and unemployment because of cross-country differences in labour markets' (Balls, 1994, p. 124). So overall wage inequality rose in both the UK and the USA after 1975, whereas in France earnings inequality fell from the mid-1970s to the mid-1980s, although it rose again subsequently.

However, there are also differences between the USA and the UK. Between 1979 and 1987, real wages of the lowest-paid 10 per cent of workers fell by 10 per cent in the USA (and by 30 per cent since 1970), whereas in the UK they rose by 10 per cent (Balls, 1994). A common view is that the lack of relative wage adjustment in most European countries has meant that the *quantity* of employment has had to adjust instead, 'partly making the European unemployment problem a "mirror image" of the increased wage dispersion in the USA' (European Commission, 1999b, p. 146). Hence Europe's poor record on unemployment raises questions not just about economic policy but also, more fundamentally, about the underlying social consensus: 'The average rate of unemployment which prevails over the course of the business cycle is a result of the particular form of social contract, whether explicit or implicit, which exists' (Ormerod, 1998).

However, the evidence is inconclusive. Nickell and Layard (1998) argue that the widening wage inequalities between differently qualified workers seen in the UK and USA are attributable to the fact that, in these countries, relative demand for skilled workers outstripped supply by far more than in other OECD countries. Hence supply and demand analysis can explain increased wage inequality without any reference to unions, minimum wages and wage inflexibility. They conclude that 'skill shifts account for only a tiny proportion of the rise in unemployment since the 1970s' (Nickell and Layard, 1998, p. 64). Furthermore, by using a more accurate measure of comparable skill levels across countries, they show that there is strong evidence in favour of a simple hypothesis in which the earnings distributions in different countries do, in fact, correspond closely to variations in the true skill distribution. Nevertheless, more rigid relative wages in Europe may help to explain lower employment and higher unemployment among particular groups such as women and younger workers (European Commission, 1999b).

Labour market institutions and practices which might have some impact on unemployment levels include: regulation of labour markets such as employment protection and labour standards; aspects of the social security system such as benefit rates, duration and work-seeking requirements; the level of geographical and occupational mobility among the workforce; and aspects of the industrial relations system including union density and coverage, and the level and type of co-ordination within unions and employers. It is misleading to consider all these features as constituting something called labour market rigidity; rather, it is a question of identifying which of these features is relevant in explaining European unemployment, and which are not (Nickell, 1997).

On the basis of regression analysis, Nickell (1997) concludes that indefinite, generous unemployment benefit in the absence of active labour market measures does raise unemployment, as do high unionisation coupled with lack of co-ordination across unions and employers, high labour taxes and poor educational standards at the lower end of the labour market. However, employment protection legislation, generous unemployment benefits coupled with pressure to take jobs, and high unionisation and union coverage accompanied by a high level of co-ordination in wage bargaining do not appear to have serious implications. Many so-called 'labour market rigidities' apply no more to high-unemployment countries than they do to low-unemployment countries. The argument that European unemployment is high because European labour markets are rigid is 'too vague and probably misleading' (Nickell, 1997, p. 73).

There is no evidence that employment protection legislation leads to higher unemployment. Strong employment protection does reduce both the inflow and the outflow into unemployment, thereby lowering the short-term unemployment rate but at the same time raising the long-term unemployment rate. Strong trade unions will only raise unemployment and lower economic growth where firms and unions do not co-ordinate centrally over wage setting, and where management and unions have adversarial rather than co-operative relations:

> Trade union wage bargaining behaviour is likely to result, *ceteris paribus*, in relatively lower employment, because union pay bargaining exerts upward pressure on wages. However, this negative effect tends to disappear or even runs positive with centralisation and co-ordination of unions and firms in the bargaining process providing a mechanism to overcome some of the externalities generated by decentralised collective bargaining, for example by avoiding leapfrogging. (European Commission, 1999b, p. 144)

Co-ordination and co-operation of this kind requires both supporting institutions and external competitive pressures. There is evidence that low structural unemployment is associated both with highly decentralised and with highly centralised wage bargaining systems. Higher unemployment is associated with intermediate systems (Calmfors and Drifill, 1988; OECD, 1997 ch.3). However, one should be careful about generalising from the experience of some smaller, highly unionised European countries – positive outcomes may be more difficult to achieve where there are larger numbers of actors (European Commission, 1999b).

As far as social security is concerned, the big difference between European and USA unemployment rates is in the level of long-term unemployment, which can be explained by the European pattern of long-term entitlements to unemployment benefit without labour-market requirements. This can be offset by active labour-market policies and a strictly operated system (Nickell and Layard, 1998). The overall tax burden is significantly higher in the EU compared with either the USA or with Japan – in the EU, the overall tax burden is 43 per cent, compared to 31 per cent in the USA and 28 per cent in Japan. The difference in terms of the tax 'wedge' – the difference between what firms have to pay, including taxes and contributions, and what employees receive, net of taxes and deductions – is greater still.

This leads to comparatively lower incentives to return to work in Europe. However, comparisons of the tax burden between Europe and elsewhere should also take account of the fact that in the USA social protection and health expenditure does not appear as a direct public sector cost, but must nevertheless be funded from payments by workers and employers. As a proportion of GDP, the amount spent on social expenditure 'is quite similar across Europe (around 27%) with the US no more than a few percentage points lower at around 24%. The difference is the way the spending is funded – whether it is paid for primarily out of taxes (as in Europe), or out of after-tax take-home pay (as in the US)' (Quintin, 1999).

Labour mobility, both occupational and geographic, plays a much greater role in adjustment to economic shocks in the USA than in Europe. Mobility in Europe was been falling in the last decades of the twentieth century, and despite the emphasis in both the SEM and EMU programmes on encouraging greater mobility, it is unlikely that there will be major changes to this pattern.

The policy implications for governments seeking to reduce unemployment are, therefore; to encourage greater competition in product markets by removing anti-competitive product market regulation; to support labour market institutions that enable co-operation and co-ordination between employers and trade unions; to encourage labour mobility; and to reform social security systems away from passive benefit receipt and towards active labour market and 'welfare to work' measures.

Defining Social Exclusion

European welfare states have also been accused of failing to respond to the challenges of social exclusion and 'new poverty'. Changes in both the economic structure and social arrangements have generated new sets of risks. Existing welfare state institutions, largely constructed in the very different social and economic circumstances of the immediate post-war period, have been unable to respond adequately to these new circumstances. In addition, the maturation of welfare systems and slower economic growth means that there has been a political reaction against further extensions to the welfare state, and moves towards retrenchment and cutbacks. Together, these factors gave rise to what has been termed 'new poverty'.

Hence, the growth of 'new poverty' was identified both with an erosion of social protection systems and new lines of social division, which reflect 'profound industrial change and ... forces that have weakened and fragmented older social and family structures and traditional forms of solidarity' (Lawson, 1995, p. 5). While economic change has brought greater opportunity and prosperity for much of the 'middle mass', for poorer groups there have been increased risks of economic and social insecurity.

Welfare states that developed in the first sixty years or so of the twentieth century, and particularly in the two decades after 1945, were based around notions of full employment and the family with a single male breadwinner. With the return of mass unemployment, greater family fragmentation, erosion of solidarity, and increased economic precariousness, the safety nets have become weaker, allowing more and different types of households and individuals to fall into poverty. The 'new poor' are thus characterised by an unexpected fall from the protection of social security systems; the suddenness of the descent into poverty; and their inability to cope and lack of skill in using the system (Room, 1990).

The term 'new poverty' refers primarily to the poverty experienced by the able-bodied of working age, in contrast to poverty in old age, and poverty associated with long-term sickness and disability. Hence 'patterns of poverty [are] changing, not just in degree but in type. If the "new poverty" exists, it is not as a replacement to the old. Rather, the use of the term makes most sense as a reference to forms of labour-market exclusion and marginalisation' (Cross, 1993, pp. 21–2). This takes the definition of new poverty close to that of social exclusion (see below). Room (1995) describes how in the first EC

Poverty Programme, there were significant differences between An-glo-Saxon and French conceptualisations of poverty. While the French were uncomfortable with the concepts of 'poverty lines', others schooled in the Anglo-Saxon tradition found the concept of social exclusion difficult to operationalise as a reference point for policy analysis.

Social exclusion is normally defined as being something conceptually distinct from poverty. Poverty refers to inadequate or unequal material resources, while social exclusion is concerned more with inadequate or unequal participation in social life (Room, 1995). This distinction is expressed in a 1989 resolution by the Council of Ministers: 'social exclusion is not simply a matter of inadequate means ... combating exclusion also involves access by individuals and families to decent living conditions by means of measures for social integration and integration into the labour market' (quoted in Duffy, 1998).

In considering social exclusion, we are therefore concerned with questions not just of up/down, top/bottom, but also of in/out – the comfortable versus the excluded (Duffy, 1998). The concept of social exclusion came originally from a primarily French tradition of social analysis, and the rapid spread of the use of the term in the later 1980s and 1990s can be ascribed to a great extent to the emphasis given to it by the European Commission and other European bodies. With widespread use, the term has become extremely ambiguous. For example, in the French tradition, social exclusion often arises from lack of access to welfare. In one of the earliest uses of the term, Lenoir (1974) referred to the 'maladapté', whether physical, mental or social, and with the administrative exclusion of certain groups from the social protection system (Duffy, 1998). In the French context, the term 'social exclusion' relates to established ideas of French identity and republican citizenship, with a strong centralised state involve-ment in the economy and society:

[French] ideology emphasises the assimilation of regional, national and religious cultures into a distinctive conception of citizenship and national civilisation actively promoted by the state. Repub-licanism is far more intolerant of diversity in public life than American pluralism ... the American term 'underclass' connotes outsiders in terms of employment, race and middle-class culture, while *exclusion* weds economic deprivation to the lack of full citizenship and not being truly 'French' in a cultural sense. (Silver, 1993 pp. 346–8)

More recently in France, social exclusion has been linked to greater 'precariousness' (*precarité*) in the labour market, a term that includes not only higher unemployment, but the growth of part-time, temporary and insecure work (Duffy, 1998).

In the UK, social exclusion has been associated not with exclusion from the welfare system, but with supposed reliance or dependency upon it. Hence, Harriet Harman, former Social Security minister, wrote about the socially excluded inhabiting 'a parallel world where income is derived from benefits, not work' (quoted in Duffy, 1998). Another minister, Peter Mandelson spoke about: 'three million people living in the worst 1,300 housing estates expressing multiple deprivation, rising poverty, unemployment, educational failure and crime. Behind these statistics ... are people who have lost hope, trapped in fatalism. They are today's and tomorrow's underclass, shut out from society' (quoted in Kleinman, 2000).

Hence, in the 'Anglo-Saxon' context, the term social exclusion comes closer to the notion of an 'underclass' and even, as in the above quote, being used interchangeably with it. More generally, the key strand of British government policy for tackling social exclusion places primary importance on *work*, and on the labour market as the primary route to social inclusion. The annual report of the British Department of Social Security (1999) states clearly: 'In order to eradicate child poverty we need to provide opportunities for their parents to work. For most people of working age, the best way to avoid poverty and social exclusion is to be in paid work' (p. 7).

The distinction between the British and the French views (and more widely between Anglo-Saxon and corporatist views) is not primarily a Left–Right distinction, but rather one based on different ideas about the relationship of the individual to the state. The social-catholic perspective that informs much of the French perspective and has been very influential on the European Commission's approach is conservative, 'workerist' and concerned only with redistribution over the life cycle and not between households (Duffy, 1998). The distinction is one of differing theoretical paradigms – poverty as a distributional issue, social exclusion as a set of relational issues, that is, inadequate social participation, lack of social integration, and lack of power (Room, 1995). Poverty research is associated with the nineteenth-century British tradition and its liberal vision of society as individuals, the role of social policy being to ensure that each has enough resources. Social exclusion is in the 'continental' tradition, starting from analysis of a status hierarchy and collectivities. Social policy is about mutual rights and obligations, rooted in a broader moral order (Room, 1995).

Can we reach an agreed and operational definition of the term 'social exclusion', distinct from poverty? 'Social exclusion is a term that has come to be widely used, but whose exact meaning is not always clear. Indeed, it seems to have gained currency in part *because* it has no precise definition and means all things to all people' (Atkinson, 1998b, p. 6). Nevertheless, Atkinson identifies three core elements, which he terms relativity, agency and dynamics. By *relativity*, he means that people are excluded from a particular society in a particular time and place; there is no equivalent to the notion of 'absolute poverty'. Exclusion can be a property of groups as well as of individuals – for example, when banks use postcodes to determine credit-worthiness. *Agency* refers to the fact that exclusion 'implies an act, with an agent or agents'. People may be excluded by the actions of others – employers, banks, government – or they may exclude themselves, for example, by refusing jobs. Finally, there is a *dynamic* element – people are excluded not just because they currently lack a job or income, but because their prospects for obtaining one in the future are low (Atkinson, 1998b, p. 8). Elsewhere, Atkinson has argued that this is the key aspect of social exclusion: 'It is not enough that there should be a fair race at the start of people's lives; the losers first time round should be offered new chances.' Moreover, a proper understanding of the dynamics of social exclusion, for example in relation to the labour market, makes it clear that inclusion is a process and not a single event: 'It is not enough to provide people with a job. Social inclusion requires that jobs provide acceptable levels of pay, coupled with dignity and future prospects. For young people entering the welfare to work programme, it should be a way station not a dead-end' (Atkinson, 2000). Hence, for Atkinson, the concept of social exclusion can be rendered meaningful and distinct from that of poverty – 'social exclusion is not simply long-term, or recurrent poverty. Social exclusion is not only a matter of *ex post* trajectories but also of *ex ante* expectations' (Atkinson, 1998b, p. 8).

The concept of social exclusion has also been criticised on a number of grounds. Levitas (1996) argues that the concept of social exclusion, whatever its origins, has now become part of a dominant discourse in which it is contrasted not with social inclusion, but rather with social integration – the latter being understood as almost synonymous with labour-market integration. In key documents, such as the European Commission's White Paper on European Social Policy, 'the over-

whelming emphasis is on paid work as the mechanism of integration, and the terms social exclusion and exclusion from the labour market are used virtually interchangeably' (Levitas, 1996, p. 9). Levitas criticises this on two grounds. First, it devalues or ignores the existence of unpaid work. Second, it strongly implies that the key division – perhaps the only division – in society is between the included and the excluded. Other sources of social and economic inequality are ignored: 'The core of my objection to this discourse is that it obscures the fact that the positions into which people are "integrated" through paid work are fundamentally unequal' (Levitas, 1996, p. 18).

Similarly, Duffy (1998) argues that the emphasis on work and job-readiness is evidence of a more neo-liberal perspective that implies 'behavioural self-exclusion', most noticeable in the UK, but emerging everywhere in Europe. Economic integration in Europe and the broader process of Globalization and free trade have meant that 'the neo-liberal perspective has grown more prominent in social policy since the Delors Presidency and the White Paper on Social Policy (Duffy, 1998)'. In both the USA and Europe, the policy environment has become tougher. The moral worth of the poor is scrutinised more closely in means-tested programmes (Lawson, 1995), and the notion of a dependency culture is never far from considerations of what social exclusion means.

Social exclusion originated as a concept derived from a very 'continental' approach to social policy and social order. It implied a corporatist welfare state, or at least a corporatist world view. Its origins lie in the specific nature of the French nation state and the tradition of republican citizenship, assimilation and inclusion of all elements to the national identity. The problem to be addressed is that of individuals who are not included or incorporated. This leaves open the question of whether such non-inclusion is the result of individual pathology, or of collective social or economic arrangements. It implies an existing status order or hierarchy, with arrangements for including all in welfare, although not on an equal basis. It further implies that a basic social division is between an excluded minority and an included majority.

As the concept has become more widespread and 'Europeanised' it has taken on more Anglo-Saxon, neo-liberal and labour-market-orientated aspects. Ironically, then, once we operationalise social exclusion, a concept with strong continental overtones, we find that it is most applicable to the Anglo-Saxon welfare states:

social exclusion of this kind is in some ways a peculiarly Anglo-American problem. At least the Anglo-American form of exclusion barely exists in the Northern parts of Europe, and in the South it is mitigated by the continued strength of the extended family. Continentals are amazed when they hear about truancy and even the right of schools to expel disruptive pupils. Other Europeans fail to understand also how it is that the country with nearly the lowest unemployment rate has the highest proportion of households with no-one employed. (Dahrendorf, 1999, pp. 3–4)

Poverty and Social Exclusion in Europe

The European Commission defines as poor those households who have disposable income below 50 per cent of the average disposable income of the country in which they reside. On this basis, the numbers living in poverty in the twelve countries of the European Union rose from 38.6 million in 1975 (12.8 per cent) to 43.9 million in 1985 (13.9 per cent). The Commission further estimated that, in the early 1990s, the numbers had risen to 50 million (including the former East Germany). By 2000, Anna Diamantopoulou, the Commissioner for Employment and Social Affairs quoted a figure for the EU15 of 65 million, 18 per cent of the population, based on a poverty line of 60 per cent of average income (Diamantopoulou, 2000b).

Poverty is not a static condition, it is dynamic. The proportion of people in permanent poverty is low – about 2–6 per cent. But this also means that a relatively large section of the population will spend a period of time in poverty. Over a 3–6 year interval this may be as high as 20–40 per cent (Quintin, 1999). The composition of those in poverty has also changed. In the late decades of the twentieth century there was increasing vulnerability of children and young people to poverty, especially in the English-speaking world, but also elsewhere. Conversely, poverty among the elderly is falling, but there is increasing inequality in the incomes of the elderly, as working life inequalities are reproduced in old age (Schulte, 1993; Lawson, 1995).

This does not mean that European welfare states are ineffective in reducing poverty. In the absence of social security, the poverty level in Europe would be almost 40 per cent – nearly 100 million people in Europe are lifted out of poverty by the welfare state (Quintin, 1999). Europe's more developed system of social protection has enabled poverty to be combated more effectively than in the USA – in general, benefit and tax systems in Europe are more effective at alleviating poverty (Franco and Pench, 2000). In continental Europe (though not in the UK) countries have been able to sustain relatively high social security budgets, partly because they are based on a more genuine insurance principle. However, throughout Europe, insurance-based systems have been weakened by the growing instability of work. As a result, changes are having to be made to help the increasing number of people without contribution-based entitlements.

The UK's social security system is less effective at preventing inequality and poverty than most 'continental' systems. There is a stronger link between long-term unemployment and social exclusion in Britain than in Germany or Sweden, for example (Clasen *et al.*, 1997). Unemployment benefit is lower in Britain, and lasts for a shorter period of time. The long-term unemployed are more likely to be unable to afford basic necessities and to be in serious debt in Britain, and social exclusion is more visible and more widespread in Britain. Labour-market schemes and training opportunities were criticised in all three countries, but especially so in the UK.

Social protection systems differ across the European Union. Examining the systems of the EU12, Schulte (1993) found that only eight of the twelve countries had a guaranteed minimum income/social assistance scheme (the four countries without such a scheme were Spain, Greece, Italy and Portugal). Room (1995) argues that the European Union and its research programmes play an important role in the politics of poverty. Questions such as the definition of poverty lines are not technical, but imply political and policy choices. The greater visibility of poverty on the political and research agendas in Italy, Germany, Spain and Greece is at least partly a result of the Commission's role in sponsoring research (Room, 1995).

The tax and benefits systems in the UK do much less to reduce income inequality than those of most other European countries (Hirsch, 1997). The UK reduces only about 40 per cent of primary poverty, while Belgium, Denmark, Sweden and the Netherlands reduce more than 70 per cent. Pre-transfer poverty is highest in the Republic of Ireland and the UK, and lowest in Belgium and Germany, while post-transfer poverty is highest in the Republic of Ireland, the UK and France (Franco and Pench, 2000).

Most importantly, however the relationship between unemployment and poverty varies significantly across European countries. In many Continental countries, the massive rise in European unemployment has not been accompanied by a corresponding rise in poverty (Atkinson, 1998b). In the USA and West Germany between the early

1970s and the early 1990s, the relationship was such that a 1 per cent rise in unemployment led to a rise in poverty of about 1 per cent. However, in Italy, France, Denmark, Finland and the Republic of Ireland, there was little or no increase in poverty, despite large increases in unemployment. Britain stands out: 'the proportion of people living in households with low income more than doubled over the period when Mrs Thatcher was Prime Minister' (Atkinson, 1998b, p. 5). Similar results are found using data from the Luxembourg Income Study. As Atkinson points out, even when unemployment does not lead to poverty and social exclusion, this does not mean that the rise in unemployment is not a serious concern. Unemployment has personal and health costs that go beyond the loss of cash income (Clark and Oswald, 1994).

Paugam (1996) looked at poverty in seven West European countries, using a mix of monetary and non-monetary indicators. He found that while there was some evidence of convergence, important differences remain. The most important of these were those that related to the strength of an individual's social connections:

> Precariousness is not correlated with weak family connections or the non-availability of a private support network in all of the countries studied. In Spain and the Netherlands, those who are without employment do not have a poorer quality of relationships with their family than those who are working. In Italy, this quality is, indeed, stronger. In these countries, along with Denmark, the general situation is one of a high level of support for individuals from family and friends, and this is equally true of those people facing social problems. By contrast, in France, Germany and Great Britain, it appears that job insecurity and unemployment are associated with impoverished social relationships. (Paugam, 1996, p. 287)

In the Southern countries of Europe, the family's traditional role remains strong. Social integration has the family unit rather than the labour market as its foundation, and so the loss of employment does not have catastrophic effects. In addition, perceptions of poverty differ considerably. In Southern Europe, poverty is seen as a permanent state by the majority of respondents to a Eurobarometer poll (Greece, 65 per cent; Portugal, 63 per cent; Italy, 55 per cent; Spain, 50 per cent), whereas in Northern Europe, this belief was much weaker (Netherlands, 17 per cent; Denmark, 20 per cent; Germany,

24 per cent). In these countries, poverty was seen as resulting from a sudden decline.

So the social relations of poverty are very different in Northern and Southern Europe. In the North, poverty often leads to what Paugam calls 'social disqualification', or what we might call 'social exclusion'. In Southern Europe, this is much less likely, because of the socially integrating effect of the family and other social support mechanisms: 'Poverty is a constituent element of the social system and even has a role to play in its regulation'. (Paugam, 1996, p. 298). While this reduces the level of social exclusion, it can also lead to social inaction, clientilism and social stagnation.

The Role of the European Union in Combating Unemployment and Social Exclusion

Increasing employment and reducing unemployment is now a priority for the EU. Much of the rhetoric from Brussels reflects the new 'welfare to work' agenda, but this is coupled with a defence of the 'European Social Model' and a reluctance to abandon existing levels of social protection and state regulation. Often it is flatly stated that there is no contradiction between, on the one hand, policies to promote competition and deregulation, and on the other, policies in support of traditional measures of social solidarity. Indeed, it is asserted that the 'European social model', far from being a burden on production, is in fact a competitive asset, a 'productive factor in economic performance' (Quintin, 1999). What this means in practice is rarely spelt out.

The shift towards an 'employment-centred' social policy is common ground between most member-states governments, the European Commission and international organisations such as the OECD. Economic growth alone is unlikely to produce large falls in OECD unemployment – so policies to reduce unemployment will remain a high priority for governments (OECD, 1998). Meeting in October 1997, OECD labour ministers agreed that social policies needed to be directed more towards job creation and reductions in welfare dependency. Subsidising employment, through the redirection of unemployment benefits to work-conditional tax credits or benefits has become the favoured policy tool. Retraining has a role, but it is relatively ineffective with regard to employment of the unskilled unemployed, while creating public-sector jobs is expensive; hence the best available option is subsidised employment 'closing the gap between what the illegal economy offers young people and what the market will pay' (Balls, 1994).

The OECD (1998) argues that social protection measures, such as minimum wages and in-work benefits should be part of an overall employment-promoting strategy, and the effects of such policies monitored. In-work benefits are better targeted than minimum wage legislation to tackle working poverty, and provide temporary earnings 'insurance' in an era of increased job insecurity. For example, in the USA, at any one time, one in six families is eligible for the Earned Income Tax Credit, but over a ten-year period two in five families will have at least one year when they qualify.

On the other hand, in-work benefits are expensive, and can lead to problems of moral hazard. That is, the net result can be taxpayer subsidisation of employers, collusion between workers and firms, or wages being driven down because of the increase in labour supply. (However, there is little direct evidence for this.) This normally conservative argument, interestingly, is echoed by some Left-wing critiques of the prevailing orthodoxy on in-work benefits. Michie and Wilkinson (1994) attack the policy option of providing taxpayer subsidy to employers to take on the unemployed, arguing that the use of public funds to subsidise the wage income of the poor is essentially a return to the 'Speenhamland' system of Poor Law used in eighteenth- and nineteenth-century Britain. They quote from Hobsbawm and Rudé (1969), who make the point rather more vividly than the technical language of moral hazard and disincentive effects:

> The distinction between worker and pauper vanished ... No measure was ever more universally popular ... employers could reduce wages at will and labourers were safe from hunger whether they were busy or slack ... The traditional social order degenerated into a universal pauperism of demoralised men who could not fall below the relief scale whatever they did, who could not rise above it. (Hobsbawm and Rude, 1969, quoted in Michie and Wilkinson, 1994, pp. 23–4)

Curiously, the switch from unemployment benefits to in-work benefits is largely advocated today on the grounds that this will *enhance* positive incentives and moral benefits. The explanation for the paradox perhaps lies in the difference between the eighteenth century agrarian economy and the modern European economies. In particular in advanced economies it is assumed that in-work benefits will apply to a relatively small proportion of the working population, with the general level of wages being relatively unaffected by the scheme.

The OECD therefore recommends a combination of minimum wage and in-work benefits, and points out that the optimum policy mix will differ across countries. Where there is a low minimum wage and a broad distribution of wages, in-work benefits are more likely. If there is a compressed earnings distribution, tax abatements and employer subsidies are more likely.

The general view of most national policy makers and international organisations is that, in the long run, raising the well-being of the poorest can only happen through increased employment opportunities and raising productivity. This implies increases in skills and competences of workers, and greater investment by firms and governments in human capital.

The European Commission and others would argue that the adoption of a European Employment Strategy in the 1990s marks an important development of the EU's role. The Strategy is founded in the Employment Title that was incorporated into the Amsterdam Treaty – employment is now an issue of 'common concern' for the Union. Each year, a set of Employment Guidelines is adopted by the member states. National Action Plans are drawn up and implementation reports compiled. According to the Commissioner responsible, the purpose of the European Employment Strategy is to deliver the structural reforms needed to obtain the full benefit in terms of employment, from the single market, the single currency and technological change (Diamantopoulou, 2000a).

The EES has four components or 'pillars': employability, entrepreneurship, adaptability and equal opportunities (Larsson, 2000). Employability refers to a new active labour market policy, involving a shift from welfare to work. Entrepreneurship means making it easier to start and run businesses, and to enable the services sector to expand. Adaptability refers to the modernisation of work organisation, meaning accepting a greater variety and flexibility of work contracts, and using the fiscal system to encourage investment in human capital. Equal opportunities are advocated, not just on equity grounds, but also to enable greater employment growth through increased female labour force participation.

What does this mean in practice? Larsson, the Director General for Employment and Social Affairs, argues that the most important commitments made by the member states are the 'ground-breaking' agreements to common measurable targets on prevention of long-term and youth unemployment, and on employability support over-all. Member states are committed to providing a job or employability support to young people before they spend six months without work and similar support for adults before they experience twelve months of unemployment (Larsson, 2000). In keeping with the 'multi-level governance' argument, he further argues that the EES is a new form of intervention, neither supra-national legislation nor inter-govern-mental co-operation, but rather a new way of working between the European and national levels. Hence 'the strategy is European, the implementation is through national policies, and the process is driven by annual reporting, by peer review, by policy recommendations and by new political commitments to higher and better employment performance.' (Larsson, 2000, p. 19). Once again, it is not entirely clear what differences the EU policies will make in practice.

What is much more clear is that whatever the commitment of the EU and the member states to greater employment as a matter of common concern, the economic policy priorities remain sound public finance and macroeconomic stability. Under the Stability and Growth Pact, member states were required to submit stability and convergence programmes giving Ecofin (meetings of European finance ministers) and the Commission information about their current and medium-term budgetary plans. These commitments might be jeopardised by spending increases consequent on population ageing and high levels of unemployment, hence the need to increase work incentives alongside other measures such as pension reform and increased participation rates (European Commission, 1999b).

Article 4.3 of the Amsterdam Treaty makes price stability and sound public finances, but not full employment, 'guiding principles' (Duffy, 1998). The Commission's study of Europe's unemployment problem (European Commission, 1999b) concludes that a strategy to tackle the 'European job malaise' will require three elements, of which the first are sound macroeconomic policies 'including in particular, continued efforts to put public finances onto a safe medium-term path so as to allow sufficient scope for fiscal stabilisation when necessary, to prepare for the costs of ageing, and to provide room for a reduction in the tax burden' (p. 152). The other elements are policies to improve the functioning of labour markets and economic reforms to improve competitiveness.

It is clear, from an analysis of Commission documents and speeches by Commissioners and senior officials, that while unemployment is the key social priority, employment policy overall is subordinate to the key economic goals of public expenditure controls and low inflation. The completion of the single market and the introduction of a single currency are the perceived routes to growth and stability. Free trade ensures optimum output, and hence full employment demand. The role of policy is to improve the supply side of the labour market; for example, through equal opportunities legislation and education and training. Hence, employability, and the shift from passive income maintenance to work-related active measures become central (Duffy, 1998).

The European Community funded three small-scale anti-poverty programmes in 1975–80, 1980–9 and 1990–4. Activities included promoting information sharing and networks, and supporting demonstration projects. A proposed fourth round was not funded because of the objections of some member states. According to Duffy (1998) the programme was influential in a number of member states in promoting the concept of social exclusion. Since then, the profile of poverty within the EU's activities has been reduced. Although the EU remains committed to reducing social exclusion, since the Delors period and the White Papers on Social Policy and on Employment and Growth, it is clear that this is within a market-orientated context, a position that is reinforced by the Amsterdam Treaty.

In a speech in September 1999, Odile Quintin of the Directorate General for Employment and Social Affairs spelt out the EU approach to social inclusion and exclusion. She stressed the principles both of economic competition and of social solidarity, claiming that there is no contradiction between them: 'the European social model is now recognised as both a productive factor in economic performance and as a mark of a cohesive society'. Once again, it was not made clear by whom this is recognised, nor in what sense the 'social model' is a productive factor. That is not to say, of course, that the case cannot be made. As we have seen, there are both theoretical arguments and empirical evidence supporting the view that, for example, income maintenance during periods of short-term unemployment helps labour market flexibility and the adaptation of the economy. Similarly, there is no evidence that employment protection legislation *per se* is associated with higher unemployment. Social policies are needed for reasons of economic efficiency as well as distributional justice. Nevertheless, a case has to be made through detailed argument, not as a blanket defence of an idealised (in both senses) European Social Model.

Quintin then lists four types of contribution of European policies to tackling social exclusion. The 'most fundamental' is the contribution of European policies to growth and employment 'that brings the increased prosperity on which our social systems depend'. Second, there is the European Employment Strategy, described above. The success of the strategy in tackling the structural failings of the European labour markets will be essential to promote social inclusion. Third, there is 'direct investment' in economic and social cohesion through the structural funds. Fourth, there is a proposed strategy for 'modernising' social protection. Finally, there are specific EU actions to help promote social inclusion, following the explicit mandate in the Amsterdam Treaty for Community action to combat social exclusion.

Conclusions

EU actions to reduce unemployment and combat social exclusion have generally been complementary to action by member-state governments. Structural Fund policies make a contribution to this, but are targeted too broadly to effect real change. To target EU budget interventions more accurately at households and individuals would raise major constitutional and federalist issues. Specific policies to target poverty and social exclusion have been small-scale.

Since the 1980s, unemployment has increased steadily in Europe. But European social security systems, particularly outside the UK, have generally been able to prevent this rise in unemployment from leading also to a rise in poverty and social exclusion. The new focus on 'employment-centred social policy' should be seen in the context of a general policy shift in this direction, among member-state governments and international organisations as well as the institutions of the EU. This is firmly within a general policy commitment to economic orthodoxy, tight control of public finances, and priority to anti-inflationary rather than full employment targets. The implication for labour-market policies is to emphasise work incentives, raising skills and qualifications, and making labour markets more flexible in general. Most actions will continue to take place at member state level, and, as we have seen, member states differ significantly in their current labour market performance and their institutions and practices. From the research evidence it is clear that improving Europe's employment performance is not simply a question of deregulating labour markets. At the same time, it is clear that some aspects of the system do little to discourage long-term unemployment.

In order to reduce unemployment, welfare-to-work policies will have a key role. In promoting greater flexibility and in devising imaginative solutions to long-term unemployment and social exclusion, Britain is generally ahead of its continental neighbours. But Britain performs poorly in any comparison of poverty and social exclusion, and particularly on issues such as the links from unemployment to social exclusion, and the extent of child poverty.

The evidence suggests that simplistic analyses of the causes of unemployment are likely to be wrong, and one-dimensional policy prescriptions likely to fail. The strong implication is that a successful policy mix will include elements from both 'Anglo-Saxon' and 'continental' policy approaches. The role of the EU will continue to be secondary to, and supportive of, policies of members-states' governments. At the same time, the EU plays a key role in the dissemination of information both about labour market performance and about the efficacy of different policy approaches. Despite the rhetoric of a supposed single 'European Social Model', it seems equally apparent that a variety of approaches will continue to be pursued within the European Union.

8

Citizens Arise? Europe and Social Citizenship

Introduction

Article 8 of the Maastricht Treaty declares ringingly that 'Every person holding the nationality of a Member State shall be a citizen of the Union.' But what – if anything – does European citizenship mean? Who is included, and who is excluded from the definition of European citizenship? Are there supranational citizenship rights that EU citizens can enforce? Does European citizenship imply a European identity, and, if so, what relationship does this have to national identity?

In this chapter, I shall explore some of these questions in relation to the future of European welfare. I look first at the meaning of relationship between citizenship and welfare. From there I examine the notion of European citizenship. Next I look at issues of legitimacy and accountability to citizens of the EU's governance arrangements, and at citizen attitudes to the EU and to welfare issues in Europe. From there I look at the implications for citizenship implicit within Europe's current 'incomplete federalism'. Finally, I draw out some conclusions and implications.

Citizenship and the Welfare State

Any discussion of citizenship must touch on three central social themes – what are the boundaries of society? Which groups belong and which do not? What entitlements do citizens have to benefits and services? T. H. Marshall (1950) famously set out a trinity of types of citizenship right – civil, political and social. He argued that 'the modern drive towards social equality is ... the latest phase of an evolution of citizenship which has been in continuous progress for some 250 years' (p. 10). Marshall divides citizenship into three parts 'dictated by history even more clearly than by logic'. The *civil* element comprises those rights necessary for individual freedom: freedoms of the person, of speech, of thought and faith; the right to own property and conclude valid contracts; and the right to justice. The key institutions are the courts of justice. The *political* element comprises the right to participate in the exercise of political power. The key institutions are parliament and local government. The *social* element refers to a whole range from 'the right to a modicum of economic welfare and security to the right to share to the full in the social heritage and to live the life of a civilised being according to the standards prevailing in the society' (ibid., p. 11). The key institutions here are the educational system and the social services. This notion of social citizenship is effectively what we mean by the welfare state and social democracy (Mann, 1996).

Each type of citizenship right has a 'formative period' corresponding, broadly, with a particular century. Hence civil rights developed in the eighteenth century; political rights in the nineteenth; and social rights in the twentieth. Marshall (1950) defined citizenship as a 'status bestowed on those who are full members of a community. All who possess the status are equal with respect to the rights and duties with which the status is endowed' (p. 28). The relationship between citizenship and social class is complex. Social class, according to Marshall, can be understood in two ways. The first sense is as a hierarchy of status expressed in terms of legal rights and established customs. Citizenship is clearly destructive to this sense of social class. However, there is a second sense of social class, which derives not from laws and customs, but from the 'interplay of a variety of factors related to the institutions of property and education and the structure of the national economy' (p 31). Here, the relationship between citizenship and social class is more complex. In its early stages, citizenship implied a diminution of the 'more unpleasant features of inequality' but this 'was not an attack on the class system. On the contrary it aimed, often quite consciously, at making the class system less vulnerable to attack by alleviating its less defensible consequences' (p. 33).

Marshall (1950) also saw that social citizenship – broadly, education plus welfare services – would itself be a source of class distinction, or social stratification. Where services are in principle universal, but in practice used by one social class (Marshall uses the example of the 'old elementary schools') the effect will be 'class-making at the same time as it was class-abating' (ibid., p. 57). Moreover, the more the education system succeeds in ignoring or destroying hereditary privilege, the more it will institute a new form of class distinction which results from the strengthening link in a modern economy between education and occupation:

> In the early stages ... the major effect is, of course, to reveal hidden inequalities – to enable the poor boy to show that he is as good as the rich boy. But the final outcome is a structure of unequal status fairly apportioned to unequal abilities ... The conclusion ... is that, through education in its relations with occupational structure, citizenship operates as an instrument of social stratification. (Marshall, 1950, p. 67)

Marshall therefore anticipated, in outline at least, the arguments of both Michael Young in the *Rise of the Meritocracy* (Young, 1958) and Esping-Andersen (1990) in his definition of the welfare state as a system of stratification. The implications for our analysis of European citizenship are twofold: first, the importance of examining the impact of citizenship in the context of the economic structure; and second, recognising the effect of citizenship as class-making as well as class-abating.

Hence Marshall's view of citizenship was a very 'English' definition – both in terms of the historical periodisation and in terms of the conception of the social element of citizenship. Marshall identified the key institutions most closely connected with the social rights of citizenship as being 'the educational system and the social services'. In this, he was in the mainstream of the Anglo-Saxon understanding of social policy as being mainly about the delivery of welfare services. Despite Marshall's interest in social class, there is no reference to the 'continental' concept of social policy as being primarily concerned with the labour market and with state-supported reconciliation between social groups.

Many critiques of Marshall have focused on the English specificity of the historical periodization he proposed. The typology in which civil rights are developed first, followed by political rights and finally social rights fits the British case, but not that of other European countries. There is a strong element of teleology in Marshall's account. Social rights are implicitly the full flowering of a gradual but inexorable increase in democracy and progress. Moreover, it is implied that each stage of citizenship development is superior to the previous one. But a comparative study of the development of citizenship and of welfare states across countries shows that a variety of situations are possible. Social rights can be instituted as part of a 'top-down' process of social control just as much as a response to democratic pressures from below, and social citizenship can be associated with authoritarian conservatism just as easily as with democratic progressivism. For example, in Germany, social rights came 'early', prior to the full development of political rights. Such a configuration is not inherently unstable (Mann, 1996).

Seen in this comparative context, the development of citizenship rights appears to be a contingent rather than an inevitable process. Mann (1996) goes further and argues that there are at least five possible strategies for the development of citizenship rights in advanced industrial countries, which he terms liberal, reformist, authoritarian monarchist, Fascist and authoritarian socialist. Each of these regimes was reasonably successful on its own terms at handling modern class struggle. So the development of citizenship rights is not 'evolutionary' – there is no single best way of institutionalising class conflict. The durability of particular regimes is not related to inherent logic or internal efficiency, but is rather a contingent outcome, driven by world politics, and in particular by success or failure in the Second World War (Mann, 1996).

More fundamentally, should 'social rights' be considered in the same category as civil and political rights? After all, civil and political rights are relatively straightforward to define, in formal terms (the right to vote, the right to trial by jury, and so on). But 'social rights' are rather more vague. Marshall (1950) states that the social element of citizenship refers to 'the whole range from the right to a modicum of economic welfare and security to the right to share to the full in the social heritage and to live the life of a civilised being according to the standards prevailing in the society' (p. 11). Such a definition – if it can be called that – is both wide-ranging and vague. Klausen (1995) argues that it is wrong to see social citizenship as equivalent to civil and political rights. Civil and political rights refer to indivisible and non-transferrable rights belonging to individuals. They are – to use the economist's lexicon – non-rival and non-excludable. One person's civil or political right does not have a significant effect on the value of another's claim.

But social rights are different. They are fundamentally about redistribution of income between social groups. Hence, social citizenship is not a question of rights at all. Rather it should be considered 'a particular paradigm of distributional politics in advanced industrial welfare states ... a suggestive metaphor for political mobilisation aimed at putting together broadly based coalitions on behalf of welfare state expansion.' (Klausen, 1995, p. 245). Social rights imply a claim on resources and legitimation of the redistributive role of the state. The language of social citizenship, in effect, enables what is fundamentally a political struggle and a philosophical argument about income redistribution and economic inequality to be dressed up in the language of legal rights and formal equality. As an ideological position, the social citizenship discourse is clearly compatible with the post-war political settlement and bi-partisan support for welfare state expansion. The revival of the discourse of social citizenship at the European level might perhaps be linked similarly to the rise of a post-Cold War ideology based around fiscal orthodoxy, economic and social convergence in Europe and an 'end to history'.

Historically, the development of citizenship was linked closely to state formation, and the concept of citizenship implies borders and barriers. Citizenship is in part about defining who is included and who excluded: 'Originally denoting residence within the protective walls of cities, citizenship defines a community by establishing who may reside within the boundaries and who may not' (Klausen, 1995, p. 249). With the development of welfare states, the importance of belonging to communities has become more important. The benefits of inclusion and the costs of exclusion are now much greater. The emergence of the nation state as the key political unit in the modern era, the development of citizenship and the expansion of the welfare state are three closely linked historical processes. This has important implications for the possibility and desirability of European citizenship, European welfare and European identity.

There is no doubt that, at least up to the time of writing, citizenship has been linked inextricably with nationality and with the nation state. Indeed, some argue that it is impossible to imagine citizenship outside the national context: 'There are no such animals as "European citizens" ' (Aron, 1974). Citizenship and the nation state are linked both in historical time and in internal consistency. The creation of the nation state is linked to the rise of modernity and the establishment of the modern contract, that is, the framework of laws and institutions (Dahrendorf, 1996). The nation state, despite its drawbacks, is the only guarantee of the rule of law, through such mechanisms as checks and balances, due process and judicial review. The nation state generalised the ancient idea of citizenship, which came to describe the rights and obligations associated with membership in a social unit, and in particular, nationality. These rights and duties are common to all members, and hence the question of how membership is defined becomes crucial. Therefore society is usually a euphemism for nation; and social analysis is 'to all intents and purposes' national analysis (Dahrendorf, 1996).

EU Citizenship Rights

How, then, should we interpret the concept of European citizenship? We can usefully divide this into two separate questions. Can we give a substantive meaning to the concept of European citizenship? And who is included, and who excluded, from the definition of European citizen?

The phrase 'European citizenship' can refer either to the specific legal status of citizenship of the European Union, or it can refer more generally to the concept of how citizenship is understood and practised in the individual member states. Citizenship is essentially a legal category – but it is the product of political and social phenomena. Over the twentieth century, conceptions of citizenship in Europe were very closely related with ideas about nationality and national identity. Generally, European states in the twenty-first century have adopted a relatively cautious approach to initial immigration coupled with a relatively open attitude towards later citizenship applications once certain criteria have been met. Partly for historical reasons, Germany has adopted the opposite approach, with relatively open doors for asylum-seekers, but a very limited concept of citizenship. Moreover, while formal citizenship is relatively similar throughout the EU, the substantive content of citizenship (in terms of benefits and so on) varies considerably. The social rights of citizenship vary considerably across member states (Garcia, 1997).

How does the principle of 'citizenship of the Union' articulate with citizenship of the individual member states? Three separate positions can be distinguished. First, it can be argued that citizenship is ineluctably and necessarily connected with nationality. Citizens belong to nations; the concept of supranational or European citizenship is at best a rhetorical device, and at worst a fraud. Second, some would suggest that European citizenship is inherently superior to citizenship based on nationality, and will in time replace it. Citizenship is seen as *progressive* – national citizenship is seen both as superior to local or regional attachments and rights, and as a logical progression from them. In a more Globalized world, it might be argued that the nation state is becoming less significant, and hence national citizenship will make way for European citizenship, perhaps itself a staging post on the way to world citizenship. A third position is to argue that European and national citizenships can coexist, Individuals in the modern world are characterised by multiple identities, so that one can be, for example, a Catalan, a Spaniard and a European all at the same time. Multiple citizenships can coexist along with multi-level governance and with multiple identities.

There is no simple answer to the question of whether citizenship is the same as nationality (Guild, 1996). A ruling by the International Court of Justice states that nationality is a legal bond, based on the 'social fact of attachment' – a genuine connection of existence, interests and sentiments, as well as reciprocal rights and duties. The creation by the Maastricht Treaty of a link between the individual and the Union via citizenship implies a host of rights attaching to the Union, exercisable by the individual. 'There is suddenly a direct link between the Union and the individual' (Guild, 1996, p. 33).

Is the EU a state, or enough of a state, for citizenship to be able to adhere to it? And second, what rights does EU citizenship under the Treaty guarantee, and do these rights amount to citizenship? We first met the question of the 'stateness' of the EU in Chapter 4. Here we can reframe the question with citizenship at its core. One way of addressing this is by looking at both the EU's view of itself, and how outsiders view it (Guild, 1996). For the European Union to have statehood, four components are necessary: the power to communicate with other governments; the power to take internal measures that affect other states; the power to contract treaties and participate in international organisations; and the power to carry out international obligations (Guild, 1996). Of these, the third is the most important.

The Community does have the power to conclude agreements, and furthermore 'perceives itself as a single entity' (Guild, 1996, p. 40), as established by Treaty and interpreted by the ECJ. The European Union lacks statehood, but perhaps statehood and citizenship can develop together. Externally, the position is clear – the outside world is willing to acknowledge the 'nationality' of the Community, at least with regard to treaty signing and enforcement. Hence the Community enjoys many of the attributes of statehood. The Maastricht Treaty has created a direct political link between member state citizens and the European Union: 'Whatever its status in international law, in its internal arrangements, the Union is now much more State-like than ever before as a result of creating a common Union citizenship' (Hall, 1999).

We must next consider the formal position of legal rights belonging to European Union citizens. What, if anything, does being a citizen of the EU add to the set of rights an individual possesses as a citizen (or indeed subject) of a member state? European citizenship was formally created by Article 8 of the Maastricht Treaty in November 1993, although some elements can be identified in earlier treaties (Meehan, 1997). Five specific rights of European citizenship, additional to those operating at member-state level can be identified (Guild, 1996; Meehan, 1997; Vranken, 1999):

- the right to free movement;
- the right to participate in municipal and European elections while resident in another member state;
- the right to diplomatic and consular protection of another EU member state while travelling outside the EU;
- the right to petition the European Parliament; and
- the right to apply to the EU Ombudsman

This is a very limited list of 'additional' rights – i.e. rights which are supplementary to the rights and duties of EU citizens by virtue of their citizenship of member states (Garcia, 1997). These European citizenship rights are legal entitlements – they are not directly redistributive (Meehan, 1997). In terms of Marshall's (1950) typology, they are in the categories of civil and political rights, and not social rights.

Do these citizenship rights make any difference? The creation of European citizenship under the Maastricht Treaty left many European citizens 'profoundly unaware or unmoved by it' (Guild, 1996, p. 2). For many, the 'European citizenship' created by the Maastricht Treaty is either not citizenship in any meaningful sense, or, at best, confers only minimal additional rights. While no-one would argue that European citizenship possesses any substantive nature in 2001, others argue that a gradual and dynamic process can build on the largely symbolic nature of European citizenship in the future. Vranken (1999) argues that the law facilitates a notion of EU citizenship that evolves both substantively through the passage of European legislation, and procedurally through actions taken by private individuals via the ECJ. European citizenship is not unitary but 'multi-dimensional', with procedural as well as substantive connotations. Meehan (1997) similarly sees a dynamic, evolving process in which the bases of citizenship are 'contested'. In her view, the relationship with nationality is contingent – also possible is a 'neo-imperial' form of citizenship in which citizenship is seen 'not only as a set of legal entitlements, but also as a moral order of conviviality and distributive justice and collective or individual welfare' (Meehan, 1997, p. 18).

Following Marshall, and Esping-Andersen, we assume that citizenship rights in a welfare state will create particular types of social stratification. The question then is: what types of stratification do 'European' citizenship rights create? A first, important point, is that European social rights are often in practice worker-based rather than citizen-based. The term 'citizenship' strongly suggests formal equality; for example, with regard to political participation, or entry and residence. However, EU citizenship does not do that (Hall, 1999). Member-state nationals residing in another EU state – what Hall calls 'inter-state citizens' – must be treated equally but are subject to 'limitations and conditions' under Article 8a of the Maastricht Treaty. So different classes of citizens are permitted in principle, and the Treaty nowhere lays down these limitations, although it is implied that these related to grounds of public policy, public security and public health. There is a fundamental right in the EU to free movement for economic purposes, but there is no right to move to look for better social assistance, although EU citizens can move in search of work and have a right to assistance for an initial period (Guild, 1996).

Furthermore, citizenship rights do not apply to third-country nationals resident in the EU. We can identify, then, at least four categories of EU residents, according to their citizenship rights:

(i)   EU citizens who are nationals of that member state;
(ii)   economically active inter-state EU citizens;
(iii)   economically non-active inter-state EU citizens; and
(iv)   third-country nationals.

Hence, even for citizens of member states, the introduction of citizenship of the Union creates new forms of stratification. But if we consider also the interaction of Union citizenship, national citizenship laws and the reality of large-scale migration into the EU from outside, the position becomes considerably more complicated. As Weil (1996) puts it, 'The Treaty of Maastricht institutes a citizenship based on inequality and national origin which creates a distinction among resident foreigners.' He gives a hypothetical example of two cousins, born in 1970, one in Paris and one in Frankfurt, to Turkish parents:

If ... the child born in Paris decides to live with his uncle in Frankfurt, for example to find a job there, he could theoretically vote in Frankfurt's city elections, despite being unable to speak German and unfamiliar with Germany and the problems of the city of Frankfurt. However, his cousin, born in Frankfurt, raised in German society and possibly able to speak only one language – German – would not be able to vote in this same election. (Weil, 1996, p. 85)

So two distinct forms of inequality for 'non-Europeans' arise from the 'constitutionalizing' of the notion of citizenship of the Union in the Maastricht Treaty. First, that differential citizenship rights can be accessed by migrants depending in which member state they are resident (lack of horizontal equity across the EU states). Second, that European social rights reproduce exclusion against residents within the EU (denizens) who are not citizens of member states. As citizenship relates closely to both nationality and national identity, the boundaries of citizenship and the 'policing' of these boundaries are central and not peripheral components of the citizenship debate.

Questions of immigration and racism are not adjuncts to the development of modern nations, but a fundamental part of that development (Silverman, 1992, p. 6). The development of European integration in the post-war period has been accompanied, paradoxically, by the increased settlement of non-Europeans in Europe. As a result, the 'foreigner' 'is no longer from elsewhere, but from here: a colleague at work, a neighbour in the same flats. The far-off has never been so close ... So the question has become how to keep the foreigner at a distance.' (de Rudder, 1982, quoted in Silverman, 1992). There are many millions of third-country migrants in Europe, who are not citizens of any European state, and hence not 'citizens of Europe'. They play an important role in Europe's economy but are often excluded in social, political and legal terms from European society. Moreover, their numbers are increasing, not only because of 'push' factors of political instability and economic stagnation in other parts of the world, but also, importantly, because of strong 'pull factors' in Europe – in particular, Europe's demographic deficit and increasing economic demand for more workers.

At bottom, there is a disjuncture between the economic and political realities around citizenship and migration. Economic liberalisation and Globalization, together with secondary economic factors such as the fall in the real cost of air travel and improved communication, imply an opening of all markets, including labour markets. This alone would imply increased labour mobility, not only within Europe, but more particularly into Europe from outside. Furthermore, the 'demographic deficit' in Europe – the fall in the birth rate, ageing population, and consequent rise in the ratio of dependants to workers – greatly increases the demand in European economies for migrant labour. A third factor is political instability in many other parts of the world, particularly in comparison with (perceived and real) political and economic stability within Europe. This leads to increased migratory demand from both political refugees and economic migrants – two categories which in any case are difficult to separate in principle and impossible in practice. There is a fundamental disjuncture between the rapid pace of economic integration, on both the European and the world scale, and much slower change in the political and legal realities.

A consideration of social citizenship takes us rapidly to fundamental issues relating to nations, nationality and federalism. We shall examine some of these in the next section. What can we conclude so far about the notion of European citizenship? First, that in practical terms it is a weak and nebulous concept. The 'citizenship of the Union' bestowed by the Maastricht Treaty is more political rhetoric than legal and social reality. However, as we saw earlier, the concept of social citizenship itself can be seen as belonging more appropriately to the arena of politics and political mobilisation than to the realm of legal rights in the strict sense. The idea of European citizenship, however weak, can itself become a force for greater integration and hence indirectly a cause of its own strengthening – citizenship and integration can develop together. This immediately raises the question of whether this is what European citizens – that is, citizens of Europe – in fact want to happen. I shall return to this in a later section.

Second, even in its weak form, European citizenship acts as an exclusionary as well as an inclusionary force. Residents within the EU member states are stratified by the emerging principle of European citizenship in a number of ways – between economically active and non-active; between those who are nationals of member states and those who are not; according to which member state non-nationals reside in; and so on. Just as attitudes towards immigration and nationality help to define the nature of national states, so too will attitudes towards immigration and diversity help to define the nature of the European Union.

Third, while it is possible logically to imagine the development of a true supranational citizenship that will complement or even replace national citizenship – as Gellner (1983) says, both nations and states are contingencies – it is difficult to see how in practice this might develop in the near future. Citizenship is tied up closely with nationality at present – a contingent development, perhaps, but a very important one. Both are closely related to notions of identity. Multiple identities are, of course, possible, and indeed may be thought of as the norm – a complex and overlapping web of local, regional, ethnic, national and other identities. 'European-ness' can be another level to this, but surely not a transcendent one. For transcendence, why stop at the boundaries of Europe, or even more parochially, at the boundaries of the EU15? Does a German feel 'European' in Spain but not in Switzerland? Does a Swede feel 'European' in Denmark but not in Norway? Moreover, the fact remains that while supranational citizenship and a supranational democracy can be imagined and perhaps even worked towards, 'to the extent that they exist at all, democratic political cultures in Europe today are closely tied to and dependent upon nation-states' (Siedentop 2000, p. 34).

Nations are artificial constructs. It is part of the business of nationalism to pretend otherwise, and in particular, to present an ahistorical, fundamentalist picture of 'the nation'. The French historian Ernest Renan put it memorably: 'Getting its history wrong is part of being a nation' (quoted in Hobsbawm, 1990, p. 12). Hobsbawm writes, 'for the purposes of analysis nationalism comes before nations. Nations do not make states and nationalisms but the other way round' (Hobsbawm, 1990, p. 10). Nationalism portrays nationality as if it were, in Gellner's words, just there, like Mount Everest. But, in reality,

Nations are not inscribed into the nature of things, they do not constitute a political version of the doctrine of natural kinds. Nor were national states the manifest ultimate destiny of ethnic or cultural groups. What do exist are cultures, often subtly grouped, shading into each other, overlapping, intertwined; and there exist, usually but not always, political units of all shapes and sizes. (Gellner, 1983, p. 49)

If nationalism begets nations, is 'supranationalism' necessary to beget 'supranations'? Does a Federal Europe require not just a supranational state, but also a logically prior political project called 'supra-nationalism'? If so, the reality of a Federal Europe will be a very long way off, as there is little evidence of 'supranationalism' of this kind as a *mass* political force in Europe.

The idea of a citizenship that has been severed from a close relationship with nationality and nationalism is inherently attractive – at least to those who do not subscribe to the mythic doctrine of the nation and the narrow version of nationalism to which it gives rise. If citizenship could be decoupled from 'the assumed need for cultural or ethnic homogeneity, then the current debates about migration and citizenship might be less heated' (Fulbrook and Cesarani, 1996, p. 214). Similarly, Klausen (1995, pp. 266–7) talks about 'decoupling' welfare policy from the state, so that citizenship 'in all its multiple meanings of nationality, political representation, and social protection, loses its exclusive focus upon state action'. Citizenship once inhered in cities, and is only contingently related to nation states. It can in principle inhere in other geopolitical entities.

This is plausible doctrine. But the elision that is sometimes made from this to the proposition that multi-level governance in the EU is somehow the expression of these multiple identities and contested notions of citizenship is not convincing. This is to confuse a real, continuing struggle over the definition and meaning of citizenship and identity in a globalizing world, with a particular set of elite-driven institutional fudges. The missing connection here is the polity, and the missing issues are those of democracy and accountability. I shall turn to these next.

Citizenship and Technocracy in the EU

In the first three decades of the post-Second World War period, partly through the effects of the expansion of northern European welfare states, citizen allegiance to national states increased alongside support for the process of European integration. These principles were not in conflict, but rather were mutually supportive. Similarly, in those European countries that in the 1970s and 1980s made the transition from dictatorship to democracy, there were simultaneously processes of strengthened national allegiance and accountability, democratic legitimacy, and a commitment to European integration.

At the same time, European integration has primarily been a policy driven by *elites*. In the main, policy has been determined in a top-down and technocratic manner. Technocratic and political elites deliberately pursued a policy of fostering economic integration as a means to the ultimate goal of political integration, to be achieved both by policy 'spillover' and through a more gradual development of 'European' ways of thinking by both masses and elites.

This emphasis on technocratic solutions, and the absence of democratic grounding to European integration, did not matter greatly during the 1950s, 1960s and 1970s. This was for three main reasons. First, post-war reconstruction and European economy recovery were successful. Economic growth during the long boom allowed for the coexistence of rising living standards for households, profitability for companies, and expanding welfare state budgets. The 'economistic' route to European integration was working. Second, the Cold War gave geopolitical significance to the creation of a regional trading bloc in Western Europe. The agendas of external security through military co-operation between Western Europe and the USA, and of internal security, through strong economies and expanded welfare states, coincided. Third, political integration, in any meaningful sense, seemed a long way off, and certainly remote from the immediate concerns of building a free trading area in Europe and strengthening democratic institutions. Hence there was no contradiction in the pursuit of European integration and support for national interests among the members of the EEC and the EC.

However, this situation began to change in the 1980s and 1990s, and now, at the beginning of the twenty-first century, a very different scenario presents itself. First, from the mid-1970s, the 'long boom' gave way to a more insecure and threatening pattern of macroeconomic change. Economic orthodoxy, as enshrined in the institutions of the EU no less than those of the national governments, now appeared to be less benign and potentially threatening to at least some groups of citizens. There was a transition from a European integration that buttressed the nation state in pursuit of income, welfare, family security and employment, to an EU that appeared to threaten the personal security and welfare of many citizens in return for 'empty platitudes about growth through competitiveness' (Milward, 1997b). In particular, it is those with less faith or less stake in the 'new' economy – older citizens; those working in agriculture, extractive and manufacturing sectors; those living in economically or geographically 'peripheral' areas – that are least enthusiastic about each new stage in European integration. With this shift in the objective (and subjective) impact of European economic integration, the previously dormant political question of mass support for elite strategies of integration, began to stir. Citizen allegiance had deepened through the expansion of welfare states, and the resulting increase in family and personal security, but this now seems threatened by the welfare consequences of a shift to a more competitive and market-orientated European social and economic space.

Second, with the removal of the Berlin Wall in 1989, and more generally, the end of the Cold War, there was a marked change, not only to the ideology of European integration, but also to the institutional mechanisms supporting it. In a bipolar world, there was strong contiguity between the political, economic, diplomatic and military aims of closer co-operation among Western European nations. After 1989, the pattern became more complex. In particular, the institutional framework of the European Union faces the challenge of incorporating the transition states of Central and Eastern Europe, and more generally coping with a future Union of twenty-five or thirty members.

Third, by the end of the 1990s, political integration in Europe was no longer a far-off aspiration, an ideal to which nominal assent could be given in the sure knowledge that no action was necessary, but increasingly a live political issue throughout the member states. This was driven both by the reality of economic integration, with a central bank and a single currency, and by the need to incorporate the transition states. Political integration became an issue of greater salience, not only to European elites, but increasingly to citizens too.

The economic reality of the euro, and the legal reality of citizenship of the Union, both imply a European government. A monetary union, with a single currency, implies not only a central bank, but also fiscal centralisation and a federal government to make federal tax-and-spend policies. Of course, it is possible, as some commentators argue, to imagine a set of governmental and financial arrangements in Europe that are unlike those that have prevailed in any previous state or federation. But they would therefore be by definition unprecedented and unique. 'Citizenship of the Union' as declared in the Maastricht Treaty, if it is to mean anything more than a vague aspiration, implies at least a 'quasi-state' in which citizenship could inhere, and against which citizens' rights and obligations could be defined.

But these economic and legal realities then run up against a political reality: is there the citizen support for a real European government of this kind? In what way would European citizens give assent to this? And what happens if the level of citizen support varies across member states, across regions, across social groups and across economic sectors? Could the movement to European integration lead not to European unity, but to increased differences across Europe?

More immediately, for Brussels to become involved in serious distributional issues and hence distributional politics, would require as a minimum: citizen support, European political parties, and a US-style legislature. None of these obtain in the EU in 2001. The type of fiscal federalism that is emerging is more akin to the Swiss experience of federation than to that of the USA (McKay 2000).

The early theorists and practitioners of European integration were technocrats, whose approach was not just anti-national – that is, attempting deliberately to transcend the national rivalries that had devastated Europe twice in the previous fifty years – but also 'anti-political' (Wallace, 1997). That is, they believed in a type of depoliticised progress in which advances were made through a disinterested, professional elite, and were strongly influenced by the French experience of a rational, top-down planning system (Wallace, 1997). The implied model of the state is one that is centralised, efficient and bureaucratic, in which power rests with the executive, where formal checks and balances play little part, and where decisions are taken away from the glare of publicity, or even the scrutiny of the legislature (Siedentop, 2000). In contrast, the British model of the state emphasises informality and 'common sense', lacks a written constitution and has an idiosyncratic (and hence non-exportable) nature; while the German model is explicitly federal and is characterised by the creation of different and separate spheres of authority, strict limits to federal government power, and a constitutional court. But it is the French model that has most influenced the form of the European Community as a whole. The French model 'is precisely what lies behind the Maastricht and Amsterdam Treaties and recent pressures to move ahead rapidly along their lines towards political integration. These developments amount to projecting something like the French state on to the rest of Europe' (Siedentop 2000, p. 107).

The technocratic and teleological attitude of the early integrationists continues to influence the policy agenda of the EU, and the modes of working of the EU institutions and functionaries. But the rest of the world has moved on. European nationalism, of the kind that prevailed for the first half of the twentieth century, is assumed by most European citizens (rightly or wrongly) to be dead and buried, and entirely remote from their own daily experience. To this extent, then, the European Union has truly become a victim of its own success (Weiler, 1995). In addition, deference to political and administrative elites has declined. Citizens have a stronger idea of their own rights, a more sceptical attitude towards governments and politicians, and an increased propensity to filter political rhetoric and ideology through the fine mesh of their own experience, and that of their families and friends. As a result of both these trends, the mode of working of European integration in its first three decades – seeking the good of all, sometimes by stealth, and almost always behind closed doors – has become not just unacceptable, but worse – anachronistic.

In the past, integration theorists have argued that the EU should not be involved in distributive issues at all. It should confine itself to situations that are 'win-win' – which is where Pareto-improvement gains are possible. Hence the EU requires a non-majoritarian mode of decision-making that will allow it to take decisions in the common interest of all with no apparent loss on the part of any actor (Majone, 1996, quoted in McAleavy and de Rynck, 1997). The objections to this are twofold. First, it assumes a level both of technical expertise and political disinterestedness within the institutions of the EU that are utopian (that is, Webbsian) in principle, and, as recent events have shown, this is far from the reality in practice. Second, it again assumes a rigid separation between efficiency issues, which should be settled by technocrats, and equity issues, which can be decided through politics. This separation, as we have seen, is not sustainable. Furthermore, the notion that European citizens are prepared to defer to technocratic wisdom for the sake of the benefits of European integration is less sustainable now than during previous phases in the integration process.

A distinction can be made between 'input-orientated' and 'output-orientated' forms of democratic legitimation (Scharpf, 1999). 'Input-orientated' refers to government *by* the people: 'Political choices are legitimate if and because they reflect the "will of the people" – that is, if they can be derived from the authentic preferences of the members of a community'. 'Output-orientated' refers to government *for* the people: 'Here, political choices are legitimate if and because they effectively promote the common welfare of the constituency in general' (Scharpf, 1999, p. 6). In general, these two aspects are complementary. Input-orientated democratic legitimation is concerned with questions of participation and consensus, while output-orientated legitimation is concerned more with the question of whether choices promote common welfare.

The danger with purely input-orientated versions of democracy is thus the well-known one of the 'tyranny of the majority' – choices that privilege some groups against others, or even lead to the oppression of minorities will still be deemed democratic if the input rule alone is applied. Scharpf (1999) argues that this danger is lessened where there is a 'thick' collective identity, arising from 'pre-existing commonalities of history, language, culture and ethnicity'. However, the EU is characterised by great diversity of these aspects, and hence a 'thin' collective identity. In this case, output-orientated legitimacy becomes more important, through its capacity 'to solve problems requiring collective solutions because they could not be solved through individual action, through market exchanges, or through voluntary co-operation in civil society' (Scharpf, 1999, p. 11). The legitimacy of output-orientated mechanisms is both 'more contingent and more limited than is true of identity-based majoritarian democracy' (ibid., p. 11). Nevertheless, the implication is that this is the most we can expect from European governance: we should accept that the 'European polity' is different from the national democracies, and can at the time of writing only aspire to output-orientated democratic legitimacy. It is therefore wrong to judge the EU by the standards of input-orientated legitimacy, as do many critics of the 'democratic deficit'.

It is only a small step from this position to legitimating a technocratic approach to European integration, in which the pursuit of the greater good of all requires the avoidance of, or occasional resistance to, what would otherwise be normal democratic procedures. Such a position implies a rather naive trust in the European Commission and the European Court of Justice:

> Through what mechanisms will benign technocrats, judges or philosopher kings in their law-making be sensitive to the changing concerns of ordinary citizens? [In Scharpf's vision] Ordinary citizens are given a very modest role. This is so, in spite of the role that citizens have actually played in the EU after Maastricht, e.g. the Danish 'no' and the new EU emphasis on transparency and bringing decisions closer to the people. (Olsen 2000, p. 315)

Europe's citizens are becoming both more affected by, and more sceptical about, European integration – and more sceptical about government in general. A technocratic, output-orientated version of European democracy looks increasingly out of step, not only with the shift to a more participatory democracy, but also with the consumer-driven market economies with which European citizens are now familiar. Citizens expect some control over inputs, at least at the level of choosing between competing elites and rival agendas (Hix, 1998). If 'Europe' looks different from this, it will not readily be identified as simply a different or even superior version of governance. More probably, it will be seen as backward, lagging, threatening, or merely self-serving. If, in addition, the democratic legitimacy of European institutions is questioned, the result will be voter resistance to further integration. This is particularly salient in relation to social policy, where already further integration is perceived as a threat to the achievements of the welfare state: 'as a consequence of the Single Market programme and of the implementation of the Maastricht and Amsterdam treaties, market integration has attained such a high level that national welfare states have turned into shields for mobilising *against* integration and communitarization' (Leibfried 2000, p. 45).

Now we can begin to see how both a single European currency and a single European citizenship contain the means to undermine their own major premises. Both have arisen as the end point of a technocrat-led process of integration in which decisions were taken away from the normal glare of democratic politics. But to the extent that these actions are successful, they not only imply a 'real' European state, they also draw attention to the undemocratic and unaccountable nature of that state. For in which country would citizens willingly agree to a national money without a democratic government, or to national citizenship without a democratic state? The political legitimacy of the EU as a polity depends not just on the efficiency of outcomes, but also crucially on the process. As Siedendop argues, to establish a real, citizen-based, accountable form of federalism in Europe would require 'a liberal doctrine of citizenship, which encourages an active sense of public duty ... Such a doctrine must focus attention on the process of government rather than merely on the outcomes of public policy-making' (Siedentop 2000, p. 41).

In practice much of the integration literature has an implicit ideology which is not only technocratic, but also teleological. It is assumed that economic and political integration are not only desirable, but also in some sense inevitable. The history of European integration can then be written as a series of advances and retreats along a defined road. The political question is not an open-ended one: 'What is the best set of arrangements for promoting both economic efficiency and social equity in Europe?' Rather, it is defined as how to advance the (noble) cause of integration, while being cognisant of the material barriers – political, economic and institutional – to achieving it. The general route, as well as the final goal, is assumed to be known.

As one example of the curious mix of the technocratic and the evangelical that comprises a key strand of writing on integration, consider the article 'Engineering the Single Currency' by T. Padoa-Schioppa (1997), originally written in 1992 in the immediate aftermath of Maastricht. Padoa-Schioppa is one of the 'fathers' of the euro, an Italian and European senior banker, an early advocate of the single currency, secretary of the Delors Committee on EMU, and a member of the Executive Board of the European Central Bank. Padoa-Schioppa's title immediately places the issue of a single currency as a technical, engineering problem. He argues that two world wars allot 'us' the goal of placing national sovereignty 'in a common order, founded on the rule of law'. He confesses himself both 'delighted' and 'astonished' when EMU was agreed at Maastricht. Rather than any immediate justification based around the costs and benefits of EMU to Europe's citizens, Padoa-Schioppa prefers to place these events in a perspective that exceeds the merely millennial: 'Europe' is apparently repairing its ancestral monetary unity which was lost around the seventh century AD. Europe is now 'retracing its steps along a path which in distant centuries led from the unity of an empire to an multiplicity of kingdoms, legal codes and currencies'. Clearly, unity and uniformity are Good Things. The alternative view – that competition and rivalry among kings, laws and monies might have certain advantages over the ornamental stasis of imperial bureaucracy, that messy diversity can create the conditions for economic development to flourish while sterile uniformity cannot – is not considered.

Padoa-Schioppa is clear that the unification of Europe will bring into existence 'a new kind of state', and sets himself the task of explaining how 'in the space of a few years, could such a momentous initiative [EMU] have been born?' (Padoa-Schioppa, 1997, p. 163). His explanation, in part, rests on leadership by a group of pro-Europe politicians, with a firm grip of power and familiarity of contacts. Many of those whom he identifies – Kohl, Mitterand, Andreotti, de Michelis, the Delors-era Commission – have subsequently become synonymous either with outright corruption or with incompetence. Tellingly, Padoa-Schioppa writes that 'the moment of clarification [that is, opening decisions up to public scrutiny] has *perhaps* arrived' (ibid., p. 172) (emphasis added). This tentative embrace of the democratic principle is in marked contrast with the effusive language with which the technocratic project of EMU is celebrated.

The Maastricht Treaty marks the end point of this stage of European integration, whose technocratic bent and secretive agendas reflect in part its Cold War origins. Since then, the divide between leaders and citizens in the EU has become 'dangerously wide' (Morgan, 1996). However, EU activities tend to 'Europeanize' increasing numbers of citizens, and hence Europe's citizens are increasingly inclined to set limits to the overall process (Morgan, 1996). What, then, is the evidence of the attitudes of European citizens to the integration process?

Citizen Attitudes to the EU

In the past, citizens' attitudes to European integration were not a major driver of the process. Citizens' attitudes to welfare, and the specific role that European institutions might play in delivering and ensuring welfare for Europeans were even less relevant. This was not because welfare issues, in the broad definition of the term, were irrelevant to Europeans, nor because they took no interest in the process of European integration. Rather it was because there was no conflict between the integration agenda on the one hand and the building of national legitimacy and personal security through the construction or further development of national welfare states on the other. The question of popular attitudes to European integration, and more specifically, popular attitudes to welfare issues in the context of European integration, generally did not arise.

Now, however, further European integration will require rather more in terms of positive assent from voters, and in this, welfare issues will be significant in the minds of voters who are now defined, both internally and externally, as European citizens. What are citizens' attitudes towards integration and welfare?

Regular comparative information is collected through the *Eurobarometer* surveys. While there are all the usual problems of 'snapshot' survey analysis, *Eurobarometer* does provide a rich source of consistent data. The following information comes from the *Eurobarometer 52* and *54* surveys, the fieldwork for which was conducted in the last quarters of 1999 and 2000, respectively (European Commission, 1999c, 2001).

First, in terms of identity, only 4 per cent of citizens in 1999 saw themselves as exclusively European; 45 per cent see themselves in terms of their nationality only; with 48 per cent declared some mixture of European and national identity. The proportion seeing themselves solely as 'nationals' varied from less than 40 per cent in France, Spain, Italy and Luxembourg, to over 60 per cent in Greece, Finland, Sweden and the UK. There is no evidence of any trend over time on this issue: 'the public generally does not become more likely to feel more European and less likely to identify with their own nation (or vice versa) from one measurement to the next' (*Eurobarometer 52*, p. 10).

Only 40 per cent of citizens in the autumn of 1999 were satisfied with the way democracy works in the EU, compared with 56 per cent who were satisfied with the way their national democracy worked. It is noticeable that satisfaction with EU democracy is lowest among countries such as Sweden, the UK and Denmark, where citizens have above-average levels of satisfaction with their national democracies. Conversely, satisfaction with EU democracy is high in countries such as the Republic of Ireland and Portugal, which have relatively low satisfaction with national democracy. In response to a question about which news items people pay attention to, the top item was news about social issues. News about the European Union was last among eight suggested topics.

Support for membership of the European Union peaked at 72 per cent in the spring of 1991. Since then, support has fallen by about 20 percentage points, although the autumn 2000 figure of 50 per cent was above the low of 46 per cent in the spring of 1997. Support was highest in Ireland, Luxembourg and the Netherlands, and lowest in the UK, Sweden, Austria and Finland. Support for EU membership is higher among better-educated groups, younger people and the higher social classes. In 1999, almost two-thirds of those who left full time education aged 20 or over support EU membership, while only 42 per cent who left aged 15 or under support it. Similar gaps are found between managers and retired people, and between younger and older citizens.

In terms of trust, all the main EU institutions received positive evaluations – that is, more people tend to trust than not to trust them. In 1999, the European Parliament received a trust rating of $+26$ percentage points, while for the European Court of Justice it was $+21$, and the Commission $+15$. Levels of trust in the European Parliament and the Commission are lowest in the UK, followed by

Sweden, Germany and Denmark. Levels of trust are highest in Ireland, Portugal and Italy.

Citizen priorities for the EU are fighting unemployment, maintaining peace and security, fighting organised crime and combating poverty and social exclusion. In 2000, 55 per cent of EU citizens supported the introduction of the euro, with 37 per cent opposing. Support for the single currency has thus fallen significantly below the 64 per cent recorded immediately prior to the launch of the euro, but at the time of writing is higher than the low 50s recorded in the early 1990s. The UK is the country most opposed, with 63 per cent against and only 21 per cent in favour, – a balance of minus 42, and then followed closely by Sweden (64 per cent against; 26 per cent in favour); Denmark (55 per cent/41 per cent); Finland (49 per cent/ 45 per cent) and Germany (44 per cent/47 per cent). As with EU membership, younger citizens, the better educated and the higher occupational groups are more likely to be in favour of the euro.

How do values and value change influence attitudes to European integration and to the 'security' aims of the welfare state? Are there differences between European societies in relation to these issues? These questions are examined by Michalski and Tallberg (1999). They argue that as European societies reach advanced stages of industrialisation, there is a shift in values towards those of a 'post-modern' society, characterised by 'a popular emphasis on democratic political institutions and individual freedom, a diminishing prestige of science, technology and rationality, and a rejection of traditional, bureaucratic and hierarchical authorities'. 'Post-modern' values are contrasted with both modern and traditional values.

On the basis of these criteria, the authors identify four 'clusters' of states in the EU (Michalski and Tallberg, 1999, p. 6). First, a 'very sceptical North': Denmark, Sweden and Finland form the most homogenous cluster, with comparable levels of economic development and social welfare, a high propensity to post-material values and a shared hostility to European integration. For example, only 13 per cent of Danes are in favour of a European government, compared with 70 per cent of Italians. The second group comprises the Benelux countries and France – here citizens feel more European and more positive towards a federal Europe than the average EU citizen, although the Netherlands and Luxembourg are more pro-Europe than the other two countries.

The third group comprises Germany and Austria. Although Austria is more Euro-sceptic than Germany as regards federalism, both countries 'display the same uneasiness in terms of acknowledging a European identity' (ibid., p. 6). The fourth cluster comprises the cohesion countries of Spain, Portugal, Greece and the Republic of Ireland. Here, values are more traditional than in other EU states. Support for the EU is high in all four countries, but is based more on the perceived economic benefits of membership than on pro-federalist sympathies or a sense of 'feeling European' – on the latter criterion they rate below the EU average.

Finally, there are two remaining countries that do not fit easily into the other categories and have opposing positions on European integration. The UK is the most Euro-sceptic country, and the British remain reluctant to transfer competencies to the EU level. In contrast, support for European integration is stronger in Italy than in any other country. Italians feel more European than any other population, and are most in favour of a transfer of powers to the EU level.

Although there is a distinction between the more traditional values of Southern Europe and those of the 'post-modern' societies of Northern Europe, the difference in values is greater between generations than between nations. The shift towards post-modern values has important consequences for popular attitudes to the EU and to further integration. The time of permissive consensus to European integration among European citizens is over. There is a general dissatisfaction with the way in which the democratic system works both on national and European level. Popular demands for more participation in the European political system are likely to grow louder – a challenge to which the Union will have to respond, or else the detachment of European citizens is likely to be further aggravated. (Michalski and Tallberg, 1999)

Citizens' demands in the 'post-modern' society differ from those in earlier periods. The EU will have to respond to this changed agenda, which highlights issues such as environmental protection; the fight against social exclusion; consumer protection; action against organised crime; and drug trafficking. Michalski and Tallberg conclude that citizens' demands for democratic participation are increasing, and hence 'It is essential that European citizens share a perception of being able to influence the policy-formation process in the EU. In a wider context, this is dependent on a general feeling of belonging to Europe. The gradual emergence of such an imagined community requires efforts both at European and national level' (Michalski and Tallberg, 1999).

The Welfare of Nations and Europe's Incomplete Federalism

Prior to 1945, citizen allegiance to the national state was driven mainly by concerns about internal and external physical security. After 1945, citizens' demands became broader and more complex, so that the key voting issues were almost always those relating to personal and family present and future income (Milward, 1997a). That is, citizen allegiance became more closely related to personal and family security – including employment, income security, health, education and other key welfare state issues. European integration, and the development of the EC/EU symbolised both types of security – physical security and national defence on the one hand, and personal security via the development of welfare states on the other. The growth of the welfare state was accompanied by a rise in national allegiance. Voters were prepared over the first three post-war decades to pay high levels of personal taxation in order to ensure a complex system of social welfare and personal benefits (Milward, 1997a). Support for European integration was *not* because a United Europe was perceived as 'better' than the nation state. There was no decline in national allegiance, but rather a rise in 'secondary' allegiance to the idea of Europe. The 'fundamental question', according to Milward (1997a), is whether the allegiance to EU institutions now is subsidiary or dependent on national and regional loyalties, or will in time replace it. Crucial to answering this question is an understanding of the extent to which support for European integration exists at the popular level – but this is 'a question from which historians have fled' (Milward, 1997a, p. 17).

In the first two or three decades after 1945, European integration was compatible with a rebuilding of national legitimacy (Milward, 1997a; Wallace, 1997). That is, there was a positive-sum game in which both national reconstruction and the building of an integrated Europe could proceed. The underlying causes of European integration can be found in the national policy choices of the post-war Western European states. The growth of Community institutions was associated with the rise or strengthening of participatory democracy and stronger policies of redistribution in the member states (Milward, 1997b). In the 1950s and 1960s, in contrast with the inter-war period, national political systems were able to deliver substantial economic growth, while welfare states strengthened national legitimacy and built citizens' loyalty (Wallace, 1997).

However, in later decades of the twentieth century the picture changed. Economic production and distribution was organised increasingly on a scale beyond that of the nation state. With the rise of 'new international migration', resident populations have become more ethnically diverse, and demographic change points to increased in-migration from outside the EU. Global media and communications have undermined the insularity of individual countries and cultures. As a result of all these changes, and others, national borders are now increasingly permeable. Electorates want the benefits of prosperity, welfare and easy access across frontiers, but without the costs in terms of a decline in national autonomy. The result of these contradictions is a series of political compromises, such as the Single European Act and the Maastricht Treaty. Both the nation and the state have lost coherence, and as a result the European nation state is now 'in retreat' (Wallace, 1997).

Equally, however, there is no evidence of any kind of linear process by which powers and responsibilities are expanded at the supranational level. The Maastricht Treaty is generally seen as the high water mark for the accelerated programme of integration of the 1980s, and some argue that the Treaty itself should be seen as a reassertion of the powers of member states (Weiler, 1995). The underlying contradiction is between the complexity and ambiguity that surrounds political integration, and the continuing and strengthening economic integration symbolised by the institution of a common currency.

The situation in 2001 might be described as incomplete federalism. Economic integration has proceeded to the point of creating a federal European Central Bank with extensive powers – and yet without any countervailing governmental institutions to provide democratic accountability. The Maastricht Treaty supposedly created a new category of European citizenship – but there is no European 'state' to which such citizenship could adhere. Both these deficits point towards the creation of a real supranational government, a European federal state. But is that what citizens would actively choose? Both the reality of the euro and the concept of European citizenship imply a European government, but a government imposed through the will of elites.

How can this be reconciled with a democratic notion of citizenship and the accountability of limited government? In contrast with the debates that preceded the creation of a federal USA, there is as yet no great debate on the *political* implications of creating a federal state in Europe (Siedentop 2000). Similarly, Weil (1996) writes:

How many experts have been consulted, how many commissions created and ministerial meetings convened [on EMU]? How many late-night negotiations regarding the range of fluctuation of various currencies within the framework of a 'snake' and then a European monetary system have been debated hotly – and to the nearest 0.25 per cent? ... Citizenship, nationality, collective identity, inter-ethnic relations – these are probably more delicate questions than money and economics. With what speed, if not offhandedness, have decisions on these subjects been made? (Weil, 1996, p. 86)

The answer that is sometimes given is that Europe does not have to address these political questions of federalism, democracy and autonomy directly, because what is evolving is a unique and novel system of 'multi-level governance' which renders such debates unnecessary. This response at best reflects muddle, and at worst a deliberate attempt to confuse. It is entirely at odds with what good government and governance should be about – that is, democracy, accountability and transparency. Modern citizens, for good or ill, are citizen-consumers. They want to know what they are getting from the government, who does what, how much they are paying, and whether it represents value for money. The current operations of the institutions of EU government fall well below the implied standards of this approach.

There is a place for ideals and idealism too, but not if that means obfuscating accountability and responsibility. In its formative years to support the European Community was to 'Do the Right Thing' – 'It was a happy state in which one could believe that long term self-interest coincided with higher values' (Weiler, 1995, p. 2). But post-Maastricht, the 'European Union can no longer serve as a vehicle for the foundational ideals' (ibid., p. 13). In part this is because of the very success of the Community, so that peace and (relative) prosperity are no longer ideals but everyday political reality.

Visions of the European future differ considerably, and the same terms (for example, Federalism) have very different connotations within different cultures and as they are used by different speakers. Supranationalism can refer to a centralised Jacobin or Bismarckian state, a top-down, elite-driven creation. Alternatively, it can mean, at least in theory, a Jeffersonian perspective in which a limited Federal government does those things, and only those, that national govern-ments cannot do well – a 'community idea' which is 'not meant to eliminate the national state but to create a regime which seeks to tame the national interest with a new discipline. The idyllic is a state of affairs which eliminates the excesses of narrow statal "national interest" ' (Weiler, 1995, p. 10). These confusions explain in part why in some countries, such as in Britain, 'Federalism' signifies an overweening centralised government, while in others, such as Germany, it symbolises precisely the opposite – the imposition of constitutional limits on government.

Conclusions

Welfare lies at the heart of our modern concept of citizenship. The development of citizenship, national identity and welfare have been closely related over the twentieth century and before. It has been a contingent relationship, but a powerful one. A single currency and a single citizenship in Europe imply a single European government, and hence a fully federal system. But the political and civil underpinning of a real notion of European citizenship barely exist. Over time, they may develop – but at the time of writing that looks a very long way off. In the absence of a real European social citizenship, the danger is that 'European welfare' will not develop in a healthy democratic manner, but only as an output-legitimised, top-down technocratic process. This is an undesirable outcome, and an avoidable one.

9

Conclusions

In this book, I set out to look at the complex, three-way relationships between European Union social policy, the social policies of the member states, and the broader process of European integration. Social policies matter: they affect the lives of hundreds of millions of citizens materially. They are also a key area for political mobilisation and political debate, and they play an important role in defining what is meant by citizenship.

I therefore began by looking at what we mean by social policy, and what in particular has been happening to the social policies of European welfare states since the 1970s. From this research, it was clear that reports of the death of the welfare state – or even its permanent 'crisis' – have been much exaggerated. What is striking is not the convergence or retrenchment of welfare states, but the consistency over time in relative levels of welfare expenditure across countries, and the continued diversity in the extent, form and content of European welfare states. There does not seem to be an unstoppable 'logic of Globalization' inexorably making all welfare states more similar and more limited; similarly, the 'logic of industrialism' did not remove differences between welfare states during the period of welfare state expansion in the three decades after 1945.

Nevertheless, there are important economic, social and demographic changes that are common to most or all countries, and which lead to similar pressures on different European welfare states. These include the restructuring of labour markets, changed patterns of fertility, changes in the gender division of labour, and an ageing population. Moreover, there are common political trends affecting the beliefs and behaviour of both voters and policy-makers. Among voters, there is greater scepticism about the ability and responsiveness of governments, and a loss of deference towards elites. Among policy-makers, there is a parallel shift towards a narrower view of the scope for government action, and conversely, a greater acceptance of the role of markets in determining patterns of production and consumption. But the key conclusion for our purposes here is that European welfare states remain distinctive – national states, national institutions and national attitudes remain the key.

In Chapter 2, I examined the 'welfare modelling business'. European welfare states retain distinctive characteristics, but can be grouped into four broad types – conservative-corporatist, social democratic, Mediterranean and Anglo-Saxon – whose members bear at least a family resemblance one to another. Furthermore, the last decades of the twentieth century have been characterised not by radical change, but rather by a 'frozen' welfare state landscape. In general, Northern European welfare states have stabilised expenditure, trimmed at the margins, and sought to manage citizen expectations downwards, while Southern European welfare states have expanded. There has been no general retrenchment, but the power and autonomy of national states have been somewhat reduced. Strikingly, several of the most extensive welfare states have recovered from economic recession and a period of welfare cutbacks, and appear to be combining economic recovery successfully with, in general, maintenance of their existing systems. On the other side, the one possible exception to these general conclusions may be the United Kingdom, where there is at least a case for arguing that the extent of changes after 1979 constitutes a regime change.

From the analysis undertaken in the first two chapters we saw that it was too simplistic to talk about a single 'European Social Model'. There is a variety of social models existing in Europe. This means that the idea that a European welfare state could arise as the logical expression of an existing, consistent European Social Model is misconceived. Should a European Social Policy seek to create a single European social model, it would have to do so either by synthesising aspects of all four models in some way, or by imposing a single model on all member states. Neither of these options is very attractive, and neither seems very likely. The term 'European Social Policy' will continue to mean a mix of national and European policies, and there will continue to be a range of European social models (plural).

One important variable is the impact of Globalization. The treatment of Globalization in this book is necessarily limited. In Chapter 3, I showed that the 'strong' version of the Globalization thesis, in which it is claimed that Globalization is destroying or undermining the welfare state is clearly wrong. Much of this argument rests on a series of misconceptions about both the effects of increased international trade and about the impact of increased trade and interdependency on welfare states. In particular, the problem of so-called 'social dumping' has generated a level of concern, and a literature, out of all proportion to the scale of the problem. In fact, one of the most significant trends in European welfare states since the 1980s has been 'social anti-dumping', as the less developed welfare states of southern Europe have sought to 'catch up' with their Northern European neighbours.

National states remain the key agents for delivering welfare to their citizens. But Globalization changes the constraints under which national states must act. This implies, not a fully-fledged European welfare state, but a complex relationship between nations, the European Union, and subnational government – that is, some form of multi-level governance.

How does the existing body of European Union social policy fit into this analysis? European social policy began as a subsidiary component of European integration. The role of social policy was to enable the process of economic integration to take place. Moreover, the original six signatories to the Treaty of Rome had broadly similar social systems. Since then, the European Union has become far more diverse, and national welfare systems have expanded enormously, both in extent and complexity. The idea of 'harmonising' such diversity has become impractical as well as undesirable. Nevertheless, in an economically integrated Europe there is, and will be, continuing pressures for co-ordination and compatibility between systems.

What the social policy of the European Union is about differs considerably from the issues on national policy agendas. Partly because of its origins, European social policy retains a focus on a specific subset of social policy issues – particularly those relating to the labour market. The major elements of social policy at national level – such as education, health and housing – have only a limited involvement at the European level. Furthermore, European social policy is mainly a regulatory activity. Direct provision of services is non-existent and fiscal policy very limited. There are inherent dangers in a mode of activity that is mainly about imposing regulations that other levels of government must enforce and often pay for. When this is combined with weak levels of accountability and transparency, the dangers are multiplied.

The way in which European social policy is developed and implemented reflects the unique nature of European governance. The European Union is more than an intergovernmental arrangement, but less than a polity. European social policy contains elements of both 'inter-governmentalism' and 'neo-functionalism'. In this context, there is a continually shifting social policy agenda, and the conditions are created for institutional opportunism by key policy actors such as the European Commission and the European Court of Justice.

Further expansion of the European social policy agenda will raise fundamental questions about the legitimacy and accountability of European institutions. For three decades and more after the Treaty of Rome, the integration process was essentially about achieving political goals through successful economic policies. This was, furthermore, against a backdrop of the Cold War and a divided Europe. In this context, questions of democracy, accountability and legitimacy took second place to an outcome-based functionalism.

But further European integration in the future, should it occur, will happen only as part of a more directly political process. 'Europe' will become more a part of everyday politics. Welfare issues – jobs, schools, health, quality of life – will form a key part of this European debate, just as they already do at national level. There is no inevitability about further integration and an expanded European welfare role. On balance, it seems likely that integration will continue, and that the role of European institutions in the social field will increase – particularly in those areas that are either at the periphery of traditionally defined national social policies, or at the boundary between economic and social concerns.

A major determinant of European social policy has been the continuing and deepening process of economic integration, leading to the introduction of the single currency in eleven member states in 1999. Economic integration has proceeded much faster than political integration, and gone much further than any compensating transnational social policy. Monetary union in the absence of a federal government and any federal fiscal mechanisms for redistribution and stabilization is a unique experiment. The European Union as it is in 2001 is bizarrely unbalanced, with no federal institutions except for a politically unaccountable central bank. The existence of a single currency and a central bank implies the creation of a European government and a fully federal system. But it is by no means clear that citizens of Europe, and not just of the most Eurosceptic countries such as the UK or Sweden, would actively wish for this.

Unemployment and social exclusion are the most important issues on the European social agenda. EU actions in these fields have been complementary to actions by member-state governments, who retain the major responsibility for reducing unemployment and tackling social exclusion. Structural fund support is still mainly area-based. Increased targeting of households and individuals would be more effective, but would raise major political and constitutional issues. Responses to unemployment and social exclusion show the continuing differences between different welfare systems within the EU. Britain has been more successful at bringing unemployment down than most continental welfare states, but its welfare system has a far worse record in preventing unemployment from turning into poverty and social exclusion. This suggests that successful European policies will need to combine elements of both 'Anglo-Saxon' and 'continental' approaches. EU actions are directed towards an 'employment-centred social policy' and aim at raising employment levels. However, in the Amsterdam Treaty, price stability and sound public finances – but not full employment – are stated to be 'guiding principles' of the Union.

Since the Maastricht Treaty, all people who are nationals of a member state have been 'citizens of the Union'. But what this means in practice is difficult to discern. Historically, citizenship has been linked closely with the nation state, and the development of *social* citizenship closely related to the creation and extension of national *welfare* states. In a narrow, legalistic sense, the concept of European citizenship is relatively thin, incorporating a small number of enforceable rights, and containing exclusionary as well as inclusionary aspects. In a wider sense, European citizenship, like a European currency, implies a European government, and in effect a Federal system. Hence it is hard to see how the notion of European citizenship can develop further without raising the same sorts of difficult constitutional and political issues raised by the single currency. The political and civil underpinnings of a real notion of European citizenship barely exist. Over time, they may develop – but at the time of writing this looks a very long way off.

For almost four decades, a functionalist engine pulled the train of European integration. But that technology is now obsolete. Further rounds of integration will require a more democratic and citizen-centred approach. More attention will need to be given to the political and constitutional underpinnings of integration – and as a result, politics may re-emerge from the shadow of economics (Siedentop, 2000). Social policy is likely to be at the centre of this process. It is social issues that drive most of the domestic policy agendas of member states. For Europeans, security is a key consideration. 'Europeans', said the French Senator, Henri Weber, 'are Americans who did not take the boat. We do not take the same risks; we have a need for greater security'. (*The Economist*, 12 February 2000). In the immediate post-war period, security meant questions of national defence, diplomacy and the avoidance of war. But in 2001, security concerns centre more on personal and family issues – jobs, education, health, housing and quality of life. Europeans look to their welfare states to promote security and protect themselves and their families against the risks of economic and social life.

Welfare will continue to be mainly a national and subnational responsibility. There is no prospect of a European welfare state taking over the financing, regulation and delivery of health care systems, social protection, schools and colleges, social housing or environmental protection from member-state governments. But the European dimension to social policy will remain, and will increase incrementally but inexorably. The questions are: what form will this European dimension take? Will it be an elite-driven technocratic and functionalist process, or will it be something more democratic, accountable and related to citizens' everyday concerns?

While a single 'European social model' does not exist, the *idea* of a European social model has been an important factor in the way European welfare states think about themselves. As we saw earlier, even in a period of supposed retrenchment, Northern European welfare states were largely maintained, and Southern European welfare states expanded. Since the 1950s, European citizens have become less deferential, more vocal, more affluent, and perhaps more 'post-modern' in their attitudes and behaviour. Europeans now live in a consumer culture and expect to exercise choice and control over most aspects of their lives. Young people in Europe in particular live in a culture that is unselfconsciously international, and in which consumer brands, for example, are true global signifiers.

Some aspects of the way in which state welfare has been provided in the past – its bureaucracy, paternalism and inflexibility – are no longer acceptable to the public. But the core idea of a welfare state, and even its extension into newer areas of concern such as the environment, consumer protection and the quality of life continues to resonate strongly with European citizens.

A narrow insistence on promoting 'Europeanism' will ultimately be self-defeating. European culture itself is a product of the interaction between Europeans and non-Europeans. The legacy of imperialism and colonialism, together with demographically and economically driven global migration means that Europe's cities are increasingly and widely ethnically mixed. One of the key challenges in the future will be how to adapt Europe's welfare systems to these changed circumstances, and how to prevent social policies becoming part of the building blocks of a 'Fortress Europe'.

For forty years, economic integration was the driving force of the European project. Over this period, by and large, economic integration was not only compatible with rising social and welfare standards, but was also a guarantee of them. Now, however, there are fears that further economic integration threatens welfare. Support for the euro appears to be grudging rather than wholehearted. – even at a time of growing prosperity in Europe. In any future recession, it is likely that support for the single currency and for economic integration generally will fall among both member state governments and citizens at large. In these circumstances, the European project may be seen as inimical to social welfare, rather than a pillar of it. It is therefore vital that the economic and social aspects of integration are closely linked, and that both are given a strong democratic foundation through greater transparency, debate and legitimacy.

Europeans will continue to want a high quality of welfare, and by and large, will be prepared to pay for it. But 'Europeans' will continue to be diverse. Integration cannot and should not eradicate the different cultures of Europe. Past and present migrations will increase Europe's ethnic and cultural mix. So welfare systems will continue to be diverse. The policy task is not to try to homogenise these differences, but to find ways of better linkage and better learning across countries and systems. In this way, European welfare will continue to increase, without the need for a European welfare state.

References

Abrahamson, P. (1992) 'Welfare Pluralism: Towards a New Consensus for a European Social Policy?', in L. Hantrais, S. Mangen and M. O'Brien (eds), *Mixed Economy of Welfare* Cross-National Research Paper No. 6, Loughborough University.

Abrahamson, P. (1999) 'The Welfare Modelling Business', *Social Policy and Administration*, 33 (4), pp. 394–415.

Adnett, N. (1995) 'Social Dumping and European Economic Integration', *Journal of European Social Policy*, 5 (1), pp. 1–12.

Alber, J. and Standing, G. 'Social Dumping, Catch-up or Convergence? Europe in a Comparative Global Context', *Journal of European Social Policy*, 10 (2), pp. 99–119.

Almeda, E. and Sarasa, S. (1996) 'Growth to Diversity', in V. George and, P. Taylor-Gooby (eds), *European Welfare Policy: Squaring the Circle* (London: Macmillan – now Palgrave).

Antonnen, A. and Sipila, J. (1996) 'European Social Care Services: Is It Possible to Identify Models?', *Journal of European Social Policy*, 6 (2), pp. 87–100.

Arestis, P. and Sawyer, M. (1996) 'Making the "Euro", Palatable', *New Economy*, 3 (2), Summer 1996, pp. 89–92.

Armstrong, H. and Taylor, J. (1985) *Regional Economics and Policy* (Oxford: Philip Allan).

Aron, R. (1974) 'Is Multinational Citizenship Possible?', *Social Research*, 41 (4), pp. 638–56.

Atkinson, A. B. (1995) 'The Welfare State and Economic Performance', LSE STICERD Discussion Paper, WSP/109.

Atkinson, A. B. (1998a) 'Can Welfare States Compete in a Global Economy?', Leicester University Public Sector Economics Research Centre Discussion Paper 98/1.

Atkinson, A. B. (1998b) 'Social Exclusion, Poverty and Unemployment', in A. B. Atkinson and J. Hills (eds), *Exclusion, Employment and Opportunity*, LSE STICERD Centre for Analysis of Social Exclusion CasEpaper No. 4.

Atkinson, A. B. (2000) 'The Economics of Social Exclusion', Speech to the BAAS Annual Festival of Science, London.

Baimbridge, M., Burkitt, B. and Whyman, P. (2000) *The Impact of the Euro: Debating Britain's Future* (London: Macmillan – now Palgrave).

Baldwin, P. (1991) *The Politics of Social Solidarity* (Oxford University Press).

Baldwin, P. (1992) 'Measurable Dynamic Gains from Trade', *Journal of Political Economy*, 100 (1), pp. 162–74.

Balls, E. (1994) 'No More Jobs for the Boys', in J. Michie and J. Grieve Smith (1994) *Unemployment in Europe* (London: Academic Press).

Bayoumi, T. and Masson, P. (1995) 'Fiscal Flows in the United States and Canada: Lessons for Monetary Union in Europe', *European Economic Review*, 39, pp. 253–75.

Bean, C., Bentolila S., Bertola G. and Dolala J. (1998) *Social Europe: One for All?*, Monitoring European Integration No. 8 (London: Centre for Economic Policy Research).

Begg, I. (1999) 'Cities and Competitiveness', *Urban Studies*, 36 (5), pp. 795–809.

Begg, I. and Mayes, D. (1991) 'Social and Economic Cohesion Among the Regions of Europe in the 1990s', *National Institute Economic Review*, November, pp. 63–74.

Begg I. and Mayes D. (1993) 'Cohesion, Convergence and Economic and Monetary Union in Europe', *Regional Studies*, 27 (2), pp. 149–65.

Blanchard, O. J. (1998) 'Discussion', *Economic Policy*, 26, pp. 248–54.

Bliss, C. (1990) 'Adjustment, Compensation and Factor Mobility in Integrated Markets', in C. Bliss, and J. Braga De Macedo (eds), *Unity with Diversity in the European Economy: The Community's Southern Frontier* (Cambridge University Press).

Borjas, G. J. and Ramey, V. A. (1994) 'The Relationship between Wage Inequality and International Trade', in J. H. Bergstrand, T. F. Cosimaro, J. W. Horck and R. G. Sheehan (eds), *The Changing Distribution of Income in an Open U.S. Economy* (Amsterdam: North-Holland).

Borjas, G. J., Freeman, R. B. and Katz, L. F. (1992) 'On the Labour Market Effects of Immigration and Trade', in G. J. Borjas and R. B. Freeman (eds), *Immigration and the Work Force: Economic Consequences for the United States and Source Areas* (University of Chicago Press).

Briggs, A. (1961) 'The Welfare State in Historical Perspective', *European Journal of Sociology*, 2, pp. 221–58.

van Buitenen, P. (2000) *Blowing the Whistle* (London: Politico's).

Buiter, W., Corsetti, G. and Roubini, N. (1993) 'Maastricht's Fiscal Rules', *Economic Policy*, April, pp. 57–100.

Burchardt, T. and Hills, J. (1997) *Private Welfare Insurance and Social Security: Pushing the Boundaries* (York: York Publishing Services).

Burchardt, T., Hills, J. and Propper, C. (1999) *Private Welfare and Public Policy* (York: York Publishing Services).

Caporaso, J. A. and Keeler, J. T. S. (1995) 'The European Union and Regional Integration Theory', in C. Rhodes and S. Mazey (eds), *The State of the Union Vol. III: Building a European Polity?* (Harlow: Longman).

Castles, F. (1982) 'The Impact of Parties on Public Expenditure', in F. Castles (ed.), *The Impact of Parties* (London: Sage).

Castles, F. (1995) 'Welfare State Development in Southern Europe', *West European Politics*, 18 (2), pp. 291–313.

Castles, F. G. and Mitchell, D. (1990) 'Three Worlds of Welfare Capitalism or Four?', Australian National University, graduate program in public policy, discussion paper no. 21.

Castles, F. and Mitchell, D. (1993) 'Worlds of Welfare and Families of Nations', in F. Castles (ed.), *Families of Nations: Patterns of Public Policy in Western Democracies* (Aldershot: Dartmouth).

Castles, F. and Pierson, C. (1996) 'A New Convergence? Recent Policy Developments in the UK, Australia and New Zealand', *Policy and Politics*, 24 (3), pp. 233–46.

Cecchini, P., Catinat, M., Jacquernin, A, and Robinson, J. (1988) *1992: The European Challenge: The Benefits of a Single Market*, Wildwood House.

Chamberlayne, P. (1992) 'Income Maintenance and Institutional Forms: A Comparison of France, West Germany, Italy and Britain 1945–1990', *Policy and Politics*, 20 (4), pp. 299–318.

Cheshire, P. (1999) 'Cities in Competition: Articulating the Gains from Integration', *Urban Studies*, 36 (5–6), pp. 843–64.

Cingolani, M. (1993) 'Dispantés Régionàles De Produit Par Tête dans La Communauté Europèene', *European Investment Bank Papers*, 19 March.

Clark, A. E. and Oswald, A. (1994) 'Unhappiness and Unemployment', *Economic Journal*, 104, pp. 648–59.

Clasen, J. and Gould, A. (1995) 'Stability and Change in Welfare States: Germany and Sweden in the 1990s', *Policy and Politics*, 23 (3), pp. 189–202.

Clasen, J., Gould, A. and Vincent, J. (1997) *Long Term Unemployment and the Threat of Social Exclusion: A Cross National Analysis of the Position of Long-term Unemployed People in Germany, Sweden and Britain* (Bristol: Policy Press).

Collier, J. (1994) 'Regional Disparities, the Single Market and EMU', in J. Michie and J. Grieve Smith *Unemployment in Europe* (London: Academic Press).

Collins, M. (1990) 'A Guaranteed Minimum Income in France?', *Social Policy and Administration*, 24 (2), pp. 120–4.

Committee of Independent Experts (1999) *First Report on Allegations Concerning Fraud, Mismanagement and Nepotism in the European Commission*, (Luxembourg: European Commission).

Cram, L. (1993) 'Calling the Tune Without Paying the Piper? Social Policy Regulation: The Role of the Commission in European Community Social Policy', *Policy and Politics*, 21 (2), pp. 135–46.

Cram, L. (1997) *Policy-making in the European Union* (London: Routledge).

Cross, M. (1993) 'Generating the "New Poverty": A European Comparison', in R. Simpson and R. Walker, *Europe: For Richer or Poorer?* (London: CPAG).

Currie, D. (1997) *The Pros and Cons of EMU* (London: HM Treasury).

Currie, D. (1998) 'Does EMU Need Political Union?', *Prospect*, June.

Dahrendorf, R. (1996) 'Citizenship and Social Class', in M. Bulmer, and A. M. Rees, *Citizenship Today: The Contemporary Relevance of T. H. Marshall* (London: UCL Press).

Dahrendorf, R. (1999) 'Answering the New Social Question, A Liberal View', DEMOS Lecture on the Welfare Society, 10 February.

Delors, J. (1985) 'Preface', in J. Vandamme (ed.), *New Dimensions in European Social Policy* (London: Croom Helm).

Department of Social Security (1999) *Opportunity for All: Tackling Poverty and Social Exclusion*, First Annual Report, Cm. 4445 (London: Stationery Office).

Diamontopoulou, A. (2000a) 'The State of the Union', Speech to the Europe Horizons Conference, 18 February.

Diamontopoulou, A. (2000b) 'New Social Trends in Europe', Speech to the Foreign Correspondents', Club of Japan, 7 March.

Dignan, T. (1995): 'Regional Disparities and Regional Policy in the European Union', *Oxford Review of Economic Policy*, 11 (2), pp. 64–95.

Ditch, J., Barnes, H., Bradshaw, J. and Kilkey, M. (1998) *A Synthesis of National Family Policies* (Brussels: DGV).

Dixon, R. J. and Thirlwall, A. P. (1975) 'A Model of Regional Growth Rate Differentials Along Kaldorian Lines', *Oxford Economic Papers*, 27, pp. 201–14).

Duffy, K. (1998) 'Combating Social Exclusion and Poverty: Social Integration in the European Union', in C. Oppenheim (ed.), *An Inclusive Society – Strategies for Tackling Poverty* (London: IPPR).

Eardley, T., Bradshaw, J., Ditch, J., Gough, I. and Whiteford, P. (1996) *Social Assistance in OECD Countries: Synthesis Report*, DSS Research Report No. 46 (London: HMSO).

Eichengreen, B. (1998a) 'European Monetary Unification: A Tour d'Horizon', Mimeo (http://emlab.berkeley.edu/users/eichengr/vines.pdf). Revised version in *Oxford Review of Economic Policy*, 14 (3), Autumn.

Eichengreen B. (1998b) 'EMU: Its Implications for Europe', Speech Delivered on the occasion of Professor Horst Siebert's birthday celebration, Kiel, Germany, 20 March, Mimeo (http://emlab.berkeley.edu/users/eichengr/siebert.pdf).

Emerson, M. (1989) *The Economics of 1992* (Oxford University Press).

Emerson, M. (1990) 'Comment', in C. Bliss and J. Braga De Macedo (eds), *Unity with Diversity in the European Economy: The Community's Southern Frontier* (Cambridge University Press).

Emerson, M. and Huhne, C. (1991) *The Ecu Report* (London: Pan Books).

Esping-Andersen, G. (1990) *The Three Worlds of Welfare Capitalism* (Cambridge: Polity Press).

Esping-Andersen, G. (1994) 'Welfare States and the Economy', in J. N. Smelser and R. Swedberg (eds), *Handbook of Economic Sociology* (Princeton, NJ: Princeton University Press).

Esping-Andersen, G. (ed.) (1996) *Welfare States in Transition* (London: Sage).

Esping-Andersen G. and Korpi W. (1984) 'Social Policy as Class Politics in Postwar Capitalism', in J. Goldthorpe (ed.), *Order and Conflict in Contemporary Capitalism* (Oxford University Press).

European Commission (1993a) *Growth, Competitiveness, Employment: The Challenges and Ways Forward into the 21st Century* (White Paper) COM (93) 700 (Luxembourg: European Commission).

European Commission (1993b) *Employment in Europe* (Luxembourg: European Commission).

European Commission (1994) *European Social Policy: A Way Forward for the Union: A White Paper* COM (94) 333 (Luxembourg: European Commission).

European Commission (1999a) *Employment in Europe 1999* (Luxembourg: European Commission).

European Commission (1999b) *The EU Economy: 1999 Review* (Luxembourg: European Commission).

European Commission (1999c) *Eurobarometer 52* (Luxembourg: European Commission).

European Commission (1999d) *Eurobarometer 54* (Luxembourg: European Commission).

Eurostat (1996) *Social Protection Expenditure and Receipts 1980–1994* (Luxembourg: European Commission).

Eurostat (2000) *Social Protection Expenditure and Receipts 1980–1997* (Luxembourg: European Commission).

Falkner, G. (1998) *EU Social Policy in the 1990s: Towards a Corporatist Policy Community* (London: Routledge).

Falkner, G. and Talos, E. (1994) 'The Role of the State within Social Policy', *West European Politics*, 17 (3).

Ferrera, M. (1996) 'The "Southern Model", of Welfare in Social Europe', *Journal of European Social Policy*, 6 (1), pp. 17–37.

Flora, P. (ed.) (1986) *Growth to Limits: The Western European Welfare States Since World War II* (New York: De Gruyter).

Franco, D. and Pench, L. R. (2000) *Reconciling the Welfare State with Sound Public Finances and High Employment*, European Commission Forward Studies Unit Working Paper.

Fulbrook, M. and Cesarani, D. (1996) 'Conclusion', in D. Cesarani and M. Fulbrook (eds), C*itizenship, Nationality and Migration in Europe* (London: Routledge).

Garcia, S. (1997) 'European Union Identity and Citizenship: Some Challenges', in M. Roche and R. van Berkel (eds), *European Citizenship and Social Exclusion* (Aldershot: Ashgate).

Garrett, G. (2000) 'Shrinking States? Globalization and National Autonomy', in N. Woods (ed.), *The Political Economy of Globalization* (London: Palgrave).

Gellner, E. (1983) *Nations and Nationalism* (Oxford: Basil Blackwell).

Giddens A. (1994) *Beyond Left and Right* (Cambridge: Polity Press).

Giddens, A. (1998) *The Third Way* (Cambridge: Polity Press).

Ginsburg, N. (1992) *Divisions of Welfare* (London: Sage).

Glennerster, H. (1995) *British Social Policy Since 1945* (Oxford: Basil Blackwell).

Glennerster, H. and Le Grand, J. (1995) 'The Development of Quasi-markets in Welfare Provision' *International Journal of Health Services*, 25 (2), pp. 208–18.

Glennerster, H. (1999) 'Which Welfare States are Most Likely to Survive?', *International Journal of Social Welfare*, 8, pp. 2–13.

Godley, W. (1997) 'The Hole in the Treaty', in P. Gowan and P. Anderson (eds), *The Question of Europe* (London: Verso).

Gold, M. (ed.) (1993) *The Social Dimension: Employment Policy in the European Community* (London: Macmillan – now Palgrave).

Goldsmith, M. (1993) 'The Europeanisation of Local Government', *Urban Studies*, 30 (4/5), pp. 683–99.

Goldthorpe, J. (1984) 'The End of Convergence: Corporatist and Dualist Tendencies in Modern Western Societies', in J. Goldthorpe (ed.), *Order and Conflict in Contemporary Capitalism* (Oxford University Press).

Golub, S. (1997) *International Labor Standards and International Trade*, IMF Working Paper 97/37.

Goodhart, C. (1996) 'European Monetary Integration', *European Economic Review*, 40 (3–5), pp. 1083–90.

Goodhart, C. (1997) 'One Government, One Money', *Prospect*, March.

Goodhart, C. and Smith, S. (1992) 'Stabilisation', Paper Presented to the Conference on 'Public Finance and the Future of Europe', London School of Economics, September, Mimeo. (Also Published in 'The Economics of Community Public Finance', *European Economy Reports and Studies*, 5, 1993.)

Gornick, J., Meyers, M. and Ross, K. (1997) 'Supporting the Employment of Mothers: Policy Variation Across 14 Welfare States', *Journal of European Social Policy*, 7 (1), pp. 45–70.

Gough, I. (1979) *The Political Economy of the Welfare State* (London: Macmillan – now Palgrave).

Gough, I. (1996) 'Social Welfare and Competitiveness', *New Political Economy*, 1 (2), pp. 209–32.

Gould, A. (1996) 'Sweden: The Last Bastion of Social Democracy', in V. George and P. Taylor-Gooby (eds), *European Welfare Policy: Squaring the Circle* (London: Macmillan – now Palgrave).

Gould, A. (1999) 'The Erosion of the Welfare State: Swedish Social Policy and the EU', *Journal of European Social Policy*, 9 (2), pp. 165–74.

Gould, S. J. (1981) *The Mismeasure of Man* (Harmondsworth: Penguin).

Guild, E. (1996) 'The Legal Framework of Citizenship of the European Union', in Cesarani and Fulbrook (eds), *Citizenship, Nationality and Migration in Europe* (London: Routledge).

Guillen, A. M. and Matsaganis, M. (2000) 'Testing the "Social Dumping" Hypothesis in Southern Europe: Welfare Policies in Greece and Spain During the Last 20 Years', *Journal of European Social Policy*, 10 (2), pp. 120–45.

Haas, E. B. (1964) *Beyond the Nation-State: Functionalism and International Organization* (Palo Alto, Calif.: Stanford University Press).

von Hagen, J. (1992) 'Fiscal Arrangements in a Monetary Union – Some Evidence from the US', in D. Fair and C. De Boissieu (eds), *Fiscal Policy, Taxes, and the Financial Systems in an Increasingly Integrated Europe* (Deventer: Kluwer).

von Hagen, J. and Hammond, G. (1998) 'Regional Insurance Against Asymmetric Shocks: An Empirical Study for the European Community', *The Manchester School*, 66 (3), pp. 331–53.

Halimi, S., Michie, J. and Milne, S. (1994) 'The Mitterand Experience', in J. Michie and J. Grieve Smith, *Unemployment in Europe* (London: Academic Press).

Hall, S. (1999) 'European Citizenship – Unfinished Business', in L. Holmes and P. Murray, *Citizenship and Identity in Europe* (Aldershot: Ashgate).

Hantrais, L. (1995) *Social Policy in the European Union* (London: Macmillan – now Palgrave).

Hantrais, L, (1996) 'Squaring the Welfare Trianagle', in V. George and P. G. Taylor-Gooby (eds), *European Welfare Policy: Squaring the Welfare Circle* (London: Macmillan – now Palgrave).

Hantrais, L. (1999) 'Socio-Demographic Change, Policy Impacts and Outcomes in Social Europe', *Journal of European Social Policy*, 9 (4), pp. 291–309.

Hantrais, L. (2000) *Social Policy in the European Union* (2nd edn) (London: Palgrave).

Harloe, M. (1995) *The People's Home* (Oxford: Basil Blackwell).

Harloe, M. and Martens, M. (1983) 'Comparative Housing Research', *Journal of Social Policy*, 13, pp. 255–77.

Heclo, H. and Madsen, H. (1987) *Policy and Politics in Sweden: Principled Pragmatism* (Philadelphia, Pa.: Temple University Press).

Hirsch, D. (ed.) (1997) *Social Protection and Inclusion: European Challenges for the United Kingdom* (York: Joseph Rowntree Foundation).

Hirschman, A. (1958) *Exit, Voice and Loyalty* (Cambridge, Mass.: Harvard University Press).

Hirst, P. (1998) 'Can the European Welfare State Survive Globalization? Sweden, Denmark and the Netherlands in Comparative Perspective', University of Wisconsin-Madison Centre for European Studies Working Paper Series, 2 (1).

Hix, S. (1998) 'The Study of the European Union II: The "New Governance", Agenda and Its Rival', *Journal of European Public Policy*, March, pp. 38–65.

Hobsbawm, E. J. (1990) *Nations and Nationalism Since 1780* (Cambridge University Press).

Hobsbawm, E. J. and Rude, G. (1969) *Captain Swing* (London: Lawrence & Wishart).

Hooghe, L. (1998) 'EU Cohesion Policy and Competing Models of European Capitalism', *Journal of Common Market Studies*, 36 (4), pp. 457–78.

Hooghe, L. and Keating, M. (1994) 'The Politics of EU Regional Policy', *Journal of European Public Policy*, 1 (3), pp. 367–93.

House of Commons Committee of Public Accounts (1999) *Financial Management and Control in the European Union*, 29th Report, Session 1998–99, Cm. 690 (London: The Stationery Office).

Huber, E. and Stephens, J. D. (1998) 'Internationalization and the Social Democratic Model: Crisis and Future Prospects', *Comparative Political Studies*, 31 (3), pp. 353–97.

Institute for Fiscal Studies (1999) *Green Budget* (London: IFS).

John, P. (1994) 'UK Sub-national Offices in Brussels: Diversification or Regionalisation?', *Regional Studies*, 28 (7), pp. 739–46.

Jordan, B. (1998) *The New Politics of Welfare: Social Justice in a Global Context* (London: Sage).

Kaldor, N. (1970) 'The Case for Regional Policies', *Scottish Journal of Political Economy*, 17, pp. 337–48.

Kastrougalos, G. (1996) 'The South-European Welfare Model: The Greek Welfare State in Search of an Identity', *Journal of European Social Policy*, 6 (1), pp. 39–60.

Katzenstein, P. J. (1985) *Small States in World Markets. Industrial Policy in Europe* (Ithaca, NY: Cornell University Press).

Kay, J. A. and Posner, M. V. (1989) 'Routes to Economic Integration: 1992 in the European Community', *National Institute Economic Review*, August, pp. 55–68.

Keynes, J. M. (1919) *The Economic Consequences of the Peace* (London: Macmillan – now Palgrave).

Klausen J. (1995) 'Social Rights Advocacy and State Building: T. H. Marshall in the Hands of Social Reformers', *World Politics*, 47 (2), pp. 244–67.

Kleinman, M. P. (1996) *Housing, Welfare and the State in Europe: A Comparative Analysis of Britain, France and Germany* (Cheltenham: Edward Elgar).

Kleinman, M. P. (2000) 'Include Me Out? The New Politics of Place and Poverty', *Policy Studies*, 21 (1) pp. 49–61.

Kleinman, M. P. and Piachaud, D. (1993) 'European Social Policy: Conceptions and Choices', *Journal of European Social Policy*, 1, pp. 1–19.

Kinnock, N. (2000) 'Reforming the Commission', Consultative Document, 18 January, Cmd. 93 1/17, European Commission.

Kloostermann, R. C. (1994) 'Three Worlds of Welfare Capitalism? The Welfare State and the Post-Industrial Trajectory in the Netherlands after 1980', *West European Politics*, 17 (4), pp. 166–89.

Krugman, P. (1991) *Geography and Trade* (Cambridge, Mass.: MIT Press).

Krugman, P. (1996) *Pop Internationalism* (Cambridge, Mass.: MIT Press).

Krugman, P. (1999) *The Accidental Theorist* (Harmondsworth: Penguin).

Krugman, P. and Venables, A. (1990) 'Integration and the Competitiveness of Peripheral Industry', in C. Bliss and J. Braga De Macedo (eds), *Unity with Diversity in the European Community* (Cambridge University Press).

Kuper, B.-O. (1994) 'The Green and White Papers of the European Union: The Apparent Goal of Reduced Social Benefits', *Journal of European Social Policy*, 4 (2), pp. 129–37.

Lange, P. (1993) 'Maastricht and the Social Protocol: Why Did They Do It?', *Politics and Society*, 21 (1), pp. 5–36.

Larsson, A. (2000) 'The European Employment Strategy: A New Field for Research', Speech to the LSE, 17 January.

Lawson, R. (1995) 'The Challenge of "New Poverty": Lessons from Europe and North America', in K. Funken and P. Cooper (eds), *Old and New Poverty: The Challenge for Reform* (London: Rivers Oram Press).

Lawson, R. (1996) 'Germany: Maintaining the Middle Way', in V. George and P. Taylor-Gooby, *European Welfare Policy: Squaring the Welfare Circle* (London: Macmillan – now Palgrave).

Le Grand, J. (1991) *Equity and Choice* (London: HarperCollins).

Le Grand, J. and Bartlett, W. (eds) (1993) *Quasi-Markets and Social Policy* (London: Macmillan – now Palgrave).

Leibfried, S. (1993) 'Towards a European Welfare State?', in C. Jones (ed.), *New Perspectives on the Welfare State in Europe* (London: Routledge).

Leibfried, S. (1994) 'The Social Dimension of the European Union: En Route to Positive Joint Sovereignty?', *Journal of European Social Policy*, 4 (4), pp. 239–62.

Leibfried, S. (2000) 'National Welfare States, European Integration and Globalization: A Perspective for the Next Century', *Social Policy and Administration*, 34 (1), pp. 44–63.

Leibfried, S. and Pierson, P. (1994) 'The Prospects for Social Europe', in A. de Swaan, *Social Policy Beyond Borders: The Social Question in Transnational Perspective* (Amsterdam University Press).

Leibfried, S. and Pierson, P. (eds) (1995) *European Social Policy: Between Fragmentation and Integration* (Washington DC: Brookings Institution).

Leira, A. (1992) *Welfare States and Working Mothers: The Scandinavian Experience* (Cambridge University Press).

Lenoir, R. (1974) *Les Exclus* (Paris: SeUIL).

Levitas, R. (1996) 'The Concept of Social Exclusion and the New Durkheimian Hegemony', *Critical Social Policy*, 16, pp. 5–20.

Lewis, J. (1992) 'Gender and the Development of Welfare Regimes', *Journal of European Social Policy*, 2 (3), pp. 159–73.

MacDougall Report (1977) 'Report of the Study Group on the Role of Public Finance in European Integration', chaired by Sir Donald MacDougall *EC Economic and Financial Series*, Nos A13 and B13.

Majone, G. (1993) 'The European Community between Social Policy and Social Regulation', *Journal of Common Market Studies*, 31 (2), pp. 153–70.

Majone, G. (1996) *Regulating Europe* (London: Routledge).

Mangen, S. (1991) 'Social Policy, the Radical Right and the German Welfare State', in H. Glennerster and J. Midgley, *The Radical Right and the Welfare State* (Hemel Hempstead: Harvester Wheatsheaf).

Mann, M. (1996) 'Ruling Class Strategies and Citizenship', in M. Bulmer and A. M. Rees, *Citizenship Today: The Contemporary Relevance of T. H. Marshall* (London: UCL Press).

Marks, G. (1992) 'Structural Policy in the European Community', in A. M. Sbragia (ed.), *Euro-Politics: Institutions and Policy-Making in the 'New'*, *European Community* (Washington, DC: The Brookings Institution), pp. 191–224.

Marshall, T. H. (1950) *Citizenship and Social Class and Other Essays* (Cambridge University Press).

Mazey, S. and Richardson, J. (1995) 'Promiscuous Policymaking: The European Policy Style?', in C. Rhodes and S. Mazey (eds), *The State of the Union Vol. III: Building a European Polity?* (Harlow: Longman).

McAleavy, P. and De Rynck, S. (1997) 'Regional or Local? The EU's Future Partners in Cohesion Policy', European University Institute Working Paper RSC No. 97/55, October.

McKay, D. (2000) 'Policy Legitimacy and Institutional Design: Comparative Lessons for the European Union', *Journal of Common Market Studies*, 38 (1), pp. 25–44.

Meehan, E. (1997) 'Citizenship and Social Inclusion in the European Union', in M. Roche and R. Van Berkel (eds), *European Citizenship and Social Exclusion* (Aldershot: Ashgate).

Melitz, J. (1994) 'Is There a Need for Community-wide Insurance Against Cyclical Disparities?', *Economic and Monetary Union*, *Economie et Statistique*, Special Issue, pp. 99–106.

Melitz, J. and Vori, S. (1992) 'National Insurance Against Unevenly Distributed Shocks in a European Monetary Union', Paper presented to Conference on 'Public Finance and the Future of Europe', London School of Economics, September, Mimeo.

Michalski, A. and Tallberg, J. (1999) 'Project on European Integration Indicators: People's Europe', Working paper, European Commission Forward Studies Unit (Mimeo).

Michie, J. and Wilkinson, F. (1994) 'The Growth of Unemployment in the 1980s', in J. Michie and J. Grieve Smith (1994) *Unemployment in Europe* (London: Academic Press).

Milward, A. S. (1997a) 'The Springs of Integration', in P. Gowan and P. Anderson (eds), *The Question of Europe* (London: Verso).

Milward, A. S. (1997b) 'The Social Bases of Monetary Union', in P. Gowan and P. Anderson (eds), *The Question of Europe* (London: Verso).

Mishra, R. (1990) *The Welfare State in Capitalist Society* (Hemel Hempstead: Harvester Wheatsheaf).

Mishra R. (1998) 'Beyond the Nation State: Social Policy in an Age of Globalization', *Social Policy and Administration*, 32 (5), pp. 481–500.

Morgan, R. (1996) 'Towards a Common European Citizenship?', *Government and Opposition*, 31 (2), pp. 241–9.

Murphy, K. M. and Welch, F. (1991) 'The Role of International Trade in Wage Differentials', in M. H. Kosters (ed.), *Workers and Their Wages: Changing Patterns in the United States* (Washington DC: AEI Press).

Myrdal, G. (1957) *Economic Theory and Underdeveloped Regions* (London: Duckworth).

Nevin, E. (1990) *The Economics of Europe* (London: Macmillan – now Palgrave).

Newton, K. (1998) 'The Welfare State Backlash and the Tax Revolt', in H. Cavanna (ed.), *Challenges to the Welfare State: Internal and External Dynamics for Change* (Cheltenham: Edward Elgar).

Nickell S. (1997) 'Unemployment and Labour Market Rigidities: Europe versus North America', *Journal of Economic Policy*, 11 (3), pp. 55–74.

Nickell, S. and Layard, R. (1998) 'Labour Market Institutions and Economic Performance', LSE Centre for Economic Performance, Discussion Paper No. 407.

Niero, M. (1996) 'Italy: Right Turn for the Welfare State?', in V. George and P. Taylor-Gooby, *European Welfare Policy: Squaring the Welfare Circle* (London: Macmillan – now Palgrave), pp. 117–35.

Obstfeld, M. and Peri, G. (1998) 'Asymmetric Shocks: Regional Non-adjustment and Fiscal Policy', *Economic Policy*, 26, pp. 205–59.

O'Connor, J. (1973) *The Fiscal Crisis of the State* (New York: St Martin's Press).

O'Donnell, R. (1992) 'Policy Requirements for Regional Balance in Economic and Monetary Union', in A. Hannequart, *Economic and Social Cohesion in Europe* (London: Routledge).

OECD (1990) *Employment Outlook 1990* (Paris: OECD).

OECD (1994) *Economic Surveys – France, 1994* (Paris: OECD).

OECD (1998) *Employment Outlook 1998* (Paris: OECD).

OECD (1999a) *Economic Survey of Germany* (Paris: OECD).

OECD (1999b) *Employment Outlook* (Paris: OECD).

OECD (2000) *Economic Surveys – France, 2000* (Paris: OECD).

Olsen, J. P. (2000) 'Political Engineering in the Name of the People?', *Journal of European Public Policy*, pp. 308–16.

Ormerod, P. (1998) 'Unemployment and Social Exclusion – An Economic View', in M. Rhodes and Y. Meny (eds), *The Future of European Welfare: A New Social Contract?* (London: Macmillan – now Palgrave).

Padoa-Shioppa (1997) 'Engineering the Single Currency', in P. Gowan and P. Anderson (eds), *The Question of Europe* (London: Verso).

Padoa-Schioppa, T. with Emerson, M. *et al.* (1987) *Efficiency, Stability and Equity* (Oxford University Press).

Panic, M. (1996) 'The Long Road to EU Unity', *New Economy*, 3 (2), Summer, pp. 68–72.

Parry, R. (1995) 'Redefining the Welfare State', in J. Hayward and E. C. Page (eds), *Governing the New Europe* (Durham: Duke University Press), pp. 374–400.

Paugam, S. (1996) 'Poverty and Social Disqualification: A Comparative Analysis of Cumulative Social Disadvantage in Europe', *Journal of European Social Policy*, 6 (4), pp. 287–303.

Perroux, F. (1950) 'Economic Space: Theory and Applications', *Quarterly Journal of Economics*, 64 (1), pp. 89–104.

Pfaller, A., Gough, I. and Therborn, G. (1990) *Can the Welfare State Compete? A Comparative Study of Five Advanced Capitalist Countries* (London: Macmillan – now Palgrave).

Pierson, C. (1991) *Beyond the Welfare State* (Cambridge: Polity Press).

Pierson, C. (1995) 'Comparing Welfare States', Review article in *West European Politics*, 18 (1), pp. 197–203.

Pierson, P. and Leibfried, S. (1995) 'Multitiered Institutions and the Making of Social Policy', in S. Leibfried and P. Pierson (eds), *European Social Policy: Between Fragmentation and Integration* (Washington DC: Brookings Institution).

van der Ploeg, F. (1991) 'Macroeconomic Policy Coordination Issues During the Various Phases of Economic and Monetary Integration in Europe', *European Economy*, Special edn, no.1.

Pollack, M. A. (1995) 'Regional Actors in an Intergovernmental Play: The Making and Implementation of EC Structural Policy', in C. Rhodes and S. Mazey (eds), *The State of the Union Vol. iii: Building a European Polity?* (Harlow: Longman).

Pollack, M. A. (1999) 'Beyond Left and Right? Neoliberalism and Regulated Capitalism in the Treaty of Amsterdam', University of Wisconsin-Madison European Research Center Working Paper (Mimeo).

PricewaterhouseCoopers (2001) *European Economic Outlook*, January (London: PricewaterhouseCoopers).

Quintin, O. (1999) 'Social Inclusion and Exclusion – European Demographic and Social Trends', Speech delivered in Brussels, 14 September.

Rees, A. M. (1996) 'T. H. Marshall and the Progress of Citizenship', in M. Bulmer and A. M. Rees, *Citizenship Today: The Contemporary Relevance of T. H. Marshall* (London: UCL Press).

Rhodes, C. and Mazey, S. (1995) 'Introduction: Integration in Theoretical Perspective', in C. Rhodes and S. Mazey (eds), *The State of the Union Vol. iii: Building a European Polity?* (Harlow: Longman).

Rhodes, M. (1995) ' "Subversive Liberalism": Market Integration, Globalisation and the European Welfare State', in *Journal of European Public Policy*, 2 (3), September, pp. 384–406.

Rhodes, M. (1998) 'Globalization, Labour Markets and Welfare States: A Future of "Competitive Capitalism"?', in M. Rhodes and Y. Meny, *The Future of European Welfare: A New Social Contract?* (London: Macmillan – now Palgrave).

Rhodes, M. and Meny, Y. (1998) *The Future of European Welfare: A New Social Contract?* (London: Macmillan – now Palgrave).

Rodrik, D. (1997) 'Sense and Nonsense in the Globalization Debate', *Foreign Policy*, Summer, pp. 19–36.

Room, G. (1990) *'New Poverty'*, *in the European Community* (London: Macmillan – now Palgrave).

Room, G. (1994) 'European Social Policy: Competition, Conflict and Integration', in R. Page and J. Baldock (eds), *Social Policy Review* (Canterbury: Social Policy Association), 6, pp. 17–35.

Room, G. (1995) 'Poverty in Europe: Competing Paradigms of Analysis', *Policy and Politics*, 23 (2), pp. 103–13.

Rosenau, J. N. and Czempiel, E.-O. (1992) *Governance Without Government: Order and Change in World Politics* (Cambridge University Press).

Rowntree Foundation (1995) *Inquiry into Income and Wealth* (York: Joseph Rowntree Foundation).

de Rudder, V. (1982) 'Vivent les ghettos?' GRECO 13 'Recherches sur les migrations internationales', 4–5, pp. 52–67.

Sachs, J. and Sala-i-Martin, X. (1989) 'Federal Fiscal Policy and Optimum Currency Areas', Mimeo, Harvard University (revised versions 'Fiscal Federalism and Optimum Currency Areas: Evidence for Europe from the United States', NBER Working Paper No. 3855, October 1991, and CEPR Working Paper No. 632, March 1992).

Sandholtz, W. and Zysman, J. (1989) '1992: Recasting the European Bargain', *World Politics*, 42 (1), pp. 95–128.

Saraceno, C. and Negri, N. (1994) 'The Changing Italian Welfare State', *Journal of European Social Policy*, 4 (1), pp. 19–34.

Scharpf, F. (1999) *The Viability of Advanced Welfare States in the International Economy: Vulnerabilities and Options*, MPIfG Working Paper 99/9 (Cologne: Max Planck Institute).

Scharpf, F. (2000) 'The Viability of Advanced Welfare States in the International Economy: Vulnerabilities and Options', *Journal of European Public Policy*, 7 (2), pp. 190–228.

Scholte, J. A. (2000) *Globalisation: A Critical Introduction* (London: Palgrave).

Schulte, B. (1993) 'Guaranteed Minimum Resources and the European Community', in R. Simpson and R. Walker (eds), *Europe: For Richer or Poorer?* (London: CPAG).

Self, P. (1993) *Government by the Market? The Politics of Public Choice* (London: Macmillan – now Palgrave).

Siebert, H. (1997) 'Labor Market Rigidities: At the Root of Unemployment in Europe', *Journal of Economic Perspectives*, 11 (3), pp. 37–54.

Siedentop, L. (2000) *Democracy in Europe* (Harmondsworth: Allen Lane).

Silver, H. (1993) 'National Conceptions of the New Urban Poverty: Social Structural Change in Britain, France and the United States', *International Journal of Urban and Regional Research*, 17 (3), pp. 336–54.

Silverman, M. (1992) *Deconstructing the Nation: Immigration, Racism and Citizenship in Modern France* (London: Routledge).

Sinn, W. (1994) 'How Much Europe? Subsidiarity, Centralization and Fiscal Competition', *Scottish Journal of Political Economy*, 4 (1), pp. 85–107.

Skelcher, C. and Stewart, J. (1993) *The Appointed Government of London*, Paper prepared for the Association of London Authorities, November.

Skocpol, T. (1992) *Protecting Soldiers and Mothers: The Political Origins of Social Policy in the United States* (Cambridge, Mass: Harvard University Press).

Skowronek, S. (1982) *Building a New American State: The Expansion of National Administrative Capacities 1877–1920* (Cambridge University Press).

Smith, G. (1999) *Area-based initiatives: The Rationale and Options for Area Targeting*, LSE Case paper 25 (London: LSE).

Smith, S. (1992) 'Financing the European Community: A Review of Options for the Future', *Fiscal Studies*, 13 (4), pp. 98–127.

Spicker, P. (1991) 'The Principle of Subsidiarity and the Social Policy of the European Community', *Journal of European Social Policy*, 1 (1), pp. 3–14.

Stephens, J. D., Huber, E. and Ray, L. (1996) 'The Welfare State in Hard Times', in H. Kitschelt, G. Marks and P. Lange (eds), *Continuity and Change in Contemporary Capitalism* (Cambridge University Press).

Streeck, W. (1999) 'Competitive Solidarity: Rethinking the "European Social Model" ', MPIfG Working Paper 99/8, September (Cologne: Max Planck Institute). (http://www.mpi-futuregen.co.uk-koeln.mpg.de/publikation/working_papers/wp99-8//wp99-8.html).

de Swaan, A. (1994) 'Introduction', in A. de Swaan (ed.), *Social Policy Beyond Borders* (Amsterdam University Press).

Taylor-Gooby, P. (1996) 'Paying for Welfare: The View From Europe', *Political Quarterly*, 67 (2), pp. 116–26.

Terhorst, P. and van der Ven, J. (1997) *Fragmented Brussels and Consolidated Amsterdam; A Comparative Study of the Spatial Organization of Property Rights* (Utrecht/Amsterdam: Royal Dutch Geographical Society).

Therborn, G. (1987) 'Welfare States and Capitalist Markets', *Acta Sociologica*, 30, pp. 237–54.

Thirlwall, A. P. (1980) 'Regional Problems as Balance of Payments Problems', *Regional Studies*, 5.

Titmuss, R. (1974) *Social Policy* (London: Allen & Unwin).

Tsoukalis, L. (1993) *The New European Economy* (Oxford University Press).

Veit-Wilson, J. (2000) 'States of Welfare: A Conceptual Challenge', *Social Policy and Administration*, 34 (1), pp. 1–25.

Visser, J. and Hemerijck, A. (1997) *A 'Dutch Miracle': Job Growth, Welfare Reform and Corporatism in the Netherlands* (Amsterdam University Press).

Vobruba, G. (1994) 'The Limits of Borders', in A. de Swaan (ed.), *Social Policy Beyond Borders* (Amsterdam University Press).

Vranken, M. (1999) 'Citizenship and the Law of the European Union', in L. Holmes and P. Murray, *Citizenship and Identity in Europe* (Aldershot: Ashgate).

Wallace, W. (1997) 'Rescue or Retreat? The Nation State in Western Europe', in P. Gowan and P. Anderson (eds), *The Question of Europe* (London: Verso).

Weale A. (1994) 'Social Policy and European Union', *Social Policy and Administration*, 28 (1), pp. 5–19.

Weale, A. (1995) 'Democratic Legitimacy and the Constitution of Europe', in R. Bellamy, V. Bufacchi and D. Castiglione (eds), *Democracy and Constitutional Culture in the Union of Europe* (London: Lothian Foundation Press).

Wedderburn D. (1965) 'Facts and Theories of the Welfare State', in R. Miliband and J. Saville (eds), *The Socialist Register 1965* (London: Merlin Press).

Weil, P. (1996) 'Nationalities and Citizenships: The Lesson of the French Experience for Germany and Europe', in D. Cesarani and M. Fulbrook (eds), *Citizenship, Nationality and Migration in Europe* (London: Routledge).

Weiler J. H. H. (1995) 'Europe After Maastricht: Do the New Clothes Have an Emperor?', Jean Monnet Working Paper, Harvard Law School, Harvard University.

von Weizsächer, R., Deharne, J.-L. and Simon, D. (1999) 'The Institutional Implications of Enlargment', report to the European Commission, 18 October.

Wes, M. (1996) *Globalisation: Winners and Losers*, IPPR Commission on Public Policy and British Business: Issue Paper No. 3.

Wilensky, H. L. (1975) *The Welfare State and Equality: Structural and Ideological Roots of Public Expenditures* (Berkeley and Los Angeles, Calif: University of California Press).

Wilensky, H. L., Luebbent, H. L., Hahn, G. M., *et al.* (1987) *Comparative Policy Research* (Berlin: Gower).

Williams F. (1989) *Social Policy: A Critical Introduction* (Cambridge: Polity Press).

Wise, M. and Gibb, R. (1993) *Single Market to Social Europe* (Harlow: Longman).

Wood, A. (1994) *North–South Trade, Employment and Inequality: Changing Fortunes in a Skill-Driven World* (Oxford: Clarendon Press).

Young, M. (1958) *The Rise of the Meritocracy 1870–2033* (Harmondsworth: Penguin).

Index

240